OUR
FIFTY
STATES

OUR FIFTY STATES

by Mark H. Bockenhauer
and Stephen F. Cunha

Foreword by Former President Jimmy Carter

NATIONAL GEOGRAPHIC
WASHINGTON, DC

TABLE OF CONTENTS

★ THE MIDWEST ★ 113 ★

★ THE SOUTHWEST ★ 165 ★

★ THE WEST ★ 185 ★

U.S. Territories ★ 232

FOREWORD

I AM SURE that every American can name a favorite place that brings spiritual comfort, a fresh outlook, peaceful and refreshing repose. I have found many such sanctuaries throughout our fifty states, in many different corners of this great country.

Growing up on a farm in southwest Georgia, I first fell in love with this part of America, and have many boyhood memories, such as hunting for arrowheads as I worked in the fields and fishing with a cane pole in a wooded creek near our home, eyes always open for snakes and an occasional otter. Much later, I recall lying on my back on the lawn of the Governor's Mansion in Atlanta watching a horde of Monarch butterflies as they migrated south.

There were times during my presidency when our family would climb to the roof of the White House to watch the Canada geese fly overhead, their faint, haunting calls just audible above the noise of the capital city at night. I have fond memories with my wife, Rosalynn, and our children of quiet moments at Camp David on a mountaintop in northern Maryland, cross-country skiing on pristine trails, and heading to Pennsylvania streams to cast for trout.

On the wild Alaska lands I was privileged to help protect, we witnessed timber wolves, musk-ox, polar bears, and a herd of caribou—100,000 strong—migrating across the land in stately grandeur.

But America's greatness comes not just from a collection of beloved corners like these, but from its diverse and vibrant whole. The richness of this land in a myriad of special places has shaped the character of our people and our history. We citizens love our country, and it is our duty and our pleasure to know it well—from "amber waves of grain" to "alabaster cities."

This book puts geographic knowledge about our country at your fingertips. Enjoy your special places, and then discover new ones. From this process, you will know even better the beauty that is America.

Jimmy Carter

Jimmy Carter is the 39th President of the United States, the recipient of the Nobel Peace Prize, and the Co-Chair, along with his wife, Rosalynn, of the Carter Center in Atlanta, Georgia.

The Fourth of July is a happy and patriotic event for these two girls (opposite). Each year Americans in all 50 states celebrate Independence Day with fireworks, parades, and picnics in honor of the freedoms that make the United States a very special place.

Cape Flattery

Seattle
Olympia ⊛ ●Tacoma
Spokane
WASHINGTON
●Yakima
Portland
Salem ⊛
Eugene
Lewiston
OREGON
Medford
Klamath Falls

Columbia

C A S C A D E   R A N G E

Great Falls ●
Helena ⊛
Butte ●
MONTANA
Billings ●

Missouri

Minot ●
Grand Forks
NORTH DAKOTA
⊛ Bismarck   Fargo

R   O   C   K   Y

Aberdeen ●
SOUTH DAKOTA
Pierre ⊛
Rapid
City
Sioux Falls

Eureka
Redding

Boise ⊛
Idaho
Falls
Pocatello ●

Snake

IDAHO

Yellowstone L.
Cody ●
WYOMING
Casper ●

Missouri

NEBRASKA
Grand
Island
Lincoln

Platte

Reno ●
Carson City ⊛
Lake Tahoe
Sacramento
San
Francisco ● Oakland
San Jose
Salinas
Fresno

GREAT
BASIN
NEVADA

Great
Salt
Lake

Ogden ●
Salt Lake City ⊛
Provo ●

UTAH

Cheyenne ⊛
Laramie ●

Fort Collins ●
○ Mt. Elbert
14,433 ft ● Boulder
4,399 m
⊛ Denver

COLORADO

S. Platte
Platte

Mt. Whitney
14,494 ft
4,418 m

Death Valley
-282 ft
-86 m

St. George ●
Lake
Powell

Grand
Junction

Colorado

Colorado Springs ●
● Pueblo

KANSAS

Bakersfield ●

Point
Conception

Los Angeles ●
Long Beach ● ● Riverside

San Diego ●

Las Vegas ●
Lake
Mead Grand Canyon

MOJAVE
DESERT

Salton
Sea

Yuma ●

Colorado

Flagstaff ●

ARIZONA

Phoenix ⊛ ● Mesa

Tucson ●

Santa Fe ⊛

Albuquerque ●

NEW MEXICO

Rio Grande

Roswell ●

Las Cruces ●
El Paso ⊛

Arkansas

Dodge
City
Wichita ●

OKLAHOMA
Oklahoma ⊛
City
Amarillo ●
Lawton ●

Lubbock ● Wichita
Falls

Red

Abilene ●
Midland ●
Odessa ●

Dallas ●
Fort
Worth

Waco ●

T E X A S

Austin ⊛

San
Antonio ●

Brazos

ALASKA

North Slope
Brooks Range
Yukon
Alaska Range
Mt. McKinley (Denali) +
20,320 ft
6,194 m
Anchorage ● ⊛ Juneau

ALEUTIAN ISLANDS
Alaska Peninsula

0   400 miles
0   400 kilometers

Kauai
Niihau   Oahu
Honolulu ⊛ Molokai
HAWAII   Lanai   Maui
Kahoolawe
Hawaii   Hilo ●

0   150 mi
0   150 km

Corpus
Christi ●
Laredo ●
Brownsville ●

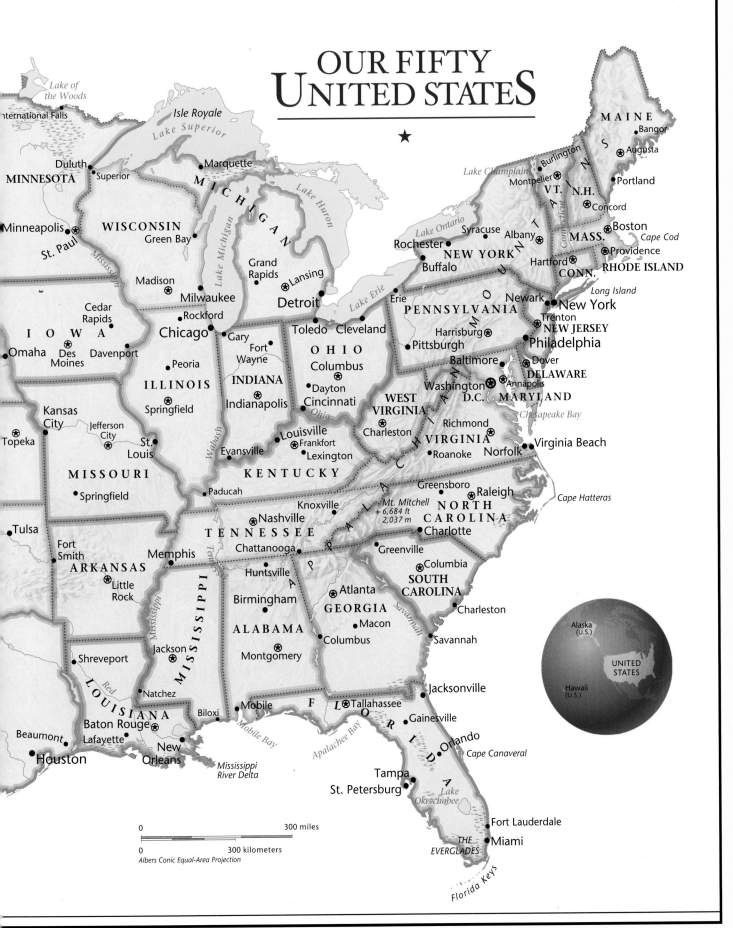

OUR FIFTY UNITED STATES

★

MINNESOTA

Lake of the Woods

International Falls

Isle Royale

Lake Superior

Duluth
Superior

Marquette

MICHIGAN

Lake Huron

Lake Michigan

WISCONSIN

Green Bay

Grand Rapids

Minneapolis
St. Paul

Madison

Milwaukee

Lansing

Detroit

Lake Erie

Erie

NEW YORK

Rochester

Buffalo

Syracuse

Albany

Lake Ontario

MAINE

Bangor

Augusta

Portland

Lake Champlain

Burlington

Montpelier

VT. **N.H.**

Concord

Boston

Cape Cod

MASS.

Providence

RHODE ISLAND

Hartford

CONN.

Long Island

Newark

New York

Trenton

NEW JERSEY

Philadelphia

PENNSYLVANIA

Harrisburg

Pittsburgh

Baltimore

Dover

DELAWARE

Annapolis

MARYLAND

Washington

D.C.

Chesapeake Bay

Cedar Rapids

I O W A

Omaha
Des Moines

Davenport

Rockford

Chicago

Gary

Fort Wayne

Peoria

ILLINOIS

Springfield

INDIANA

Indianapolis

Toledo

Cleveland

O H I O

Columbus

Dayton

Cincinnati

Ohio

Louisville

Frankfort

Lexington

WEST VIRGINIA

Charleston

Richmond

VIRGINIA

Roanoke

Norfolk

Virginia Beach

Kansas City

Jefferson City

Topeka

St. Louis

Evansville

KENTUCKY

Wabash

MISSOURI

Springfield

Paducah

Knoxville

Greensboro

Raleigh

Cape Hatteras

Mt. Mitchell
+ 6,684 ft
2,037 m

NORTH CAROLINA

Charlotte

Tulsa

Nashville

T E N N E S S E E

Chattanooga

Greenville

Fort Smith

Memphis

Huntsville

Columbia

SOUTH CAROLINA

ARKANSAS

Little Rock

Birmingham

Atlanta

GEORGIA

Charleston

MISSISSIPPI

ALABAMA

Macon

Montgomery

Columbus

Savannah

Jackson

Shreveport

Red

LOUISIANA

Natchez

Biloxi

Mobile

F L O R I D A

Tallahassee

Jacksonville

Beaumont

Lafayette

Baton Rouge

New Orleans

Houston

Mississippi River Delta

Mobile Bay

Apalachee Bay

Gainesville

Orlando

Cape Canaveral

Tampa

St. Petersburg

Lake Okeechobee

THE EVERGLADES

Fort Lauderdale

Miami

Florida Keys

Alaska (U.S.)

UNITED STATES

Hawaii (U.S.)

0   300 miles

0   300 kilometers

Albers Conic Equal-Area Projection

WASHINGTON, D.C.

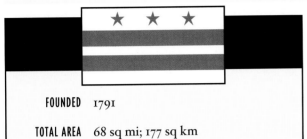

FOUNDED	1791
TOTAL AREA	68 sq mi; 177 sq km
LAND AREA	61 sq mi; 159 sq km
POPULATION	570,898
POPULATION DENSITY	9,359 people per sq mi
MAJOR RACIAL/ ETHNIC GROUPS	60.0% African American; 30.8% white; 2.7% Asian; .3% Native American. Hispanic (any race) 7.9%.
INDUSTRY	government, services, tourism

WOOD THRUSH   AMERICAN BEAUTY ROSE

Did you know?

No buildings in Washington, D.C., can be higher than the United States Capitol.

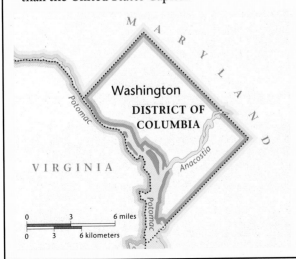

THE NATION'S CAPITAL. To the people of the United States it is a place of symbol and power like no other. It is the seat of the U.S. government where decisions are made that affect not only the country but the world. It is a magnet for tourists, who come to see its splendid monuments and museums, and home to 571,000 ordinary citizens.

In 1790 Northern and Southern leaders agreed on a capital location somewhere along the Potomac River, but it was President Washington who chose the exact spot the following year. He selected French architect Pierre L'Enfant to design a grand city on land originally donated by Maryland and Virginia. Congress used Maryland's share but gave back Virginia's land in 1846.

Washington ranks among the world's great capital cities, but life in the District is not everywhere so grand. From a high of more than 800,000 people in the 1950s, population has declined, as many have chosen to leave the high costs, congestion, and crime of District life. Hundreds of thousands of commuters work in the city but live—and spend their money—in surrounding states. City leaders are working to find ways to improve life for all its residents, but without a voting representative in Congress, change is slow and often difficult. Still, Washington, D.C.—a city honoring the Father of Our Country and a district named for Columbus—is a source of pride for all Americans.

The United States Capitol (opposite) anchors the District of Columbia and the nation. Atop its dome, the imposing Statue of Freedom stands nearly 308 feet (94 m) above ground level. The west entrance overlooks the National Mall, with its monuments and museums, and the White House, where the President lives.

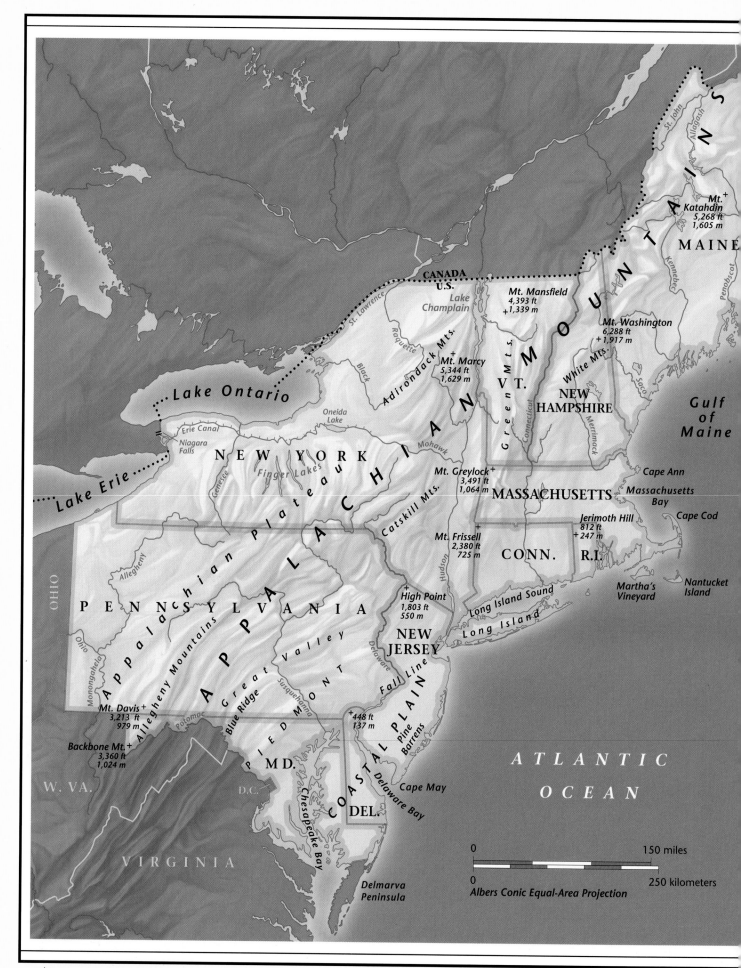

CANADA
U.S.

Lake Champlain

Mt. Mansfield
4,393 ft
+1,339 m

Mt. Washington
6,288 ft
+1,917 m

MAINE

Mt.+
Katahdin
5,268 ft
1,605 m

St. John

Allagash

Kennebec

Penobscot

St. Lawrence

Raquette

Black

Adirondack Mts.

Mt. Marcy
5,344 ft
1,629 m

Green Mts.

VT.

White Mts

NEW
HAMPSHIRE

Merrimack

Saco

Gulf
of
Maine

Lake Ontario

Oneida
Lake

Erie Canal

Niagara
Falls

NEW YORK

Finger Lakes

Genesee

Mohawk

Mt. Greylock+
3,491 ft
1,064 m

MASSACHUSETTS

Cape Ann

Massachusetts
Bay

Lake Erie

Appalachian Plateau

Catskill Mts.

Mt. Frissell
2,380 ft
725 m

CONN.

Jerimoth Hill
812 ft
+247 m

R.I.

Cape Cod

PENNSYLVANIA

Appalac

APPA

Allegheny

OHIO

Ohio

Monongahela

Mt. Davis +
3,213 ft
979 m

Backbone Mt. +
3,360 ft
1,024 m

Allegheny Mountains

Great

Valley

Blue Ridge

PIEDMONT

Susquehanna

Potomac

LACHIAN

Hudson

APPALACHIAN MOUNTAINS

High Point
1,803 ft
550 m

Delaware

NEW
JERSEY

Fall Line

Long Island Sound

Long Island

Martha's
Vineyard

Nantucket
Island

+448 ft
137 m

Pine
Barrens

W. VA.

D.C.

MD.

COASTAL PLAIN

DEL

Chesapeake Bay

Delaware Bay

Cape May

ATLANTIC
OCEAN

VIRGINIA

Delmarva
Peninsula

0   150 miles

0   250 kilometers

Albers Conic Equal-Area Projection

The Northeast

RETREATING GLACIERS helped shape this crumpled landscape. The forested mountains, fertile valleys, navigable rivers, and excellent harbors attracted settlers. Over time, the northeast has become the country's most densely populated region. The ancient Appalachian Mountains, stretching from Maine to southwestern Maryland and beyond, form the geologic backbone. The chief ranges—the White Mountains and Green Mountains of New Hampshire and Vermont, the Catskills of New York, and the Alleghenies and Blue Ridge of Pennsylvania and Maryland—provide mineral wealth, timber resources, and recreational playgrounds. Croplands and towns fill the valleys. Rivers flowing east out of the mountains onto the flat Atlantic Coastal Plain help power the industry and commerce of some of the country's oldest and largest cities from Boston to Baltimore. Waterways flowing west link the region to the Great Lakes and the Mississippi Valley.

St. Croix

Desert
nd

Ancient Wilderness Meets Modern Megalopolis

THIS COMPACT LANDSCAPE of rocky coastline, fertile valleys, and rolling mountains inspired local author Emily Dickinson to "think New Englandy." The North-east's rich history of self-governing began in the 1500s (and perhaps much earlier) when five Native American tribes agreed to mutual trade and peaceful treaties under the Iroquois Confederacy. The original Mohawk, Oneida, Onondaga, Cayuga, and Seneca tribes thrived by hunting, fishing, collecting berries, and trading these and other resources with nearby tribes.

In 1620 the first European colonists arrived and began gradually displacing the Indians. Employing "Yankee ingenuity" and a strong dose of Puritan work ethic, America's colonial economy literally sprang from the earth. Trees cut from the dense forests provided ample wood to craft into homes, barns, and ships. On this newly cleared land, settlers raised corn, wheat, and livestock. They also tapped maple trees for tasty syrup. From the mountains to the coastal plain, they harnessed water to drive mills—initially to grind flour and mill lumber

and then, as the economy developed, to power textile factories. Although most people farmed, whalers, fishermen, ship builders, barrel makers, blacksmiths, and shop keepers all played important roles in this emerging economy.

For two centuries, waves of immigrants helped propel the Northeast into the center of American manufacturing and trade. By the early 1800s, cities and family farms dominated the region. An expanding network of post roads built to deliver mail, canals, and railroads linked the growing population and their markets. Ports such as Philadelphia and Baltimore became key centers of international trade.

Throughout the 19th century, the Northeast was a global industrial powerhouse. Coal, railroads, and labor powered vast iron/steel works and manufactured goods. Although during the Civil War the Border States had some Southern leanings, the Northeast was the core of the Union, and its rich resources and industrial might eventually overwhelmed the South.

During the 20th century, the economy began to change. Rapidly expanding cities such as New York, Boston, and Hartford swallowed up farms, while many factories relocated to the South and abroad, where land and labor cost less. As manufacturing declined, the Northeast was reborn into a powerful center of international business. Today, suburbs link cities into a giant interconnected metropolitan area—called a megalopolis—that stretches from Boston to Baltimore and Washington, D.C., and that is home to one in five Americans. Cities and transportation routes mirror those first built during colonial times. The region's cities and suburbs still welcome new waves of immigrants from home and abroad, who arrive seeking jobs in banking, insurance, education, technology, and other service businesses.

Gigantic traffic jams, sprawling suburbs, trees damaged by acid rain, and polluted rivers are signs of a population struggling to cope with its own success. Yet, squeezed between the farms and cities are stunning remnants of the dense forests once inhabited by various native peoples. Tourism is providing new jobs as people flock to some of America's largest parks and seashores. Researchers are working to find ways to rebuild the dwindling oyster population in Chesapeake Bay. Elsewhere, the return of moose and black bear hint that some of this ancient wilderness will flourish alongside a modern megalopolis.

> "I never saw an autumnal landscape so beautifully painted....It was like the richest rug imaginable spread over an uneven surface."
>
> HENRY DAVID THOREAU

Far from bustling Northeast cities, a lone canoeist finds solitude on a lake in the Adirondack Mountains. Every autumn, shortened days and falling temperatures turn the green leaves of these hardwoods flaming shades of red, orange, and yellow.

CONNECTICUT

★ *Constitution State* ★

YANKEE QUALITY IS ASSURED. The word "Yankee" probably started out as *Jankes (Yahn kes)*, a name the Dutch used to make fun of the tradespeople they competed with in the New World. By the Revolution, people were happy to call themselves Yankees. With a long tradition of excellence and leadership in politics, seafaring, inventions, and insurance, Connecticut Yankees have plenty of reasons to be proud.

The Dutch were the first to scout the coast in 1614, but it was English colonists from Massachusetts, led by Thomas Hooker and others, who established a series of permanent settlements, including Hartford in 1635. The Pequots, the most powerful of several native groups, attacked settlements that they saw as a challenge to their regional power. In 1637, the Pequot threat was largely eliminated by soldiers who burned a native fort, killing hundreds of Indians. Competing colonies, centered at Hartford and New Haven, joined together in the 1660s. By then, Connecticut—from an Algonquin term for "on the long tidal river"—was a colony chartered by the English king.

Critical ideas about a government "by the people" came from Connecticut. The early Hartford community's Fundamental Orders, based on a sermon by Thomas Hooker, became law in 1639, giving people the right to elect government officials. Nearly 150 years later the Connecticut Compromise was adopted at the Constitutional Convention. By providing that each state would be represented by two Senators, it ensured that states with small populations would be fairly represented in the new nation's Congress. Connecticut became the fifth state in early 1788, with Hartford as its capital.

The state has hummed with industry since colonial times, beginning with clocks, tin pots and pans, and silverware by the 1740s. Fertile

1635

Minister Thomas Hooker and a group of followers founded Hartford. He preached that government should be by consent of the people.

1793–1825

Just as his cotton gin revolutionized the South, Eli Whitney's concept of mass production revolutionized industry in the North.

1839–1840

The ruling that freed the slaves of the Amistad was a landmark decision, recognizing the right of all people to rebel against injustices.

Present day

Groton, home to the U.S. Naval Submarine Base, is where the country's newest nuclear attack sub, the Virginia-*class, is built.*

This restored whaling ship at Mystic Seaport (opposite) is part of the state's maritime history. Connecticut shipyards produced warships for the British in colonial days, whalers in the 1800s, clipper ships and steamers into the 20th century, and submarines today.

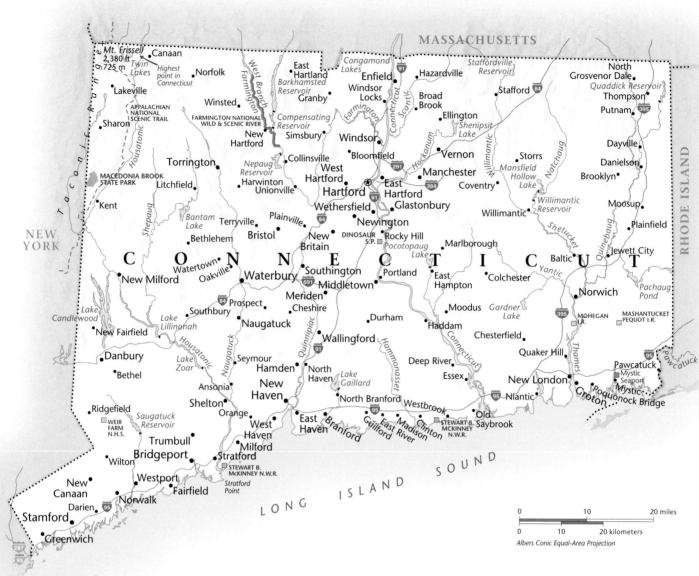

MASSACHUSETTS

Mt. Frissell
2,380 ft
725 m
Twin
Lakes

Highest
point in
Connecticut

Canaan

Norfolk

Lakeville

Sharon

APPALACHIAN
NATIONAL
SCENIC TRAIL

Winsted

FARMINGTON NATIONAL
WILD & SCENIC RIVER

New
Hartford

Simsbury

Collinsville

West
Branch
Farmington

East
Hartland

Barkhamsted
Reservoir

Granby

Compensating
Reservoir

Congamond
Lakes

Enfield

Windsor
Locks

Hazardville

Broad
Brook

Ellington

Staffordville
Reservoir

Stafford

Shenipsit
Lake

North
Grosvenor Dale

Quaddick Reservoir

Thompson

Putnam

Dayville

Torrington

MACEDONIA BROOK
STATE PARK

Litchfield

Kent

Nepaug
Reservoir

Harwinton

Unionville

Bantam
Lake

Bethlehem

Terryville

Plainville

Windsor

Bloomfield

West
Hartford

Vernon

Manchester

Coventry

Hockanum

Storrs

Mansfield
Hollow
Lake

Willimantic

Willimantic
Reservoir

Danielson

Brooklyn

Moosup

Plainfield

NEW
YORK

Housatonic

Taconic Trail

Shepaug

CONNECTICUT

Watertown

Oakville

Bristol

New
Britain

DINOSAUR
S.P.

Rocky Hill

Pocotopaug
Lake

Marlborough

Baltic

Jewett City

Pachaug
Pond

New Milford

Waterbury

Southington

Middletown

Portland

East
Hampton

Colchester

Yantic

Norwich

Lake
Candlewood

Lake
Lillinonah

Southbury

Prospect

Meriden

Cheshire

Durham

Moodus

Gardner
Lake

Chesterfield

MOHEGAN
I.R.

MASHANTUCKET
PEQUOT I.R.

New Fairfield

Naugatuck

Quinnipiac

Wallingford

Haddam

Quaker Hill

Danbury

Lake
Zoar

Seymour

Hamden

North
Haven

Lake
Gaillard

Deep River

Essex

New London

Pawcatuck

Bethel

Ansonia

New
Haven

North Branford

Westbrook

Niantic

Mystic
Seaport

Mystic

Ridgefield

WEIR
FARM
N.H.S.

Saugatuck
Reservoir

Shelton

Orange

West
Haven

East
Haven

Branford

Guilford

East River

Madison

Clinton

STEWART B.
McKINNEY
N.W.R.

Old
Saybrook

Groton

Poquonock
Bridge

Trumbull

Bridgeport

Stratford

Milford

STEWART B.
McKINNEY N.W.R.

Stratford
Point

Wilton

Westport

Fairfield

LONG ISLAND SOUND

New
Canaan

Darien

Norwalk

Stamford

Greenwich

Hartford

East
Hartford

Wethersfield

Glastonbury

Newington

RHODE ISLAND

Housatonic

Naugatuck

Hammonasset

Connecticut

Thames

Shetucket

Quinebaug

Natchaug

Willimantic

Scantic

Farmington

Pawcatuck

0   10   20 miles
0   10   20 kilometers
Albers Conic Equal-Area Projection

Building on a successful tradition of firearms manufacturing, Connecticut became a center of defense contracting in World War II. Today, submarines, jet aircraft components, helicopters, and more contribute to the nation's military. Sikorsky Aircraft Corporation, based in Stratford, has made helicopters since 1939. Here, the crew of the U.S. Air Force Sikorsky HH-60 Pave Hawk practices aerial maneuvers.

Connecticut River Valley farmlands grew plenty of corn, beans, and tobacco, and its coastal waters produced seafood. During the Revolution, cannon, cannonballs, and shot for muskets rolled from ironworks to American fighting ships and army units, starting a long tradition of military manufacturing and defense support. Connecticut inventors provided revolutionary ideas in industry. Eli Whitney came up with the idea of interchangeable parts, which made mass production possible. Samuel Colt invented the repeating pistol in 1836, and Charles Goodyear found a method of vulcanizing, or strengthening, rubber in 1844.

Connecticut's trade and shipbuilding also flourished in the 1800s. At mid-century, whaling was a huge enterprise. Though the industry soon declined, Connecticut's ties to the sea have not. New London is home to the U.S. Coast Guard Academy, while just across the Thames River is Groton, site of the U.S. Naval Submarine Base. Sea connections helped launch another key activity. After the Revolution, some state businessmen helped a shipowner by "insuring" his vessel and cargo. They agreed to pay for lost cargo in return for a share of the profits if the voyage was successful. Thus was born the U.S. insurance business.

In the late 20th century, many New York City-based companies moved their headquarters to Connecticut. This brought many high-paying, white-collar jobs, but it did little to help old industrial cities, which began to lose jobs by the 1970s. The state government has begun efforts to revitalize cities and has enacted policies to limit sprawl and preserve the state's scenic rural areas. Connecticut fights to keep its industrial jobs and attract more technology business. These are good Connecticut Yankee ideas likely to ensure success and keep the state a leader.

CONNECTICUT
Constitution State

STATEHOOD	January 9, 1788; 5th state
CAPITAL	Hartford
LARGEST CITY	Bridgeport Population 140,104
TOTAL AREA	5,543 sq mi; 14,357 sq km
LAND AREA	4,845 sq mi; 12,548 sq km
POPULATION	3,483,372
POPULATION DENSITY	714.3 people per sq mi
MAJOR RACIAL/ ETHNIC GROUPS	81.6% white; 9.1% African American; 2.4% Asian; .3% Native American. Hispanic (any race) 9.4%.
INDUSTRY	transportation equipment, metal products, machinery, electrical equipment, printing and publishing, scientific instruments, insurance
AGRICULTURE	nursery stock, dairy products, poultry, eggs, shellfish

ROBIN

MOUNTAIN LAUREL

Did you know?

1. Mark Twain lived in Hartford for many years. While there, he wrote several of his books, including *Huckleberry Finn.*
2. Connecticut sent so many supplies to the Continental and Union Armies during the Revolutionary and Civil Wars that it became known as the Provision State.
3. Connecticut was first governed under a document called the Fundamental Orders, which later served as a model for the U.S. Constitution. For this reason, Connecticut is called the Constitution State.
4. Old Newgate, in East Granby just north of Hartford, was the first state prison in America. Originally a copper mine, it was used to house Loyalists to the King during the Revolutionary War.
5. The first fully operational steel mill in the U.S. opened in Simsbury in 1728.

DELAWARE

★ *First State* ★

"A JEWEL AMONG STATES," said Thomas Jefferson about Delaware. Though the second smallest state in area, its economic importance has long been huge. Favorable laws for starting and operating businesses have attracted a variety of enterprises. More than half of the country's largest companies call themselves Delaware corporations—even if their offices in the state are just on paper. Delaware's place in the nation's history is oversize, too. When the time came to approve the U.S. Constitution, Delaware was at the head of the line. The First State signed on December 7, 1787.

Barrier island beaches stretch for 28 miles (45 km) along Delaware's southeastern Atlantic coast. Spanning its southernmost border with Maryland is the Cypress Swamp, home of one of the northernmost stands of cypress trees in the country. Northward, the state's shoreline faces the Delaware Bay. Salt marshes here provide nesting sites for birds and breeding grounds for shellfish. In the south, farms grow soybeans and corn, which help feed the quarter-billion broiler chickens produced annually. A wide variety of vegetables and fruits are grown for processing or transporting from "truck farms" to nearby cities. In the north, where the state narrows to less than 10 miles (16 km) in width, the Chesapeake and Delaware Canal links the two great bays. More than 60 percent of Delaware's population lives in this largely urban and industrial region.

When Henry Hudson sailed into Delaware Bay in 1609, Lenni-Lenape, Nanticoke, and Minqua peoples lived there. The next year, English ship captain Samuel Argall named a point of land Cape De La Warr, for the governor of Virginia. Later, the bay, river, and state all took the name Delaware. Dutch, Swedish, and English interests competed for control of the region. New Sweden, a small colony of Swedes

1638

The Swedish and Finnish pioneers who founded New Sweden were skilled woodsmen who built the first log cabins in the New World.

1802–early 1900s

This E.I. du Pont mill, which made gunpowder during the War of 1812, developed into Delaware's giant chemical industry.

1951

The Delaware Memorial Bridge opened in 1951, providing a faster and more direct route to New Jersey and New York.

Present day

Delaware has been a leader in coastal conservation since 1971 when it passed laws protecting its beaches from polluting industries.

Du Pont family wealth supports schools, roads, and public projects across Delaware. Winterthur, once a private du Pont estate, is now a world-famous garden, museum, and study center for Americana. Its latest feature is a fantasy garden for children (opposite).

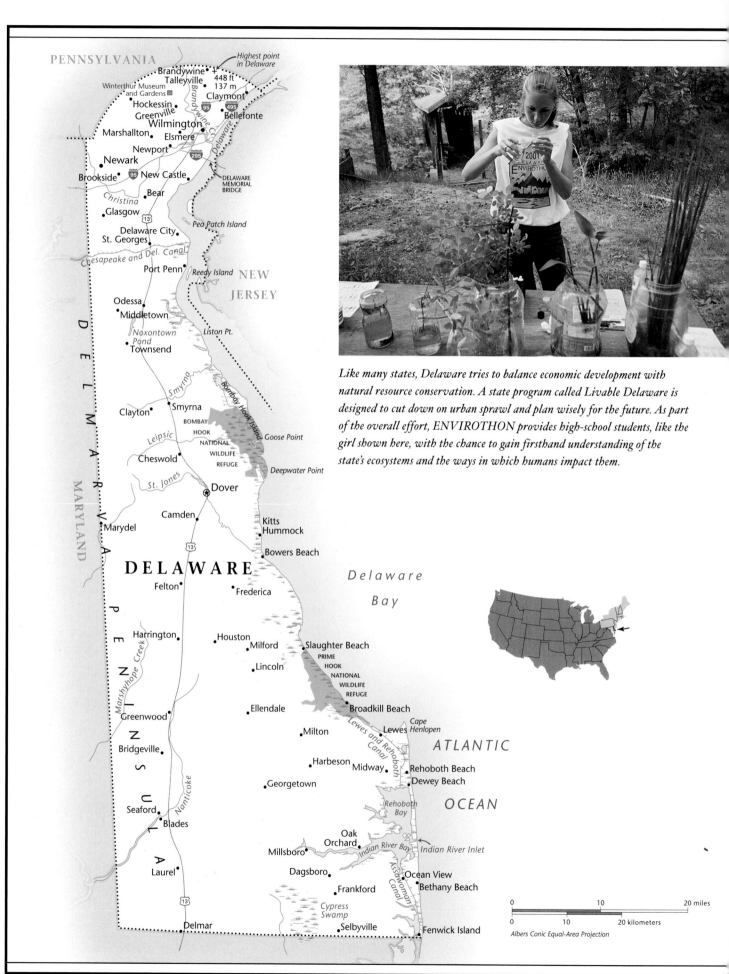

PENNSYLVANIA

Highest point in Delaware
+ 448 ft
137 m

Brandywine
Talleyville
Claymont
Winterthur Museum and Gardens
95
495
Bellefonte
Hockessin
Greenville
Wilmington
Marshallton
Elsmere
Newport
295
Newark
95
New Castle
Brookside
DELAWARE MEMORIAL BRIDGE
Bear
Christina
Glasgow
13
Delaware City
St. Georges
Pea Patch Island
Chesapeake and Del. Canal
Port Penn
Reedy Island

NEW
JERSEY

Odessa
Middletown
Noxontown Pond
Liston Pt.
Townsend

Smyrna
Clayton
Smyrna
BOMBAY HOOK NATIONAL WILDLIFE REFUGE
Leipsic
Goose Point
Cheswold
St. Jones
Deepwater Point

M
A
R
Y
L
A
N
D

Dover
Camden
Marydel
13
Kitts Hummock
Bowers Beach

DELAWARE

Felton
Frederica

Delaware Bay

Harrington
Houston
Milford
Slaughter Beach
PRIME HOOK NATIONAL WILDLIFE REFUGE
Lincoln
Marshyhope Creek
Ellendale
Broadkill Beach
Greenwood
Milton
Lewes
Cape Henlopen
Bridgeville
Harbeson
Midway
Rehoboth Beach
Georgetown
Dewey Beach

ATLANTIC

Rehoboth Bay

OCEAN

Seaford
Nanticoke
Blades
Oak Orchard
Indian River Bay
Indian River Inlet
Millsboro
Laurel
Dagsboro
Ocean View
Frankford
Bethany Beach
Cypress Swamp
Delmar
Selbyville
Fenwick Island

P
E
N
I
N
S
U
L
A

0   10   20 miles
0   10   20 kilometers
Albers Conic Equal-Area Projection

Like many states, Delaware tries to balance economic development with natural resource conservation. A state program called Livable Delaware is designed to cut down on urban sprawl and plan wisely for the future. As part of the overall effort, ENVIROTHON provides high-school students, like the girl shown here, with the chance to gain firsthand understanding of the state's ecosystems and the ways in which humans impact them.

and Finns, was founded in 1638. A Dutch force from New Amsterdam took over in 1655, and the English finally secured the area in 1674. Eight years later, it was made part of Pennsylvania. Over time, Delaware began to operate like, then finally became, an independent colony. Its population was split between Loyalists and those wanting independence, but Delaware voted to break away.

Industry came to northern Delaware in the person of a French immigrant named Éleuthère Irénée du Pont de Nemours, who opened a gunpowder factory on Brandywine Creek in 1802. Water powered Wilmington-area mills that made flour, paper, and cloth. Though some landowners in its southern counties used slaves, Delaware stayed in the Union. But pro-Southern feelings grew during the Civil War, and Delaware did not approve the U.S. Amendments securing racial equality until 1901. Integration of schools in the 1950s and housing in the 1960s was difficult here.

Delaware continued its industrial growth in the 20th century, and thousands of European workers moved in to take factory jobs. Spurred on by the demands of two world wars, oil refineries were built, as were shipyards, auto-making plants, and metal-working factories. The creek-side gunpowder mill grew into one of the world's top chemical companies. Among the many products staff at the DuPont Company invented and manufactured was the world's first human-made fiber—nylon—in 1935. Today, Delaware enjoys better economic conditions than many states and has added 11,000 jobs since 2000. But two centuries of industrial pollution have made environmental clean-up a top state priority. Also underway are attempts to save remaining natural areas from development. These efforts will take time, money, and dedication, but Delaware, the "Small Wonder," can make it happen.

DELAWARE
First State

STATEHOOD	December 7, 1787; 1st state
CAPITAL	Dover
LARGEST CITY	Wilmington Population 72,503
TOTAL AREA	2,489 sq mi; 6,447 sq km
LAND AREA	1,954 sq mi; 5,060 sq km
POPULATION	817,491
POPULATION DENSITY	413.3 people per sq mi
MAJOR RACIAL/ ETHNIC GROUPS	74.6% white; 19.2% African American; 2.1% Asian; .3% Native American. Hispanic (any race) 4.8%.
INDUSTRY	food processing, chemicals, rubber and plastic products, scientific instruments, printing and publishing, financial services
AGRICULTURE	poultry, soybeans, nursery stock, corn, vegetables, dairy products

BLUE HEN CHICKEN   PEACH BLOSSOM

Did you know?

1. A portion of the Delaware-Pennsylvania border is the only rounded boundary in the United States.
2. Delaware's nickname, First State, refers to the fact that it was the first state to ratify the U.S. Constitution.
3. In 1880 the country held the first Miss United States pageant in Delaware. Inventor Thomas Edison was one of the judges.
4. During the Revolutionary War, a company of soldiers under Captain Jonathan Caldwell amused themselves by staging cockfights with their captain's blue hen chickens. The men distinguished themselves in several key battles and became known as the Blue Hen's Chickens. The state bird symbolizes this fighting spirit.
5. Delaware is sometimes called the Diamond State. This nickname can be traced back to Thomas Jefferson, who called Delaware a jewel among states because of its strategic position along the Atlantic coast.

MAINE

★ *Pine Tree State* ★

COASTLINE AND PINE. Maine is known especially for these, and both have helped make the state what it is today. Evergreen forests reach right down to the Atlantic shore, along the rocky, 3,478-mile- (5,596-km-) long ocean edge of the Pine Tree State.

Massive Ice Age glaciers left Maine's jagged coastline with perhaps 1,100 islands, big and small. Sculpted by the moving ice and then partly submerged by rising sea level as the huge sheets of ice melted, once-onshore hilltops became offshore islands.

While Viking Leif Ericson probably visited the coast here about A.D. 1,000, the English and French definitely began scouting it in the 1500s. Maine is believed to have taken its name from English explorers who called the shore the "maine-land" to set it apart from the many islands. Several English communities were founded along the southern coast by 1623. After

decades of ownership disputes, Massachusetts gained control of the territory of Maine by 1677. The French gave up all claims after the French and Indian War in 1763, but many French settlers stayed and played a key role in the economy's development. Treaties cost the Algonquin-speaking peoples most of their land.

Maine's people, like other Americans, hated what they saw as unfair British rule and taxes. Thousands of men joined the fight for freedom. After the Revolution, Maine's population grew quickly. Eventually, people wanted to separate from Massachusetts, and in 1819 they voted to do just that. In a "package deal" known as the Missouri Compromise, made between anti-slavery and pro-slavery states, Maine entered the Union "slave free" as the 23rd state in 1820. (Missouri entered as a slave state the next year.)

Logging, shipping, and shipbuilding in Maine grew from the 1600s onward. The

1498

John Cabot probably reached the Maine coast in 1498, claiming it for England. Conflicting claims with the French ended in 1763.

1809–1891

A strong voice against slavery, Hannibal Hamlin served as Lincoln's first Vice President and supported freedom for slaves.

1942–1945

During World War II, Maine shipyards built 236 Liberty Ships to haul grain, ore, munitions, and troops to our Allies in Europe.

Present day

Lobsters are at the heart of Maine's seafood industry. The state supplies more than half of the nation's total harvest.

Lighthouses have long helped sailors avoid disaster from pounding surf and strong tides along Maine's dangerous coast. The Portland Head light (opposite), built in 1791, is no longer operated by a keeper. Its light is electronically controlled.

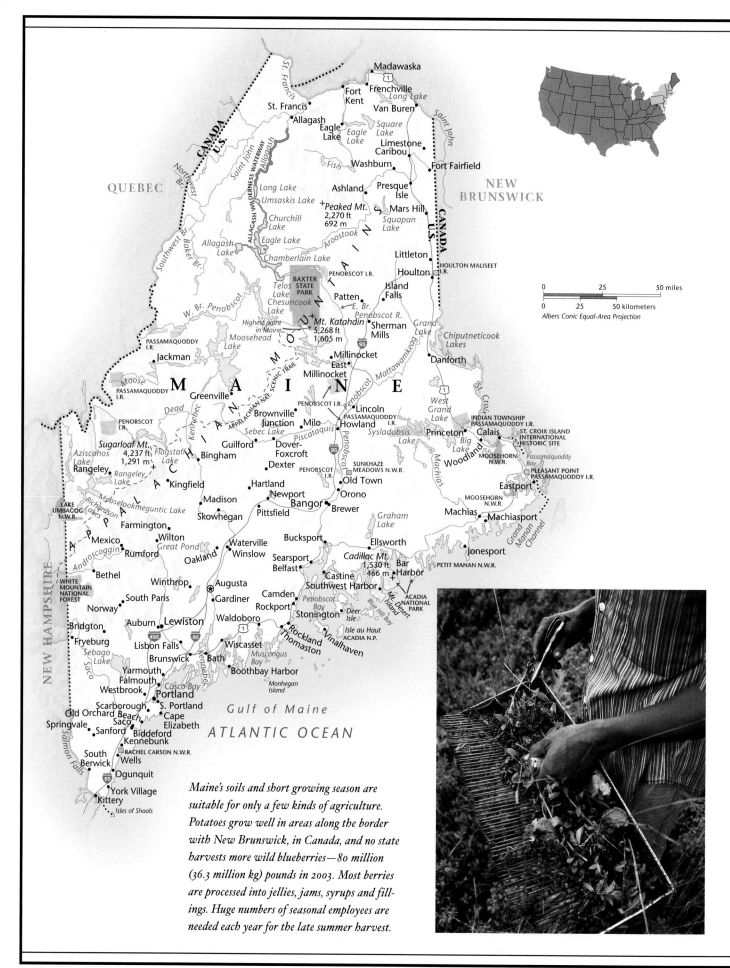

MADAWASKA

Fort Kent · Frenchville
St. Francis · *Long Lake* · Van Buren
Allagash
Eagle
Lake · *Eagle
Lake* · *Square
Lake* · Limestone
Caribou
Washburn · Fort Fairfield
Ashland · Presque
Isle
+ *Peaked Mt.
2,270 ft
692 m* · Mars Hill
*Squapan
Lake*

QUEBEC

NEW
BRUNSWICK

Littleton
Houlton
HOULTON MALISEET
I.R.
PENOBSCOT I.R.
Island
Falls
Patten · *E. Br.
Penobscot R.*
*Grand
Lake* · *Chiputneticook
Lakes*
Telos
Lake
Chesuncook
Lake · BAXTER
STATE
PARK
+ Mt. Katahdin
5,268 ft
1,605 m · Sherman
Mills
*Highest point
in Maine* · Danforth
Moosehead
Lake · Millinocket
East
Millinocket
Jackman · *West
Grand
Lake*
M   A   I   N   E

Greenville · Lincoln
Brownville
Junction · Milo · Howland
Guilford · Dover-
Foxcroft · Princeton · Calais
Bingham · Dexter · *Syladobsis
Lake* · INDIAN TOWNSHIP
PASSAMAQUODDY I.R.
Woodland
Big
Lake · ST. CROIX ISLAND
INTERNATIONAL
HISTORIC SITE
MOOSEHORN
N.W.R.
Sugarloaf Mt.
4,237 ft
1,291 m · *Flagstaff
Lake* · Hartland
Newport · Old Town
Orono
Kingfield · Madison · Bangor · Brewer · *Passamaquoddy
Bay*
PLEASANT POINT
PASSAMAQUODDY I.R.
Rangeley · Pittsfield · *Graham
Lake* · Machias
Machiasport
Farmington · Skowhegan · Bucksport · Ellsworth · Eastport
LAKE
UMBAGOG
N.W.R. · Wilton · Waterville · Searsport · *Cadillac Mt.
1,530 ft
466 m* · Bar
Harbor · MOOSEHORN
N.W.R.
Mexico · Rumford · Winslow · Belfast · Castine
Southwest Harbor · ACADIA
NATIONAL
PARK
Bethel · Oakland · Jonesport
PETIT MANAN N.W.R.
WHITE
MOUNTAIN
NATIONAL
FOREST · Winthrop · Camden · Stonington
Norway · South Paris · Augusta · Gardiner · Rockport · *Penobscot
Bay* · *Deer
Isle* · Vinalhaven
Bridgton · Auburn · Lewiston · Waldoboro · Rockland
Thomaston · *Isle au Haut
ACADIA N.P.*
Fryeburg · Lisbon Falls · Wiscasset
Brunswick · Bath · *Muscongus
Bay*
Yarmouth · Boothbay Harbor
Falmouth · *Monhegan
Island*
Westbrook · Portland
Scarborough · S. Portland
Old Orchard Beach · Cape
Elizabeth
Springvale · Saco
Sanford · Biddeford

NEW HAMPSHIRE

Gulf of Maine
ATLANTIC OCEAN

South
Berwick
Wells
Ogunquit
York Village
Kittery
Isles of Shoals
RACHEL CARSON N.W.R.
Kennebunk

*Maine's soils and short growing season are
suitable for only a few kinds of agriculture.
Potatoes grow well in areas along the border
with New Brunswick, in Canada, and no state
harvests more wild blueberries—80 million
(36.3 million kg) pounds in 2003. Most berries
are processed into jellies, jams, syrups and fill-
ings. Huge numbers of seasonal employees are
needed each year for the late summer harvest.*

0   25   50 miles
0   25   50 kilometers
Albers Conic Equal-Area Projection

tallest, straightest white pines were perfect for the masts of sailing ships. When two centuries of cutting took most of these giants, loggers turned to woods such as oak and maple to make other products. Using river power, textile and shoe-making industries grew in the mid-1800s—though many mills moved south in the early 1900s. By then, Maine's rivers were harnessed for hydroelectric power, especially for paper and pulp mills. Shipbuilding cities like Bath and Portland, using first wood and then steel, launched thousands of vessels for military and merchant use and for fishing and lobstering, too.

Largest of the six New England states in area, Maine has the lowest population density of any state east of the Mississippi River. Most "Mainers" live near the coast in a string of communities that arc from the New Hampshire border to Bangor. The state's northern two-thirds are, in Henry David Thoreau's words, "all mossy and moosey" and much less populated. The cool, moist climate and shallow soils make much of the state's lands unsuitable for crops. Areas in the Aroostook River Valley have some of the best soils, and they make Maine a big potato producer. Food processing has grown in importance, as has tourism.

Like other New England states, Maine has lost industrial jobs, such as in paper mills. Even so, Maine remains a big producer of paper and wood products, while working to preserve its forests. As a pioneer in restoring free-flowing waterways, Maine removed the 160-year-old Edwards Dam in Augusta to allow salmon and other fish to ascend the Kennebec River. The state works hard to build "new economy" businesses, such as the making of computer components. People increasingly see that sustaining state environments will pay off with a prosperous future.

MAINE
Pine Tree State

STATEHOOD	March 15, 1820; 23rd state
CAPITAL	Augusta
LARGEST CITY	Portland Population 63,882
TOTAL AREA	35,385 sq mi; 91,646 sq km
LAND AREA	30,862 sq mi; 79,931 sq km
POPULATION	1,305,728
POPULATION DENSITY	41.9 people per sq mi
MAJOR RACIAL/ ETHNIC GROUPS	96.9% white; .7% Asian; .6% Native American; .5% African American. Hispanic (any race) .7%.
INDUSTRY	health services, tourism, forest products, leather products, electrical equipment, food processing, textiles
AGRICULTURE	seafood, potatoes, dairy products, poultry and eggs, livestock, apples, blueberries, vegetables

CHICKADEE   WHITE PINE CONE AND TASSEL

Did you know?

1. Former governor Percival Baxter donated the land that makes up Baxter State Park to be "kept and remain in the Natural Wild State."
2. Sunrise in the lower 48 states occurs first at West Quoddy Head, the easternmost point of land on the mainland of the United States.
3. The French colony of Acadia, which was first settled in 1604—three years before the first British colony at Jamestown—included part of what is now Maine. One third of the state's population is of French descent and 7 percent are French speaking.
4. Maine covers nearly as much area as the other five New England states combined.
5. Acadia is the only national park in New England. The park's Cadillac Mountain is the highest point along the Atlantic coast of North America.

MARYLAND

★ *Old Line State* ★

"SAVE THE BAY!" Heard across Maryland and beyond, this slogan reminds people to care for their beautiful Chesapeake Bay. This estuary, largest in the country, is the state's greatest economic and environmental resource. Both Maryland's history and its future are tied to this vast yet vulnerable arm of the Atlantic Ocean.

Splitting Maryland almost in half, the Chesapeake separates the Atlantic Coastal Plain from the state's strip of Piedmont and oddly shaped Appalachian panhandle. Fed by the Susquehanna and other rivers, the bay has offered passage and protection for ships since colonial times. Here lie the state's main seaports, Baltimore and Annapolis. Watermen have long made their living from the bay's rich populations of oysters, blue crabs, and fish.

In 1608 John Smith became the first European to chart the bay. George Calvert, whose title was Lord Baltimore, received a grant from English King Charles I for the northern part of the Virginia Colony. His son settled Maryland in 1634, naming the area in honor of the king's wife, Queen Henrietta Maria. Planters in some Tidewater areas used slaves to farm tobacco. Such labor was not needed on small, mixed-crop and wheat farms to the east, north, and west. When the Revolution came, most Marylanders supported it. The Treaty of Paris, which ended the war, was signed in 1783 in the statehouse in Annapolis. The building was used as the new nation's capitol for a nine-month period beginning that same year. Maryland became the seventh state in 1788. Three years later it donated land for the building of a federal city in the District of Columbia.

Maryland grew quickly in the 19th century. A fine harbor and many waterfalls to power industry resulted in Baltimore's rise as a major East Coast port. Key road and canal routes

1634

Maryland's first settlement, St. Marys City, near the Potomac's confluence with the Chesapeake, was founded by Leonard Calvert.

1814

Watching Fort McHenry defend Baltimore in the War of 1812 inspired Francis Scott Key to write "The Star-Spangled Banner."

1862

The Battle of Antietam, on September 17, 1862, was the costliest day of the Civil War in terms of lives lost.

Present day

Harborplace, which opened in 1980 as a tourist, cultural, and business center, has brought new life to the port of Baltimore.

The Hooper Strait Lighthouse and an oyster-dredging skipjack (opposite) are among the symbols of Chesapeake Bay life that are preserved at the Chesapeake Bay Maritime Museum in St. Michaels. The skipjack was named the state boat in 1985.

MARYLAND
The Old Line State

STATEHOOD	April 28, 1788; 7th state
CAPITAL	Annapolis
LARGEST CITY	Baltimore Population 638,614
TOTAL AREA	12,407 sq mi; 32,133 sq km
LAND AREA	9,774 sq mi; 25,314 sq km
POPULATION	5,508,909
POPULATION DENSITY	558.4 people per sq mi
MAJOR RACIAL/ ETHNIC GROUPS	64.0% white; 27.9% African American; 4.0% Asian; .3%Native American. Hispanic (any race) 4.3%.
INDUSTRY	real estate, federal government, health services, business services, engineering services, electrical and gas services, communications, banking, insurance
AGRICULTURE	poultry and eggs, dairy products, nursery stock, soybeans, corn, seafood, cattle, vegetables

NORTHERN (BALTIMORE) ORIOLE   BLACK-EYED SUSAN

Did you know?

1. Maryland's nickname stems from praise its "troops of the line" earned from George Washington during the Revolutionary War.
2. The Maryland State House in Annapolis is the oldest state capitol still in continuous use for meetings of the state legislature.
3. The first successful passenger balloon flight in the U.S. took place in Baltimore on June 24, 1784. The only person onboard was 13-year-old Edward Warren.
4. In 1860 Baltimore had more free African Americans than any other major U.S. city. The Chesapeake Marine Railway and Dry Dock Company, founded in 1869, was operated by African Americans. Today, Prince George's County is one of the wealthiest predominantly black communities in the country.

The Chesapeake and Ohio Canal, built between 1828 and 1850, stretches for 184.5 miles (297 km) from Georgetown, in the District of Columbia, west to Cumberland, Maryland. Bedrock and tough competition from the railroads stopped the digging and ended the original vision of the canal as a link between the Atlantic and the Ohio Valley. The canal was used mostly for hauling Appalachian coal east in barges until 1924. Today, it is a national historic park, where tourists (above) can travel back in time.

linked it to the state's far-western reaches and beyond, and the Baltimore & Ohio Railroad began service in 1836. As the Civil War loomed, Maryland was divided on the issue of slavery. It stayed in the Union as a Border State, seeing many skirmishes and some major battles.

In the post-war period, Maryland became a bustling rail and ship transport center reconnecting North and South. Steelmaking, shipbuilding, and aircraft manufacturing attracted more workers during the two world wars. Nearly 90 percent of all Marylanders now live in the 35-mile- (56-km-) long corridor between D.C. and Baltimore, which has become a huge swath of suburban homes, shopping centers, and office parks. The state boasts

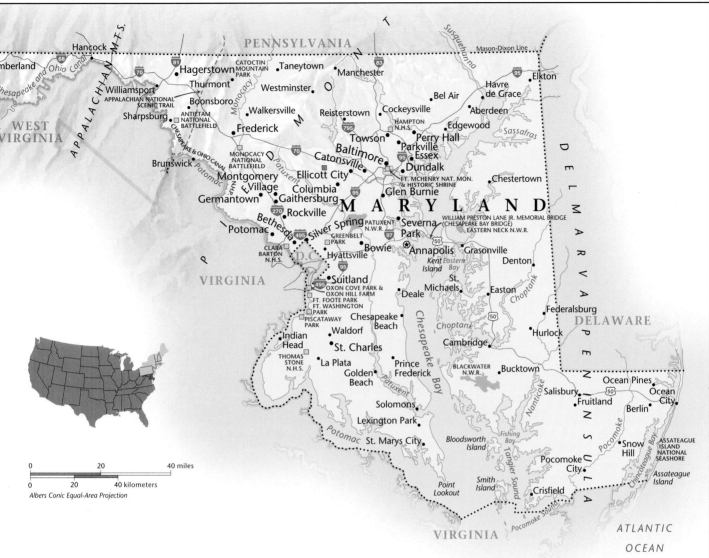

more than 50 major federal research facilities and has become a magnet for high-tech businesses. Traffic clogs roadways, despite the huge numbers of Maryland commuters who carpool and ride mass transit. Though more than a third of the state is still forested and agriculture—led by poultry raising—remains important, more and more land is being shifted to urban uses.

Tourists and residents alike sail, fish, swim, bird-watch, and simply soak up sun and sea breezes on Chesapeake Bay. The Bay Bridge has enabled easier travel both to Eastern Shore fishing villages and to Ocean City beaches along the state's Atlantic coast. But the mighty Chesapeake is in danger. Runoff from farm fields, backyards, and parking lots drains billions of gallons of pollutants into the estuary. Oysters, which serve as natural filters to clean the bay's waters, have declined dramatically. Between 1885 and 2003, the state's annual oyster harvest fell from 15 million bushels to 15 thousand bushels. Amazingly, the Chesapeake still supports a wide array of wildlife, plus a variety of jobs for Maryland residents. Millions of migrating birds feed here, and the state harvests more blue crabs than any other. Efforts now focus on reducing runoff, upgrading sewage treatment plants, and slowing suburban sprawl. Research to rebuild oyster populations advances. If all goes well, Maryland's people will one day be able to say, "We saved the bay!"

MASSACHUSETTS

★ *Bay State* ★

NEW LIFE, NEW IDEAS. That's what the Pilgrims wanted when they voyaged across the Atlantic in 1620. Landing first near the tip of Cape Cod, then crossing the bay to a mainland spot they named Plymouth, these settlers eventually found a better life. New ideas arose when they set down rules to govern themselves—the Mayflower Compact. Ever since, Massachusetts ideas have had enormous influence on American life—in government, education, business, and culture.

The Bay State's best-known feature is Cape Cod, curling like an arm around its large bay. This and many landscapes were shaped as gigantic glaciers pushed south. The Connecticut River Valley was scooped out, and then later filled in with fertile soils. Thin soils elsewhere limit farming. Ice sheets piled up sandy ridges, which remain today as Cape Cod and the famous islands Nantucket and Martha's Vineyard. West of the coastal plain rise rolling mountains, including the Berkshires.

The Pilgrims' new home became known as Massachusetts, after one of the groups of Algonquin-speaking peoples who lived there. Following a terrible first winter, the Pilgrims owed their lives to Native Americans who showed them how to plant corn and beans and otherwise survive. Other immigrants settled nearby, including communities of the Massachusetts Bay Colony that later became Salem and Boston by 1630. Here, political freedoms and representative government were begun, though everyone still had to be a Puritan.

Conflict had a role in colonial history here, too. Relations between settlers and native peoples began on friendly terms, but over time grew hostile. King Philip, chief of the Wampanoag people, declared war on the colonists in 1675 to protect his people and homeland.

1620

The men aboard the Mayflower *signed the Mayflower Compact, agreeing to write and obey "just and equal laws" in the new land.*

1775

The first battles of the American Revolution were fought in Lexington and Concord, where 95 Americans and 273 British died.

1800s

The state became a center of the textile, woolen, and tanning industries, which often hired women and immigrants at low pay.

1991–Present

The "Big Dig," a huge, almost-completed highway-tunnel project in Boston, will spur economic vitality and ease congestion.

The Old State House (opposite), built in 1713, was a center of political life in 18th-century Boston. The lion and unicorn are symbols of British authority, as was the council chamber of the royal governors inside.

MASSACHUSETTS
Bay State

STATEHOOD	February 6, 1788; 6th state
CAPITAL	Boston
LARGEST CITY	Boston Population 589,281
TOTAL AREA	10,555 sq mi; 27,336 sq km
LAND AREA	7,840 sq mi; 20,306 sq km
POPULATION	6,433,422
POPULATION DENSITY	819.9 people per sq mi
MAJOR RACIAL/ ETHNIC GROUPS	84.5% white; 5.4% African American; 3.8% Asian; .2% Native American. Hispanic (any race) 6.8%.
INDUSTRY	electrical equipment, machinery, metal products, scientific instruments, printing and publishing, tourism
AGRICULTURE	fruits, nuts and berries, nursery stock, dairy products

CHICKADEE

MAYFLOWER

Did you know?

1. The country's first planned industrial community was built around a complex of textile mills beginning in 1821. By the 1840s Lowell was a leading industrial center in America.
2. Lake Webster's Algonquin name is Lake Chargoggagoggymanchauggagoggchaubunagungamaug, which reportedly means "You fish on your side; I fish on my side; nobody fish in the middle."
3. The U.S.S. *Constitution* ("Old Ironsides"), the oldest, fully commissioned ship in the U.S. Navy, is permanently docked at Charlestown Navy Yard.
4. Massachusetts is the home of the country's first institute of higher learning (Harvard, 1636), its first printing press (Cambridge, 1638), its first post office (Richard Fairbanks's tavern, Boston, 1639), and its first ironworks (Saugus, 1650).

Hundreds died on both sides until, eventually, the colonists won. After decades of changes in how they governed the colonies, the English combined Plymouth and Massachusetts Bay in 1691. Later, the colonists helped the British win the French and Indian War, which ended in 1763. Shipping became a huge business, including the trading of slaves. Colonists up and down the Atlantic coast grew frustrated over control of trade and other rights by faraway England. In April 1775, British troops and colonists fought the opening battles of the Revolutionary War at Lexington and Concord. Many early battles took place in Massachusetts before action shifted south. Great leaders, such as early patriots John and Samuel Adams, made lasting impacts on the new nation. Massachusetts became the sixth state in 1788, with Boston as its capital.

Hardships caused by a law halting trade with European countries and then the War of 1812 brought huge changes for the state. Textile mills sprouted along state rivers, beginning with Lowell in 1814. Massachusetts's ties to the sea grew stronger. Shipping flourished in ports like Boston and Salem. Whalers sailed from New Bedford and Nantucket for decades until the 1860s. The state contributed nearly 150,000 men and many ships to the Union effort in the Civil War. Industrialization increased for the rest of the century. By 1900 Massachusetts produced half the shoes made in America, as well as woolens and other clothing. The 20th century brought difficulties with labor strife and jobs leaving the state. World

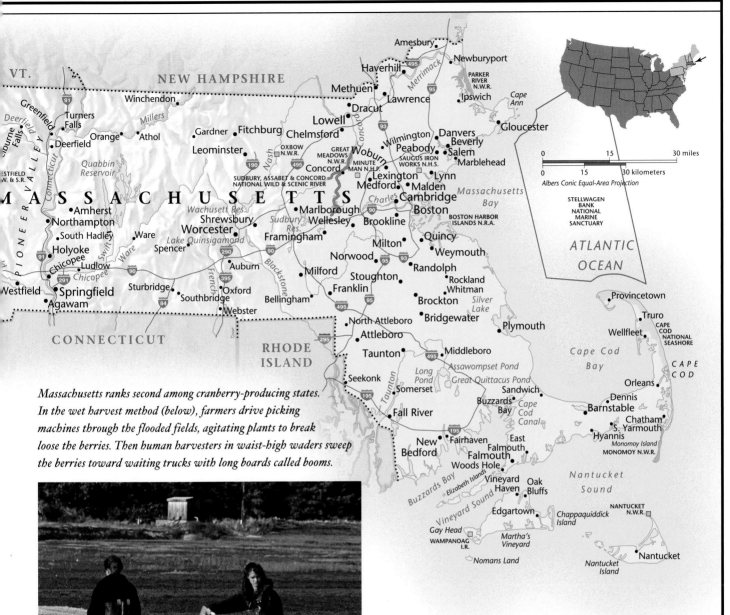

VT.

NEW HAMPSHIRE

Amesbury
Newburyport
Haverhill
PARKER RIVER N.W.R.
Methuen
Ipswich
Cape Ann
Lawrence
Dracut
Gloucester
Winchendon
Lowell
Greenfield
Turners Falls
Millers
Chelmsford
Wilmington
Danvers
Gardner
Fitchburg
Peabody
Beverly
Orange
Athol
Deerfield
Leominster
OXBOW N.W.R.
Salem
Marblehead
Woburn
SAUGUS IRON WORKS N.H.S.
Quabbin Reservoir
GREAT MEADOWS N.W.R.
MINUTE MAN N.H.P.
Concord
Lynn
M A S S A C H U S E T T S
SUDBURY, ASSABET & CONCORD NATIONAL WILD & SCENIC RIVER
Lexington
Medford
Malden
Cambridge
Massachusetts Bay
Wachusett Res.
Amherst
Marlborough
Boston
Northampton
Shrewsbury
Sudbury Res.
Wellesley
Brookline
BOSTON HARBOR ISLANDS N.R.A.
Worcester
Framingham
South Hadley
Ware
Lake Quinsigamond
Spencer
Milton
Quincy
Holyoke
Weymouth
Chicopee
Auburn
Norwood
Randolph
Ludlow
Chicopee
Milford
Stoughton
Rockland
Whitman
Springfield
Sturbridge
Franklin
Brockton
Silver Lake
Westfield
Agawam
Southbridge
Oxford
Bellingham
Bridgewater
Plymouth
Webster
North Attleboro
Middleboro
CONNECTICUT
Attleboro
Provincetown
RHODE ISLAND
Taunton
Assawompset Pond
Truro
CAPE COD NATIONAL SEASHORE
Wellfleet
Cape Cod Bay
Seekonk
Long Pond
Great Quittacus Pond
Sandwich
CAPE COD
Somerset
Buzzards Bay
Orleans
Dennis
Barnstable
Fall River
Cape Cod Canal
Chatham
S. Yarmouth
New Bedford
Fairhaven
East Falmouth
Hyannis
Monomoy Island
MONOMOY N.W.R.
Falmouth
Woods Hole
Nantucket Sound
Vineyard Haven
Oak Bluffs
Buzzards Bay
Elizabeth Islands
NANTUCKET N.W.R.
Vineyard Sound
Edgartown
Chappaquiddick Island
Gay Head
WAMPANOAG I.R.
Martha's Vineyard
Nantucket
Nomans Land
Nantucket Island

ATLANTIC OCEAN

STELLWAGEN BANK NATIONAL MARINE SANCTUARY

0   15   30 miles
0   15   30 kilometers
Albers Conic Equal-Area Projection

Massachusetts ranks second among cranberry-producing states. In the wet harvest method (below), farmers drive picking machines through the flooded fields, agitating plants to break loose the berries. Then human harvesters in waist-high waders sweep the berries toward waiting trucks with long boards called booms.

War II sparked shipbuilding and other war-materials business, but by the 1960s the shift from old industries to high-tech research and products, like computers and electronics, was underway. Thousands of new jobs have recently been created.

Though there are many positives, Massachusetts's 6.4 million people face challenges, too. It's a crowded and expensive place. Boston is choked with the traffic and sprawl of modern urban life. There is a shortage of affordable housing and a wealth of traffic congestion. Whatever the problems, it seems certain Massachusetts will seek—and most likely find—new ideas to solve them.

NEW HAMPSHIRE

★ Granite State ★

THE GRANITE STATE. Though named for hard rock formations under the state, the nickname also reflects New Hampshire's strong feelings about liberty. First of the British colonies to become self-governing, it's no surprise that the state motto, written by Revolutionary War hero John Stark, declares "Live Free or Die."

The Appalachians form New Hampshire's backbone. Highest of the Northeast's peaks is 6,288-foot (1,917-m) Mount Washington, in the Presidential Range of the White Mountains. Famed for fearsome winter storms, a weather station atop the mountain once recorded winds of 231 mph (372 kph)! The Connecticut River flows out of the mountains to form most of the state's boundary with Vermont. More than four-fifths of the state is forested with spruce, fir, maple, oak, beech, and other trees. White-tailed deer abound, as do black bear and moose.

A short but important 18-mile (29-km) coastline stretches between Maine and Massachusetts.

To this shore came the English, founding their first settlements in 1623 along the Piscataqua River near present-day Portsmouth and Dover. Nearby communities Hampton and Exeter were soon established, and New Hampshire was made a royal colony in 1679. Long-running boundary disputes were settled with Massachusetts in the 1740s, with New York in the 1790s, and with Canada in 1842. Settlers and Abenaki peoples got along at first, but greater numbers of newcomers caused increased conflicts over hunting grounds and fishing rights. Native resistance ended by the close of the French and Indian War in 1763.

New Hampshire's patriotic colors showed early. A key event—which some consider the first strike in the fight for independence—was the taking of gunpowder from an English fort at

1777

Native son General John Stark's victory at the Battle of Bennington, in Vermont, was a turning point in the Revolution.

1850S

Mills producing lumber, paper, textiles, and woolens industrialized the state. It became a leader in child labor laws.

1944

World attention focused on the state when President Franklin Roosevelt hosted a global economic conference at Bretton Woods.

2004

Every four years, New Hampshire's tradition of holding the first presidential primary election draws national attention.

New Hampshire's spectacular fall colors attract busloads of tourists from across the country to places like Marlow (opposite). Its trademark white-steepled church and town hall are typical of rural New England towns.

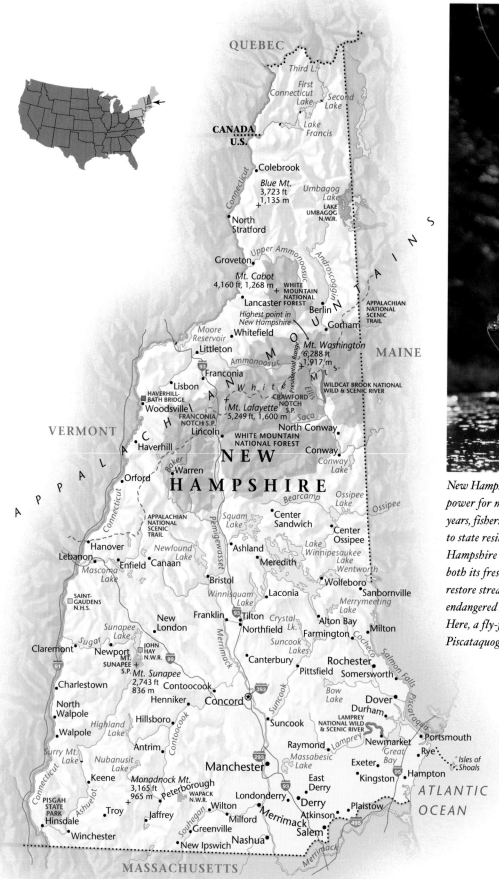

QUEBEC

Third L.

*First
Connecticut
Lake*

*Second
Lake*

*Lake
Francis*

CANADA
U.S.

● Colebrook

Blue Mt.
3,723 ft
+ 1,135 m

*Umbagog
Lake*

**LAKE
UMBAGOG
N.W.R.**

● North
Stratford

Connecticut

Upper Ammonoosuc

Androscoggin

Groveton ●

Mt. Cabot
4,160 ft, 1,268 m +

**WHITE
MOUNTAIN
NATIONAL
FOREST**

● Lancaster

Berlin ●

**APPALACHIAN
NATIONAL
SCENIC
TRAIL**

*Highest point in
New Hampshire*

Whitefield ●

● Gorham

*Moore
Reservoir*

Mt. Washington
6,288 ft
+ 1,917 m

● Littleton

Ammonoosuc

Presidential Range

MAINE

Franconia ●

White

Mts.

Lisbon ●

**HAVERHILL-
BATH BRIDGE**

Woodsville ●

Mt. Lafayette
+ 5,249 ft, 1,600 m

**CRAWFORD
NOTCH
S.P.**

Ellis

**WILDCAT BROOK NATIONAL
WILD & SCENIC RIVER**

**FRANCONIA
NOTCH S.P.**

Saco

VERMONT

Lincoln ●

**WHITE MOUNTAIN
NATIONAL FOREST**

North Conway ●

Haverhill ●

Baker

Warren ●

**NEW
HAMPSHIRE**

Conway ●

*Conway
Lake*

Orford ●

Bearcamp

*Ossipee
Lake*

Ossipee

**APPALACHIAN
NATIONAL
SCENIC
TRAIL**

Center
Sandwich ●

Center
Ossipee ●

*Squam
Lake*

Pemigewasset

Hanover ●

*Newfound
Lake*

Ashland ●

*Lake
Winnipesaukee*

Lebanon ●

Canaan ●

Meredith ●

Wentworth

Enfield ●

Bristol ●

Wolfeboro ●

*Mascoma
Lake*

Sanbornville ●

**SAINT-
GAUDENS
N.H.S.**

*Winnisquam
Lake*

Laconia ●

*Merrymeeting
Lake*

Sugar

*Sunapee
Lake*

Franklin ●

Tilton ●

*Crystal
Lk.*

Alton Bay ●

Milton ●

New
London ●

Northfield ●

Farmington ●

Cocheco

Claremont ●

**JOHN
HAY
N.W.R.**

*Suncook
Lakes*

Merrimack

Newport ●

**MT.
SUNAPEE
S.P.**

Mt. Sunapee
2,743 ft
836 m +

Contoocook ●

Canterbury ●

Rochester ●

Salmon Falls

Charlestown ●

Henniker ●

Concord ⊛

Pittsfield ●

Somersworth ●

North
Walpole ●

Hillsboro ●

Suncook

*Bow
Lake*

Dover ●

Piscataqua

Walpole ●

*Highland
Lake*

Durham ●

Antrim ●

Contoocook

Suncook ●

**LAMPREY
NATIONAL WILD
& SCENIC RIVER**

*Surry Mt.
Lake*

Raymond ●

Lamprey

Newmarket ●

Portsmouth ●

*Nubanusit
Lake*

*Massabesic
Lake*

*Great
Bay*

Rye ●

Keene ●

Monadnock Mt.
3,165 ft
+ 965 m

Manchester ●

Exeter ●

Kingston ●

*Isles of
Shoals*

Peterborough ●

East
Derry ●

Hampton ●

**WAPACK
N.W.R.**

Wilton ●

Londonderry ●

Derry ●

ATLANTIC
OCEAN

**PISGAH
STATE
PARK**

Ashuelot

Troy ●

Jaffrey ●

Milford ●

Atkinson ●

Plaistow ●

Hinsdale ●

Southegan

Greenville ●

Salem ●

Winchester ●

New Ipswich ●

Nashua ●

Merrimack

MASSACHUSETTS

*New Hampshire's rivers have provided industrial
power for more than two centuries. In recent
years, fisheries have proven increasingly valuable
to state residents and visitors alike. New
Hampshire takes pride in the wide variety of
both its fresh- and saltwater fishing. Efforts to
restore stream habitats and to restock the
endangered Atlantic salmon are underway.
Here, a fly-fisher tries his luck on the
Piscataquog River near Manchester.*

0   10   20 miles
0   10   20 kilometers
Albers Conic Equal-Area Projection

Portsmouth by a band of the colony's men in late 1774. Six months before the Declaration of Independence, New Hampshire declared its freedom from England on January 5, 1776. The state was the ninth and deciding state to approve the U.S. Constitution in mid-1788. New Hampshire was strongly against slavery. During the Civil War, it supported the Union with troops and supplies.

Industrialization started up early. The textile and woolen industries threaded their way through the Merrimack River Valley. Manchester's massive Amoskeag Mills stretched along the river and canals below its original power source, Amoskeag Falls. By 1915 this single company employed 17,000 workers—many from Canada, Ireland, Greece, and Poland—in 30 mills and turned out 50 miles (80 km) of finished cloth per hour! Change came when many mills slowed or closed due to major labor strikes and competition from lower-cost mills in Southern states. World War II helped the state rebound from the Great Depression. New businesses replaced old industries by the 1980s. Portsmouth, Nashua, and other cities benefit from their closeness to Boston, attracting high-technology companies that take advantage of an educated, skilled workforce. Some traditional state work is still strong. The Portsmouth Naval Shipyard repairs nuclear submarines; maple trees are still tapped for syrup; and forests still supply wood products and pulp to mills.

Natural resources have long been important to the state's economy. Conservation measures protecting river headwaters and large tracts of woodland have been in place since the early 1900s, and four-season tourism has begun to play a larger role in the state. Today, state residents understand that natural resources sustained can be even more valuable than those removed.

NEW HAMPSHIRE
Granite State

STATEHOOD	June 21, 1788; 9th state
CAPITAL	Concord
LARGEST CITY	Manchester Population 108,398
TOTAL AREA	9,350 sq mi; 24,216 sq km
LAND AREA	8,968 sq mi; 23,227 sq km
POPULATION	1,287,687
POPULATION DENSITY	142.2 people per sq mi
MAJOR RACIAL/ ETHNIC GROUPS	96.0% white; 1.3% Asian; .7% African American; .2% Native American. Hispanic (any race) 1.7%.
INDUSTRY	machinery, electronics, metal products
AGRICULTURE	nursery stock, poultry and eggs, fruits and nuts, vegetables

PURPLE FINCH

PURPLE LILAC

Did you know?

1. The famous naturally carved granite profile known as The Old Man of the Mountain in Franconia Notch State Park was destroyed by a rock slide in 2003. For centuries it served as a rugged symbol of the state.
2. The first strike organized by women workers in the United States occurred in December 1828. Several hundred workers walked out of the Dover Cotton Factory to protest new management policies that forbid them to talk on the job, reduced wages from 58 cents a day to 53 cents, and docked them a fourth of a day's wage if they arrived after the morning bell stopped ringing.
3. New Hampshire was named by Captain John Mason after his home county of Hampshire in England.
4. In 1963 New Hampshire became the first U.S. state to adopt a legal lottery in the 20th century. Since it started, the lottery has raised more than 850 million dollars to aid education.

NEW JERSEY

★ *Garden State* ★

CROSSROADS OF THE EAST. New Jersey's location has placed it squarely in the middle of Atlantic coast action for four centuries. Benjamin Franklin called it a "barrel tapped at both ends," referring both to its abundant farm production and to its position between New York City and Philadelphia.

The Dutch set up their first trading post here near present-day Jersey City in 1618 as part of New Netherland. They surrendered the land to England in 1664, and it was renamed New Jersey after the English Channel Isle of Jersey. Following decades of legal tug-of-war between leaders from New York City and Philadelphia, New Jersey became its own royal colony in 1738. It was in the thick of things during the Revolution, with more than 90 battles fought here, including important victories at Trenton, Princeton, and Monmouth. New Jersey was the third state to ratify the Constitution in late 1787, and Trenton was made its capital three years later.

By the 19th century, the state was in the middle of the industrial revolution. There was still farming, but factories produced textiles, shoes, bricks, and more. Roads were built, canals dug, and rail lines laid down. New Jersey gave soldiers, supplies, and monetary support to the Union during the Civil War. The war fueled industries and attracted thousands of European immigrants. Most factory workers crowded into Newark and other northern cities, often living in poverty. Manufacturing eventually declined— as did the health of New Jersey's urban neighborhoods. Riots broke out in Newark in 1967, calling attention to the need for change.

New Jersey's economy has turned increasingly to a wide range of service and trade businesses. The state has long been a top research center. Manufacturing has not died, though:

1524—early 1600s

The Lenni-Lenape, a peaceful farming people, greeted a succession of Europeans who came ashore in what is now New Jersey.

1778

George Washington honored Mary Ludwig Hays McCauly (Molly Pitcher) for her bravery at the Battle of Monmouth.

1879

Thomas Edison, the "Wizard of Menlo Park," is credited with more than 1,000 inventions, including the electric light bulb.

Present day

Though service industries have begun to dominate, the manufacture of drugs and chemicals continue to be key industries.

Tourists first came to Atlantic City by train in 1854. It enjoyed a century of popularity until other destinations drew visitors away. In the past two decades, the city has been revitalized. Its celebrated Boardwalk (opposite) of Monopoly fame is once again a favorite stroll.

Food processing has long been a healthy part of the Garden State's economy. The Joseph A. Campbell Preserve Company, now the Campbell Soup Company, began selling canned soups from its Camden plant in 1869. The National Biscuit Company, (Nabisco), has produced a wide variety of crackers, cookies, and snacks since 1898. Though now owned by a firm based in New York City, production facilities, like this Fairlawn bakery (above), still turn out herds of animal crackers in New Jersey.

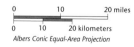

0   10   20 miles
0   10   20 kilometers
Albers Conic Equal-Area Projection

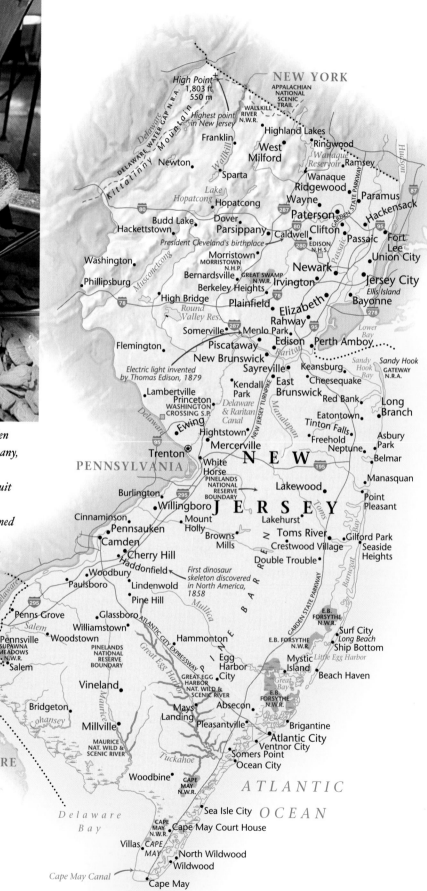

NEW YORK

High Point
1,803 ft.
550 m
Highest point in New Jersey

APPALACHIAN NATIONAL SCENIC TRAIL

WALLKILL RIVER N.W.R.

Franklin
Newton
Sparta
Highland Lakes
West Milford
Ringwood
Ramsey
Wanaque Reservoir
Wanaque
Ridgewood
Wayne
Paramus
Hackensack
Budd Lake
Hackettstown
Dover
Parsippany
Caldwell
President Cleveland's birthplace
EDISON N.H.S.
Clifton
Passaic
Fort Lee
Union City
Washington
Morristown
MORRISTOWN N.H.P.
Paterson
Newark
Jersey City
Phillipsburg
Bernardsville
Berkeley Heights
GREAT SWAMP N.W.R.
Irvington
High Bridge
Plainfield
Elizabeth
Bayonne
Round Valley Res.
Rahway
Somerville
Menlo Park
Edison
Perth Amboy
Flemington
Piscataway
New Brunswick
Sayreville
Keansburg
Sandy Hook Bay
Sandy Hook
GATEWAY N.R.A.
Electric light invented by Thomas Edison, 1879
Kendall Park
East Brunswick
Cheesequake
Red Bank
Long Branch
Lambertville
Princeton
WASHINGTON CROSSING S.P.
Delaware & Raritan Canal
Eatontown
Tinton Falls
Freehold
Asbury Park
Neptune
Ewing
Hightstown
Mercerville
Belmar
Trenton
White Horse
Manasquan

PENNSYLVANIA

PINELANDS NATIONAL RESERVE BOUNDARY
Lakewood
Point Pleasant
Burlington
Willingboro
Cinnaminson
Mount Holly
Lakehurst
Pennsauken
Browns Mills
Toms River
Gilford Park
Camden
Crestwood Village
Seaside Heights
Cherry Hill
Double Trouble
Haddonfield
First dinosaur skeleton discovered in North America, 1858
Woodbury
Lindenwold
Paulsboro
Pine Hill
Penns Grove
Salem
Glassboro
Williamstown
E.B. FORSYTHE N.W.R.
Surf City
Long Beach
Pennsville
SUPAWNA MEADOWS N.W.R.
Woodstown
Hammonton
E.B. FORSYTHE N.W.R.
Ship Bottom
Salem
PINELANDS NATIONAL RESERVE BOUNDARY
Egg Harbor City
Mystic Island
Beach Haven
GREAT EGG HARBOR NAT. WILD & SCENIC RIVER
Vineland
E.B. FORSYTHE N.W.R.
Bridgeton
Absecon
Mays Landing
Pleasantville
Brigantine
Millville
Atlantic City
MAURICE NAT. WILD & SCENIC RIVER
Ventnor City
Somers Point
Ocean City

DELAWARE

Woodbine
CAPE MAY N.W.R.

ATLANTIC OCEAN

Delaware Bay
Sea Isle City
CAPE MAY N.W.R.
Cape May Court House
Villas
CAPE MAY
North Wildwood
Wildwood
Cape May Canal
Cape May

NEW JERSEY

PINE BARRENS

GARDEN STATE PARKWAY

New Jersey still has 10,000 firms producing a vast array of products.

New Jersey boasts a wide range of landscapes. Its northern third, covered by glaciers 20,000 years ago, is hilly, rocky, and spotted with lakes and wetlands. Ancient 35-mile- (56-km-) long Kittatinny Mountain lines its northwest edge. From Sandy Hook to Cape May, the Jersey Shore sports some of the Atlantic coast's best beaches. Most of southern New Jersey is low coastal plain that supports a people-light, wildlife-heavy region called the Pine Barrens. Called "barren" only because it wasn't good for farming, its forests, bogs, and swamps are home to more than a thousand plant and animal species. In 1978 Congress set aside 1.1 million acres (445,344 ha) as the first national reserve. This wilderness survives in the country's most densely populated state. Despite the state's overall urban and industrial character, dozens of different kinds of fruits and vegetables are grown on nearly 10,000 farms that give it the nickname Garden State. New Jersey ranks in the top five states in output of blueberries, cranberries, peaches, head lettuce, and bell peppers. Produce is either trucked fresh to regional cities or processed in factories.

All ten of New Jersey's largest cities are within 30 miles (48 km) of New York City or Philadelphia. In New Jersey, as across the U.S., people have chosen for decades to leave cities and build suburbs. The state's Smart Growth Plan and other strategies have made it a national leader in efforts to slow this sprawl and protect farmlands. By the end of 2003, a total of 120,000 acres (48,583 ha) of croplands had been preserved. By working to balance the needs of its cities, countryside, and connections to its neighbors, New Jersey seeks a lasting and vital middle ground.

NEW JERSEY
Garden State

STATEHOOD	December 18, 1787; 3rd state
CAPITAL	Trenton
LARGEST CITY	Newark Population 277,000
TOTAL AREA	8,721 sq mi; 22,588 sq km
LAND AREA	7,417 sq mi; 19,211 sq km
POPULATION	8,638,396
POPULATION DENSITY	1,158.1 people per sq mi
MAJOR RACIAL/ ETHNIC GROUPS	72.6% white; 13.6% African American; 5.7% Asian; .2% Native American. Hispanic (any race) 13.3%.
INDUSTRY	machinery, electronics, metal products, chemicals
AGRICULTURE	nursery stock, poultry and eggs, fruits and nuts, vegetables

AMERICAN GOLDFINCH

VIOLET

Did you know?

1. Beneath the Pine Barrens lie aquifers that hold 17 trillion gallons (64 trillion kl) of fresh water.
2. The first dinosaur skeleton found in North America was excavated at Haddonfield in 1858. It was named Hadrosaurus in honor of its discovery site.
3. Cape May became the nation's first seaside resort in 1761. It was named by the Dutch sea captain Cornelius Jacobsen Mey, who explored the region in 1620. In recognition of its well-preserved Victorian houses it was named a National Historic Landmark City in 1976.
4. Famed inventor Thomas Edison filed for more than 400 patents from his laboratory in Menlo Park. During the seven years he worked there, his achievements included perfecting the light bulb and the telephone, inventing the phonograph (record player), and inventing the multiplex telegraph.
5. Early settlers mined the bogs of the Pine Barrens for iron to make nails, kettles, and cannonballs.

NEW YORK

★ *Empire State* ★

GATEWAY TO A NATION. New York has long been America's front door, welcoming millions of people from all over the world to new homes. Now the largest Northeast state in both area and population and long the nation's chief commercial center, New York fits the Empire State nickname given to it by George Washington.

The Appalachians and Adirondacks arc across the state's eastern half, while the Alleghenies rise in the west. Glaciers scooped out Lakes Ontario and Erie as well as the narrow Finger Lakes. Long Island is a great ridge of sand and rock left behind by retreating ice. Western lowlands and broad valleys carved by the Mohawk and Hudson Rivers offer fertile croplands.

Long before Europeans walked its lands, the powerful Iroquois Confederacy and Algonquin-speaking peoples lived here. In 1609 French explorer Samuel de Champlain explored the lake that today bears his name, and Englishman Henry Hudson explored the river now named for him. Acting on Hudson's reports, a Dutch company set up the New Netherland colony, including a settlement near present-day Albany and another on the island of Manhattan. The colony was taken over by the English in 1664 and renamed for England's Duke of York. New York was the site of many conflicts in the French and Indian War. Split loyalties among the Iroquois then and during the American Revolution cost them dearly. They had lost most of their land by the time New York became the 11th state in 1788.

New York City has been the nation's most populous city ever since the first U.S. Census in 1790. The key factor in its 19th-century growth was the digging of the Erie Canal, which by 1825 connected it—via the Hudson River—with Lake Erie and western lands beyond. Vast waves of immigrants flowed to and through New York City. Many newcomers stayed on, making the

1626

Peter Minuit, governor-general of New Amsterdam, bought Manhattan Island for goods worth about 60 Dutch guilders ($24).

1825

The opening of the Erie Canal linked the Atlantic and the Great Lakes, bringing prosperity to New York cities along its route.

1892–1954

More than 17 million people entered the U.S. through Ellis Island (now shared with New Jersey) between 1892 and 1954.

2001

The attack that killed almost 2,800 people and destroyed the World Trade Center changed forever everyday life in America.

Standing nearly 1,453 feet (443 m) tall, the Empire State Building (opposite) has been a towering symbol of New York City since it was completed in 1931. From the tower's 86th-floor observation deck, visitors can see New York and four neighboring states!

The Niagara River is known for its magnificent waterfalls—American, Bridal Veil, and Horseshoe—along the New York-Ontario border. Known collectively as Niagara Falls, they are visited each year by roughly 12 million people. Each minute, an average of 40 million gallons (152 million liters) of water thunder 175 feet (53 m) over its ledges of limestone and shale.

city a "melting pot" of peoples and cultures. African Americans moved to the city from the South in the decades after the Civil War, and the Harlem neighborhood grew into a focal point for black cultural life. Already the nation's leading trade center, New York soon sewed up the top spot in U.S. textile and clothing manufacturing, too. Printing and publishing boomed, and Wall Street in Manhattan became the country's financial hub. The 20th century saw New York City grow into an international stage for theater, television, film, advertising, and music recording. And the United Nations has been headquartered in the city since 1946.

New Yorkers call almost all of the state north of New York City "Upstate," and it's a different world from "The City." A quarter of state lands are devoted to agriculture, including dairy farming, fruits, and vegetables. Only Vermont taps more sugar maples for syrup. Industrial cities include Buffalo, Schenectady, Syracuse, and Utica. Rochester is known for photographic and optical equipment. Tourism is huge in the state, too, with both urban and natural areas drawing visitors year-round.

Today, the state of New York ranks third in population, with the New York City metropolitan area one of the biggest on Earth, with more than 21 million people. Both the city and state are working to rebound from the enormous impacts of the 9/11 terrorist attack. While New York's role as a commerce capital remains, its old industries face long-term decline. The state works to attract new industry and to clean up its natural environments. By 2009, the 400th anniversary of Hudson's voyage, the state plans to restore the long-polluted Hudson River. In New York City's harbor, the Statue of Liberty stands as a beacon of freedom and an invitation to people everywhere.

NEW YORK
Empire State

STATEHOOD	July 26, 1788; 11th state
CAPITAL	Albany
LARGEST CITY	New York City Population 8,084,316
TOTAL AREA	54,556 sq mi; 141,299 sq km
LAND AREA	47,214 sq mi; 122,283 sq km
POPULATION	19,190,115
POPULATION DENSITY	405.8 people per sq mi
MAJOR RACIAL/ ETHNIC GROUPS	67.9% white; 15.9% African American; 5.5% Asian; .4% Native American. Hispanic (any race) 15.1%.
INDUSTRY	printing and publishing, machinery, computer products, finance, tourism
AGRICULTURE	dairy products, cattle and other livestock, vegetables, nursery stock, apples

EASTERN BLUEBIRD   ROSE

Did you know?

1. New York is the only state that borders both the Atlantic Ocean and the Great Lakes.
2. Many men of the Mohawk tribe have a seeming lack of fear of heights that makes them especially suited to working as riveters on steel bridges and skyscrapers. The Empire State Building, the George Washington Bridge, and Rockefeller Center are among the many structures they have helped build.
3. Adirondack State Park is the largest state park in the country. It is almost as big as Yellowstone, Yosemite, Grand Canyon, and Olympic National Parks combined.
4. The Finger Lakes, a series of glacially carved lakes in upstate New York, bear the names of various Native American tribes, including the Seneca, Cayuga, and Canandaigua. The region is second only to California in the production of grapes.

PENNSYLVANIA

★ *Keystone State* ★

THE KEYSTONE STATE. To a builder, the keystone is at the center of an arch, the stone that binds the others together. Pennsylvania was key to the nation's successful start, and a major force in holding the Union together during its toughest time.

William Penn's heavily forested colony was named for his father, Admiral William Penn. (*Sylvania* is a Latin word meaning "woodlands.") In 1682, the younger William brought 500 settlers who believed in religious freedom and a fair government to form this 12th of the 13 English colonies. Penn treated Native Americans with respect, signing a fair treaty with Delaware chiefs. In 1701, the colony's Charter of Privilege gave its elected assembly greater power than any other in the English world. Though Penn was a Quaker, people of other religions were welcome. The colony expanded farther west, too. There, settlers met resistance from native peoples and the French. These conflicts did not end until 1763, after the French and Indian War.

Pennsylvania's lands were packed with resources above and below ground. Beech and maple uplands plus lowlands of oak and hickory made up "Penn's woods." Fertile valley soils, especially in the southeast, proved perfect for grain and dairy farming. Coal, iron, limestone, and oil supplied the minerals for industry. The many rivers and streams—and later a link to Lake Erie—offered water power and transportation.

Wealthy, populous Pennsylvania took center stage in the move to gain independence. Representatives from the 13 Colonies met in Philadelphia to adopt the Declaration of Independence, which local resident Benjamin Franklin helped draft. Pennsylvania became the second state in 1787. In the next century, the stately merchant city of Philadelphia became a brawny industrial giant—Workshop of the

1682

William Penn founded his colony in 1682 on land west of the Delaware River granted to him by King Charles I in a charter.

1863

At Gettysburg, the Union withstood "Pickett's Charge," stopping the South's advance. This was the turning point in the Civil War.

1870–1970S

Pittsburgh grew to be a steel powerhouse. By 1900, the city's mill workers turned out two-thirds of the country's steel.

1979

The near-disaster at the Three Mile Island nuclear power plant near Harrisburg stopped all U.S. development of nuclear plants.

Though a crack ended its ringing days, no symbol of freedom could ring truer than the Liberty Bell—Philadelphia's top attraction. While London-made, it became clearly American when it was rung at the first public reading of the Declaration of Independence.

"Penn's woods" are wildlife-rich. One of the largest deer populations in the country and thousands of black bears live along its forested ridges. Elk, once eliminated from the state, have made a difficult and finally successful return. But the state's best-known animal is the world's most famous groundhog. In a playful 117-year tradition, Punxsutawney Phil (left) sees his shadow on February 2, 2004. His prediction: six more weeks of winter!

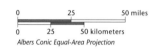

0   25   50 miles
0   25   50 kilometers
Albers Conic Equal-Area Projection

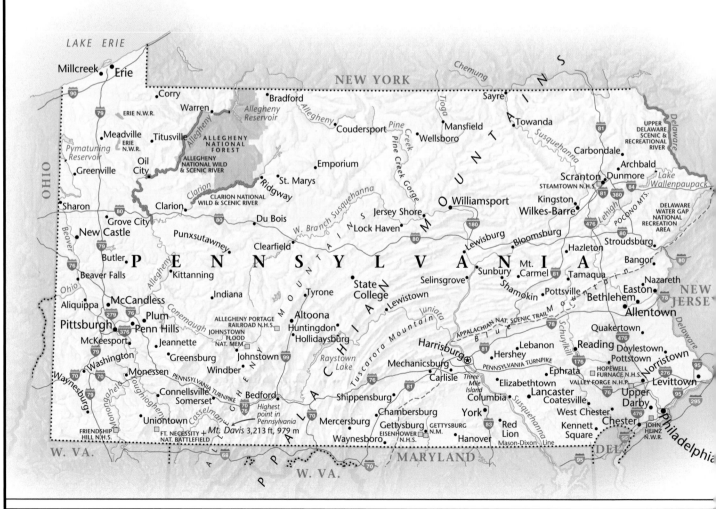

World. It launched steamships, rolled out locomotives, and milled textiles, clothing, paper, and more. Immigrants came from Ireland, Germany, and elsewhere. Located at the junction of three rivers, Pittsburgh used in-state coal and Great Lakes iron ore to make iron and later steel. Other cities boomed, too, making a thousand different products. The state contributed huge volumes of material and tens of thousands of soldiers to the Civil War.

After the war the industrial boom continued, and waves of immigrants poured in from Europe and the rural South to work in the state's mines and factories. Owners became wealthy, but life was tough and often dangerous for workers. To gain safer working conditions and better pay, labor unions were formed, leading to violent strikes in the late 1800s and early 1900s. Though industrial success continued through the two world wars, the steel industry began to decline. Less coal was needed as the steel business moved overseas, where it could be made more cheaply.

Today, Pittsburgh's mills are gone, but the city still has advanced manufacturing—plus world-class medical and life sciences research. Philadelphia is becoming a center for information technology and financial services. But Pennsylvania is still a mining and industrial force, ranking fourth in coal production and fifth in steel output. It's an agricultural state, too, with 50,000 farms producing dairy products, fresh vegetables, and eggs. Tourists increasingly find the state's rural landscapes, plentiful wild spaces, and key historic sites unbeatable destinations. Though Pennsylvania is a different fit now from when Penn and Franklin walked its cobblestones, the Keystone State still has a key place in the workings of the nation.

PENNSYLVANIA
Keystone State

STATEHOOD	December 12, 1787; 2nd state
CAPITAL	Harrisburg
LARGEST CITY	Philadelphia Population 1,492,231
TOTAL AREA	46,055 sq mi; 119,283 sq km
LAND AREA	44,817 sq mi; 116,075 sq km
POPULATION	12,365,455
POPULATION DENSITY	275.2 people per sq mi
MAJOR RACIAL/ ETHNIC GROUPS	85.4% white; 10.0% African American; 1.8% Asian; .1% Native American. Hispanic (any race) 3.2%.
INDUSTRY	machinery, printing and publishing, forest products, metal products
AGRICULTURE	dairy products, poultry and eggs, mushrooms, cattle, hogs, grains

RUFFED GROUSE

MOUNTAIN LAUREL

Did you know?

1. Edwin Drake launched the petroleum industry when he drilled the first oil well in 1859 at Titusville.
2. During the American Revolution, the Liberty Bell was moved from Philadelphia to Allentown. It was returned after the British evacuated Philadelphia.
3. Hershey is known as the Chocolate Capital of the World. Among its most popular candies are Hershey's Kisses. Between its factory in Hershey and the one in Oakdale, California, the company can turn out 33 million of these candies each day.
4. The first federal building whose construction was specifically authorized by the Constitution was the U.S. Mint. Philadelphia was selected for the site because, when construction began in 1792, it was the nation's capital. It is believed that some of the silver used in making the first silver coins was donated by President George Washington, who lived a few blocks from the mint at the time.

RHODE ISLAND

★ *Ocean State* ★

SMALL SPACE, SPECIAL PLACE. Rhode Island is the smallest state in area—tinier than some *counties* in other states—but it's founded on freedoms still revered across the nation. There's much that makes Rhode Island special.

The Dutch explored the coastline in 1614—possibly giving it the name *Roodt Eylandt* (Red Island)—but it was Roger Williams who began white settlement there in 1636. Forced to leave Massachusetts because he disagreed with its Puritan leaders, Williams wanted to create a place of religious freedom. He obtained land along a large bay from the Narragansett people, naming his community Providence. Other like-minded people later established Newport, Portsmouth, and Warwick. The settlements joined together for protection. Over time, relations with the Indians worsened. King Philip's War ended native resistance to white settlement in 1676.

Rhode Island steered an independent course as a colony, avoiding outside affairs. But the people soon realized that such connections were needed and began trading their harvests and catches for goods from other colonies and countries. In the 1700s, Newport emerged as the leading port in the very profitable "triangle trade," in which ships carrying lumber to the West Indies returned with molasses for making rum. Rum was then sent to Africa in exchange for slaves. In the 1780s a state law banned the slave trade and provided for the gradual emancipation of children of slaves.

In the first years of the United States, Rhode Island's independent attitude kept it from signing the Constitution. It pressed for greater freedom of worship and other rights, for slavery to be abolished, for changes in trade rules and in taxes, and for a method of representation in Congress that was not based on

1636

Roger Williams founded Rhode Island and Providence Plantations and also wrote America's first document separating church and state.

1793

Samuel Slater's use of water to power a cotton mill started the industrial revolution in the U.S. and New England's textile empire.

1890s

The Breakers was one of several "cottages" built in Newport by wealthy business barons from New York in the 1890s.

Present day

Providence's worn-out harbor area has been revitalized by an award-winning urban renewal project called Waterplace Park.

Historical home of the America's Cup yacht races, Newport still hosts sailing crews from across the globe. Here, the crew of the Spirit of Rhode Island *enjoys a sun-splashed day on the water.*

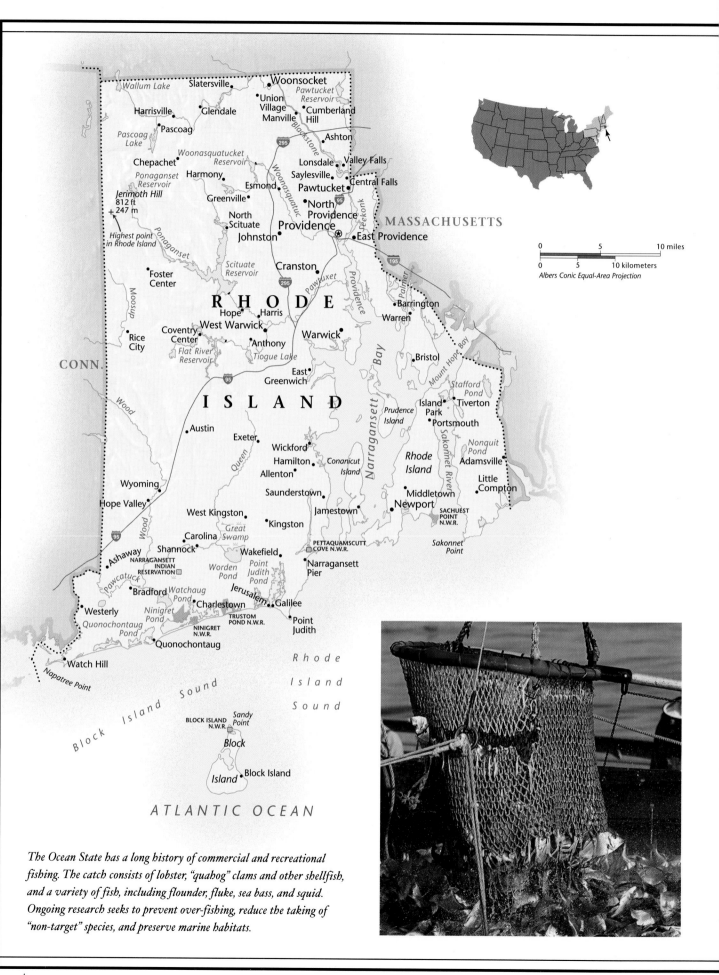

Wallum Lake
Slatersville
Woonsocket
Pawtucket
Reservoir
Harrisville
Glendale
Union
Village
Cumberland
Manville
Hill
Pascoag
Lake
Pascoag
Ashton
Chepachet
Woonasquatucket
Reservoir
Lonsdale
Valley Falls
Ponaganset
Reservoir
Harmony
Saylesville
Central Falls
Esmond
Pawtucket
Jerimoth Hill
Greenville
North
812 ft
Providence
+ 247 m
North
Scituate
MASSACHUSETTS
Highest point
in Rhode Island
Providence
Johnston
East Providence

R H O D E

Foster
Center
Scituate
Reservoir
Cranston
Barrington
Moosup
Warren
Hope
Harris
Bristol
West Warwick
CONN.
Rice
City
Coventry
Center
Anthony
Warwick
Flat River
Reservoir
Tiogue Lake
Mount Hope Bay
Wood

I S L A N D

East
Greenwich
Stafford
Pond
Austin
Island
Park
Tiverton
Exeter
Wickford
Prudence
Island
Portsmouth
Nonquit
Pond
Hamilton
Conanicut
Island
Rhode
Island
Adamsville
Wyoming
Allenton
Little
Compton
Hope Valley
Saunderstown
Middletown
West Kingston
Jamestown
Newport
SACHUEST
POINT
N.W.R.
Carolina
Kingston
Great
Swamp
PETTAQUAMSCUTT
COVE N.W.R.
Sakonnet
Point
Ashaway
Shannock
Wakefield
NARRAGANSETT
INDIAN
RESERVATION
Worden
Pond
Point
Judith
Pond
Narragansett
Pier
Bradford
Watchaug
Pond
Jerusalem
Galilee
Westerly
Ninigret
Pond
Charlestown
Point
Judith
Quonochontaug
Pond
TRUSTOM
POND N.W.R.
NINIGRET
N.W.R.
Quonochontaug
Rhode
Watch Hill
Island
Napatree Point
Sound
Block Island Sound

BLOCK ISLAND
N.W.R.
Sandy
Point
Block
Block Island
Island

ATLANTIC OCEAN

*The Ocean State has a long history of commercial and recreational
fishing. The catch consists of lobster, "quahog" clams and other shellfish,
and a variety of fish, including flounder, fluke, sea bass, and squid.
Ongoing research seeks to prevent over-fishing, reduce the taking of
"non-target" species, and preserve marine habitats.*

population alone. With the addition of the Bill of Rights and the provision that each state would have two Senators in Congress plus a number of Representatives based on state population, Rhode Island finally signed the Constitution in 1790 and became the 13th state.

Rhode Island had what was needed to be a leader in the new U.S. economy: wealth from trade, power from its rivers, and cheap labor. Dozens of textile mill towns prospered, attracting immigrants first from Ireland, England, and Scotland and later from Italy and Portugal. Providence, linked by sea and rail, became Rhode Island's biggest commercial center. Newport developed as a vacation spot for the wealthy. In spite of its cotton-trade ties to the South, the state's anti-slavery stand made it a Union supporter in the Civil War.

Textiles began a gradual decline that continued into the 20th century. Labor strikes caused by a gap between wealthy business owners and poor workers developed in the 1920s. Tough times continued during the Depression. World War II helped the state's economy, but it suffered later when military bases were closed in the 1970s.

In recent years, Rhode Island has seen economic improvement. It has a thriving jewelry and silverware industry and manufactures electronics, scientific instruments, machines, and some textiles. Like other old industrial states, Rhode Island is switching to a more service-based economy. Biotechnology is growing, and the state is working to preserve the environment of Narragansett Bay, source of much of its wealth. The Ocean State also looks to expand tourism, drawing visitors with its rich history and a variety of water sports. No place in this small state is more than a half-hour drive from the ocean or bay—something special that no big state can match.

RHODE ISLAND
Ocean State

STATEHOOD	May 29, 1790; 13th state
CAPITAL	Providence
LARGEST CITY	Providence Population 175,901
TOTAL AREA	1,545 sq mi; 4,002 sq km
LAND AREA	1,045 sq mi; 2,706 sq km
POPULATION	1,076,164
POPULATION DENSITY	1,023.7 people per sq mi
MAJOR RACIAL/ ETHNIC GROUPS	85.0% white; 4.5% African American; 2.3% Asian; .5% Native American. Hispanic (any race) 8.7%.
INDUSTRY	health services, business services, silver and jewelry products, metal products
AGRICULTURE	nursery stock, vegetables, dairy products, eggs

RHODE ISLAND RED

VIOLET

Did you know?

1. The Rhode Island Red was one of the first chicken breeds developed to increase the quality and quantity of egg and meat production.
2. In colonial times, Providence was an important port in the Triangle Trade, which centered on slaves, sugar products—especially molasses—and rum. The Sugar Act of 1764 threatened Rhode Island's economy and caused the colony to be among the first to push for an end to British rule.
3. The Quonset hut takes its name from Quonset Point, the Naval Air Station on Narragansett Bay where this type of structure was first built.
4. The rights guaranteed to all Americans in the First Amendment to the Constitution, including freedom of religion, speech, and assembly, were among the rights promised much earlier to settlers in Rhode Island by Roger Williams, the colony's founder.

VERMONT

★ *Green Mountain State* ★

GREEN MOUNTAIN MAJESTY. When the French explorer Samuel de Champlain viewed a ridge of a long, forest-cloaked dividing range, he called it *vert mont*—"green mountain." Ever since, these granite and green slopes of the northern Appalachians have defined the region. Still four-fifths wooded and split north to south by rugged lines of peaks, Vermont proudly wears its nickname: Green Mountain State.

The only New England state without direct access to the Atlantic, Vermont has a freshwater sea instead: Lake Champlain. Shared with New York and Quebec, the glacially-carved, 120-mile- (193-km-) long lake is the sixth-largest in the country. Vermont has plentiful water elsewhere, too. Among its many rivers, the Connecticut forms the state's long eastern boundary. Vermont's northern location and high ridges bring heavy snows during cold winters. Cool, short summers and poor, rocky soils limit most agriculture to lake and river lowlands.

The French traded in the area and built their first settlement in 1666, but it did not last. In 1724 the English founded Fort Dummer near present-day Brattleboro. The two empires fought over Vermont, with the French retreating to Canada at the close of the French and Indian War in 1763. Shaped like a rocky wedge between New York and New Hampshire, Vermont once divided those colonies. Each wanted the territory, and they actually fought over Vermont. Among the battlers was fiercely proud Ethan Allen, who at first led efforts to join these lands to New Hampshire. But once the Revolutionary War began, he and his Green Mountain Boys switched to fight the British. Allen's daring capture of Fort Ticonderoga sparked early war efforts by patriots all across New England and beyond.

1609

Samuel de Champlain, with the aid of Huron people, was the first European to explore the region, claiming it for France.

1775

Ethan Allen and his Green Mountain Boys won fame by capturing Fort Ticonderoga, on Lake Champlain, from the British.

1811–1850s

Merino sheep imported from Spain gave rise to woolen mills and made the breed the state's chief livestock animal until the 1850s.

Present day

Tourism is now a top state business. This snowboarder competed in the 2001 Winter X-Games, which attracted huge crowds.

It's county fair time in Tunbridge, a classic New England small town (opposite). In Vermont such communities are known for their tradition of "town meetings"—gatherings where every citizen can have a say in local issues, such as education and taxes.

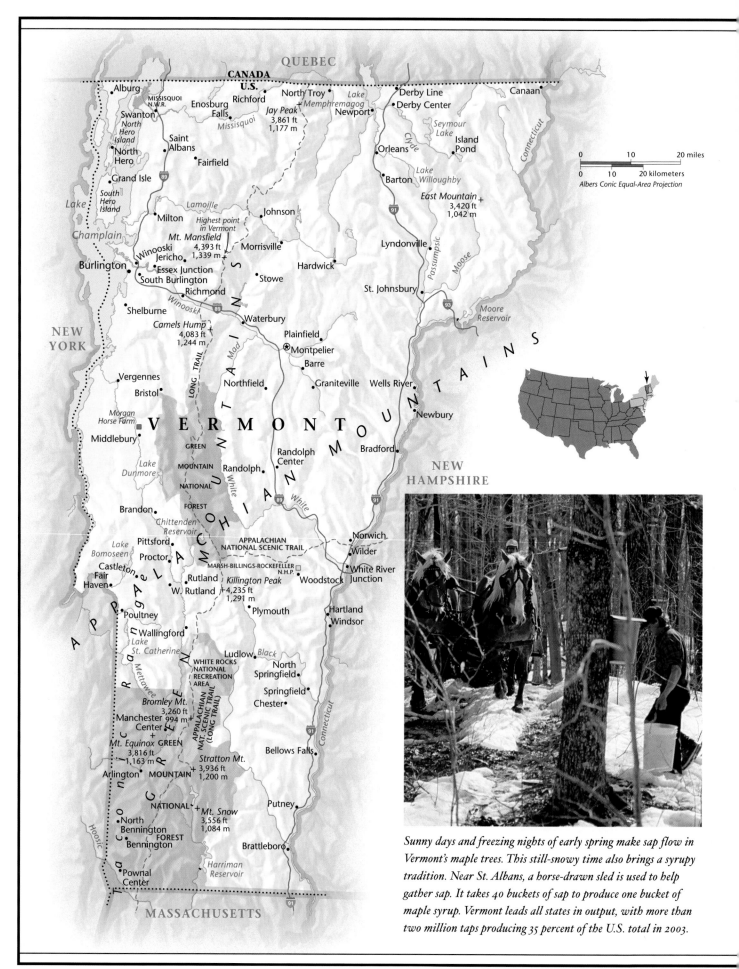

QUEBEC

CANADA
U.S.

Alburg
Richford
North Troy
Derby Line
Canaan

MISSISQUOI N.W.R.
Enosburg Falls
Lake Memphremagog
Derby Center

Swanton
Missisquoi
Jay Peak
3,861 ft
1,177 m
Newport

North Hero Island
Saint Albans
Seymour Lake

North Hero
Fairfield
Orleans
Island Pond

Grand Isle
Barton
Lake Willoughby

Lamoille
Johnson
East Mountain +
3,420 ft
1,042 m

Lake Champlain
Milton
Highest point in Vermont
Mt. Mansfield
4,393 ft
1,339 m +
Morrisville
Lyndonville
Moose

Burlington
Winooski
Jericho
Hardwick
Passumpsic

Essex Junction
Stowe
St. Johnsbury

South Burlington
Richmond
Waterbury

Shelburne
Winooski
Plainfield
Moore Reservoir

NEW YORK
Camels Hump
4,083 ft
1,244 m
Mad
Montpelier
Barre

Vergennes
Northfield
Graniteville
Wells River

Bristol
Randolph Center
Newbury

Morgan Horse Farm
V E R M O N T   M o u n t a i n s

Middlebury
GREEN
Randolph
Bradford

Lake Dunmore
MOUNTAIN
White
NEW HAMPSHIRE

Brandon
NATIONAL
White

FOREST
Chittenden Reservoir

Pittsford
APPALACHIAN NATIONAL SCENIC TRAIL
Norwich
Wilder

Proctor
MARSH-BILLINGS-ROCKEFELLER N.H.P.
White River Junction

Castleton
Rutland
Killington Peak
+ 4,235 ft
1,291 m
Woodstock

Fair Haven
W. Rutland
Hartland
Windsor

Poultney
Plymouth

Wallingford
Lake St. Catherine
Ludlow
Black
North Springfield

WHITE ROCKS NATIONAL RECREATION AREA
Springfield
Chester

Mettawee
Bromley Mt.
3,260 ft
994 m
APPALACHIAN NAT. SCENIC TRAIL (LONG TRAIL)

Manchester Center
Mt. Equinox GREEN
3,816 ft
1,163 m
Stratton Mt.
+ 3,936 ft
1,200 m
Bellows Falls

Arlington MOUNTAIN

NATIONAL + Mt. Snow
3,556 ft
1,084 m
Putney

North Bennington
FOREST
Hoosic

Bennington
Brattleboro

Pownal Center
Harriman Reservoir

MASSACHUSETTS

Sunny days and freezing nights of early spring make sap flow in Vermont's maple trees. This still-snowy time also brings a syrupy tradition. Near St. Albans, a horse-drawn sled is used to help gather sap. It takes 40 buckets of sap to produce one bucket of maple syrup. Vermont leads all states in output, with more than two million taps producing 35 percent of the U.S. total in 2003.

Vermonters' independent attitudes caused them to declare freedom not just from British rule in 1777, but from all their neighbors, too. After some talk of joining with Canada, Vermont joined the U.S. as the 14th state in 1791. Montpelier became its capital in 1805. Stability brought more immigrants to Vermont, and sheep farming and woolen mills proved successful for the first half of the 19th century. Railroads arrived in 1849 to help tranport Vermont resources.

Vermont's geology plays a key role in its economy. The world's largest granite quarry (east of Barre) and the largest underground marble quarry (near Danby) produce building stone. Above ground, Vermont's green treasures include hardwoods for furniture and softwoods for pulp and paper. Milk and cheese are produced from dairy herds grazed on mountain pastures. For years, tourists have enjoyed the state's country roads, hiking trails, water activities, and winter sports. In recent decades, computer and other high-tech companies have found Burlington and other Vermont cities fine spots to locate operations.

Vermonters have traditionally blazed their own path in politics, and ideas born here often led the country. Vermont's 1777 constitution banned slavery and gave the vote to all men even if they did not own land—two ideas that were way ahead of their time. By 1970 Vermont was a national leader in environmental legislation. Today the state struggles to balance environmental protection and economic growth. Recent problems include an increase in part-time residents who bring money to the state but reduce its rural nature, the loss of dairy farms, and pollution. Success in preserving Vermont's natural resources will safeguard opportunities for future generations of Green Mountain boys and girls.

VERMONT
Green Mountain State

STATEHOOD	March 4, 1791; 14th state
CAPITAL	Montpelier
LARGEST CITY	Burlington Population 39,466
TOTAL AREA	9,614 sq mi; 24,901 sq km
LAND AREA	4,845 sq mi; 23,956 sq km
POPULATION	619,107
POPULATION DENSITY	66.7 people per sq mi
MAJOR RACIAL/ ETHNIC GROUPS	96.8% white; .9% Asian; .5% African American; .4% Native American. Hispanic (any race) .9%.
INDUSTRY	health services, tourism, finance, real estate, computer components, electrical parts, printing and publishing, machine tools
AGRICULTURE	dairy products, maple products, apples

HERMIT THRUSH

RED CLOVER

Did you know?

1. Almost three-quarters of Vermont's electricity is generated by the nuclear power plant at Vernon, south of Brattleboro, along the Connecticut River.
2. From 1777 until it became a state in 1791, Vermont had its own postal and monetary systems.
3. Morgan horses, an American breed known for its stamina, vigor, and all-purpose usefulness, have been raised on farms throughout Vermont since just after the Revolution. The First Vermont Cavalry rode Morgans in the Civil War, and Confederate General Stonewall Jackson's horse "Little Sorrel" was a Morgan.
4. The Long Trail is a 265-mile- (412-km-) long hiking trail that runs along the ridges of the Green Mountains for the entire length of the state.
5. Vermont has never been heavily populated. Today, only Wyoming has fewer residents.

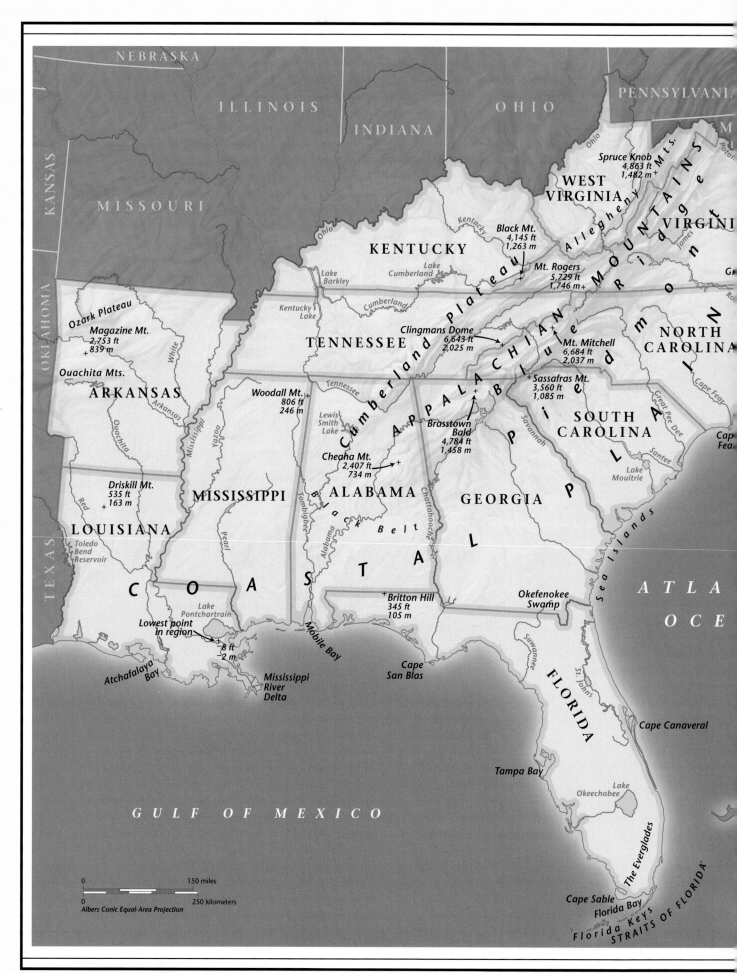

NEBRASKA

ILLINOIS

INDIANA

OHIO

PENNSYLVANIA

KANSAS

MISSOURI

WEST
VIRGINIA

Ohio

Spruce Knob
4,863 ft
1,482 m +

Allegheny Mts.

VIRGINI

KENTUCKY

Kentucky

Black Mt.
4,145 ft
1,263 m

Mt. Rogers
5,729 ft
1,746 m +

OKLAHOMA

Ozark Plateau

Magazine Mt.
2,753 ft
+ 839 m

Ouachita Mts.

*Lake
Barkley*

*Lake
Cumberland*

Cumberland

TENNESSEE

*Kentucky
Lake*

Clingmans Dome
6,643 ft
2,025 m

Mt. Mitchell
6,684 ft
2,037 m

NORTH
CAROLINA

Great Pee Dee

Cape Fear

White

ARKANSAS

Arkansas

Tennessee

Woodall Mt.
806 ft
246 m +

*Lewis
Smith
Lake*

Sassafras Mt.
3,560 ft
1,085 m

SOUTH
CAROLINA

Cap
Fea

Ouachita

Mississippi

Yazoo

Brasstown
Bald
4,784 ft
1,458 m

Savannah

Santee

*Lake
Moultrie*

Driskill Mt.
535 ft
+ 163 m

Red

MISSISSIPPI

ALABAMA

Cheaha Mt.
2,407 ft
734 m +

GEORGIA

Chattahoochee

LOUISIANA

Pearl

Black

Belt

Sea Islands

ATLA
OCE

Toledo
Bend
Reservoir

C   O   A   S   T   A   L

Britton Hill
345 ft
105 m

Okefenokee
Swamp

TEXAS

*Lake
Pontchartrain*

Lowest point
in region

−8 ft
−2 m

Mobile Bay

Suwannee

Cape
San Blas

FLORIDA

Cape Canaveral

Atchafalaya
Bay

Mississippi
River
Delta

Tampa Bay

*Lake
Okeechobee*

GULF   OF   MEXICO

The Everglades

0   150 miles

0   250 kilometers

Albers Conic Equal-Area Projection

Cape Sable
Florida Bay

Florida Keys

STRAITS OF FLORIDA

The Southeast

ROUNDED MOUNTAINS, big rivers, and fertile plains characterize the Southeast. Southern ranges of the Appalachians—the Allegheny, Blue Ridge, and Cumberland Plateau—form a divide through the region. Streams flowing west of this divide join and enlarge the mighty Mississippi. Those draining east cross the Piedmont to a coastal plain that wraps around the southern tip of the Appalachians to Louisiana's Gulf Coast—a watery world of meandering rivers, deltas, swamps, and barrier islands.

West of the Mississippi the Ouachita Mountains and Ozark Plateau overlook Arkansas. The Florida peninsula is built on a limestone foundation punctuated by numerous lakes, sinkholes, islands, and America's most famous swamp—the Everglades. Throughout the Southeast needle-leaf, broadleaf, and mixed forests thrive in a mostly mild climate where rainfall occurs in every month.

Tradition and Change Between Two Coasts

ABUNDANT natural resources have always shaped how people live in this well-watered land. Native Cherokee, Shawnee, Choctaw, and Seminole tribes thrived by hunting in the forest, fishing, and gathering fruits, nuts, and berries that appear to grow everywhere. Many tribes also planted the "three sisters"—corn, squash, and beans.

Europeans arrived from three directions. Spain's Ponce de León reached Florida in 1513. By 1565 the Spanish had founded the first permanent colony in America at St. Augustine, Florida—55 years before the Pilgrims landed in Massachusetts. In 1673 two Frenchmen, missionary Jacques Marquette and explorer Louis Joliet, paddled down the Mississippi River to the mouth of the Arkansas River. Within a decade France claimed the entire area drained by the Mississippi River. The English colonized Virginia in the early 1600s and slowly extended settlements south to Georgia by the 1730s. Although the Europeans were few in number, their guns and "Old World" diseases such as smallpox devastated Indian populations.

The colonists quickly took advantage of the natural resources. They planted tobacco on the fertile coastal lands, mined rich deposits of coal and iron ore in the Appalachians, and turned marshlands into rice fields. The rivers plus Atlantic and Gulf waters were chock-full of fish, while the broadleaf and pine forests yielded plenty of game and timber. Along the fall line, where Appalachian streams tumble from the Piedmont onto the Atlantic Coastal Plain, water-powered factories helped cities such as Richmond and Raleigh prosper.

Spanish and French control of the Southeast dwindled in the late 1700s. After frontiersman Daniel Boone blazed the Wilderness Road across the Appalachians in 1775, American farmers migrated into the Kentucky, Ohio, and Tennessee River Valleys. Elsewhere the rise of tobacco and cotton created a plantation economy dependent upon slave labor. East of the Appalachians fine seaports promoted trade with the Northeast and Europe, while areas west of the mountains turned to the Ohio and Mississippi Rivers. To open lands for settlers in the 1830s, the government forced thousands of Native Americans westward along what became known as the Trail of Tears.

By 1850 a diverse mix of people of European heritage firmly controlled this thriving region. However, by 1861 tensions over slavery between northern and southern states erupted in Civil War. All the states in this region except Kentucky and West Virginia seceded from the Union to form the Confederacy. The Union victory after four years of war left most of the region in ruins for the next half century.

By the 1930s two events changed the Southeast. The first was a 1920s plague of boll weevils that devastated cotton crops and forced farmers to diversify. The second was the Tennessee Valley Authority, which built dams to control flooding and provide power. The abundant electricity coupled with nonunion labor and air-conditioning attracted northern-based companies and people—a process that still continues.

Today, crops like Georgia peaches, Louisiana rice, and Florida oranges are known worldwide. The region also produces varied products such as Arkansas chickens, Kentucky racehorses, North Carolina timber, and oil along the Gulf Coast. Sandy coastal beaches attract visitors. Cities such as Atlanta, New Orleans, Miami, and Raleigh-Durham are leaders in business, research, and tourism.

All this development has brought water shortages, pollution, and crowded commutes, but it is also a sure sign that the Southeast is thriving again.

> "...Louisiana bayous,... sun, cotton fields, lonesome roads, train whistles in the night,...."
>
> LANGSTON HUGHES, *"Music at Year's End,"* The Chicago Defender, *January 9, 1943*

A shady lane of stately oak trees stretches to the white columns and porches of this restored Louisiana plantation home (above). Built in 1839, the mansion provides a glimpse into the lifestyle of wealthy Southerners before the Civil War brought lasting change.

ALABAMA
★ Heart of Dixie ★

"OH, I WISH I was in the land of cotton, old times there are not forgotten!" So begins the famous song, "Dixie," a favorite of Confederate troops as they battled to maintain their way of life. Today, Alabama's nickname is Heart of Dixie, which fits as well in today's South as when the state anchored the Confederate States of America.

The Spanish explored the region in the 1500s, but it was the French who established the first permanent European settlement along Mobile Bay in 1702. They named the region for Indians who called themselves "Alibamu." The British won control of the land after the French and Indian War, but lost it to the U.S. after the Revolution. Andrew Jackson's defeat of Creek warriors in the War of 1812 and the rising demand for cotton spurred immigration from Tennessee and Georgia. The Territory of Alabama was formed in 1817 and became a state two years later. Native Americans were forced to relocate to Oklahoma during the 1830s.

Alabamans settled a state of mostly low, rolling plains. The rugged southern reaches of the Cumberland Plateau and the Appalachian Mountains stretch into the northeast. Except for the Tennessee River, which arcs through Alabama's northern districts, most rivers flow from northeast to southwest, emptying into Mobile Bay. Spanning the middle is the Black Belt, a band of rich, dark soil that made cotton Alabama's chief crop. Wealthy landowners, using slaves for labor, established big plantations in fertile bottomlands. They led the state to secession from the Union in 1861.

The Confederacy's government was formed in Montgomery, which acted as its capital for a time. Selma was a center of ammunition manufacture, and Mobile was a critical port. The Civil War cost 15,000 Alabama soldiers their

1813–1814

Defeated after the massacre of settlers at Fort Nims, the Creek people were forced to give up their lands to the U.S. government.

1880

Alabama's iron and steel industry was launched with the opening of Birmingham's first blast furnace, Alice No. 1.

1955

When Rosa Parks refused to give up her bus seat to a white man in Montgomery, her arrest was a key event in the civil rights movement.

Present day

U.S. Space Camp, in Huntsville, is one of several NASA programs that provide jobs and revenue for the state.

Cave-dwelling peoples lived for nearly 8,000 years in the rugged region around DeSoto Falls (opposite) in northeastern Alabama. Named for Spanish gold seeker Hernando de Soto, who trekked through in 1540, it is part of Little River Canyon National Preserve.

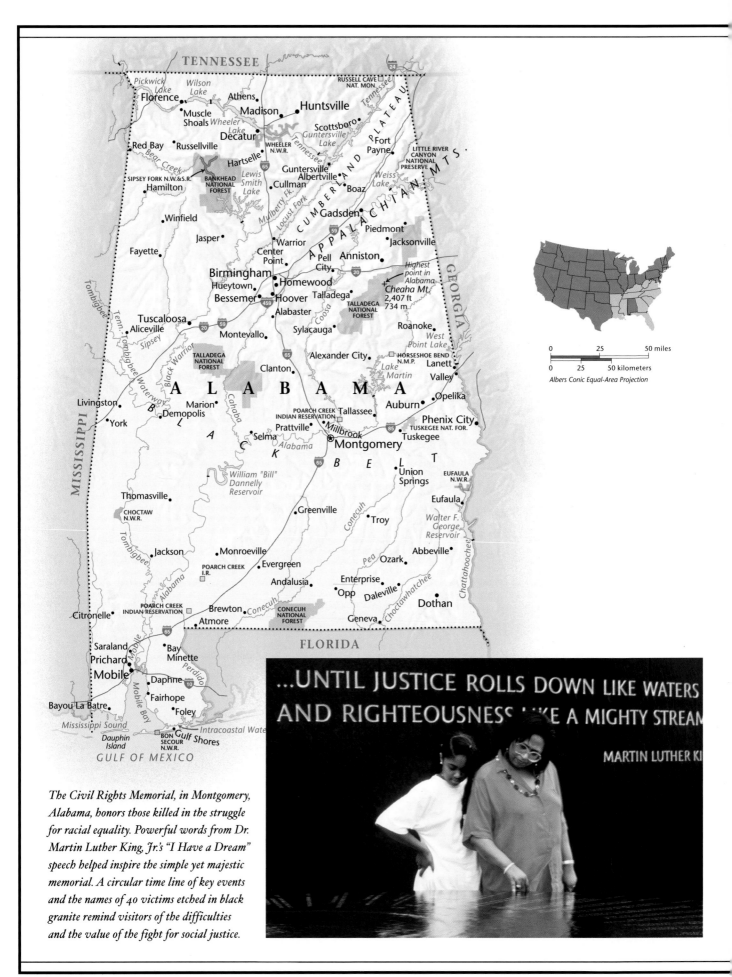

TENNESSEE

Pickwick Lake
Wilson Lake
Florence
Athens
Muscle Shoals
Madison
Huntsville
Wheeler Lake
Decatur
Scottsboro
Guntersville Lake
Fort Payne
RUSSELL CAVE NAT. MON.
Red Bay
Russellville
WHEELER N.W.R.
Hartselle
LITTLE RIVER CANYON NATIONAL PRESERVE
Bear Creek
BANKHEAD NATIONAL FOREST
Guntersville
Albertville
Boaz
SIPSEY FORK N.W.&S.R.
Lewis Smith Lake
Cullman
Hamilton
Weiss Lake
Winfield
Mulberry Fk.
Gadsden
Piedmont
Jasper
Locust Fork
Warrior
Jacksonville
Fayette
Center Point
Pell City
Anniston
Birmingham
Hueytown
Homewood
Highest point in Alabama
Bessemer
Hoover
Talladega
Cheaha Mt. 2,407 ft 734 m
Alabaster
TALLADEGA NATIONAL FOREST
Tuscaloosa
Aliceville
Montevallo
Sylacauga
Roanoke
Tenn-Tombigbee
Sipsey
West Point Lake
TALLADEGA NATIONAL FOREST
Clanton
Alexander City
HORSESHOE BEND N.M.P.
Lanett
Livingston
Marion
Lake Martin
Valley
A L A B A M A
York
Demopolis
POORCH CREEK INDIAN RESERVATION
Tallassee
Auburn
Opelika
Black Warrior
Prattville
TUSKEGEE NAT. FOR.
Phenix City
Selma
Millbrook
Tuskegee
Alabama
Montgomery
William "Bill" Dannelly Reservoir
B E L T
Union Springs
EUFAULA N.W.R.
Thomasville
Greenville
Eufaula
CHOCTAW N.W.R.
Conecuh
Troy
Walter F. George Reservoir
Tombigbee
Jackson
Monroeville
Pea
Ozark
Abbeville
POORCH CREEK I.R.
Evergreen
Andalusia
Enterprise
Daleville
Dothan
Alabama
Opp
Choctawhatchee
Citronelle
POORCH CREEK INDIAN RESERVATION
Brewton
Conecuh
CONECUH NATIONAL FOREST
Geneva
Chattahoochee
Atmore
FLORIDA
Saraland
Bay Minette
Prichard
Mobile
Daphne
Bayou La Batre
Fairhope
Foley
Mississippi Sound
BON SECOUR N.W.R.
Gulf Shores
Intracoastal Wate
Dauphin Island
GULF OF MEXICO

MISSISSIPPI
GEORGIA

0   25   50 miles
0   25   50 kilometers
Albers Conic Equal-Area Projection

The Civil Rights Memorial, in Montgomery, Alabama, honors those killed in the struggle for racial equality. Powerful words from Dr. Martin Luther King, Jr.'s "I Have a Dream" speech helped inspire the simple yet majestic memorial. A circular time line of key events and the names of 40 victims etched in black granite remind visitors of the difficulties and the value of the fight for social justice.

...UNTIL JUSTICE ROLLS DOWN LIKE WATERS AND RIGHTEOUSNESS LIKE A MIGHTY STREAM

MARTIN LUTHER KI

lives. Post-war Reconstruction brought corrupt governments and the persistence of racial inequalities and injustices. It also saw the rise of Birmingham as the "Pittsburgh of the South" as railroads carried Alabama coal, iron ore, and limestone to the city's steel mills. But it took a tiny insect to spark a transformation in the economy.

In the 1920s the boll weevil destroyed the cotton harvest. Together with declining soil fertility caused by planting cotton year after year, the weevil infestation forced farmers to finally break away from a single crop. Cotton is still important, but so are peanuts, sweet potatoes, pecans, chickens, and pond-raised catfish. Vast stands of oak and pine support a giant forest-products industry. Beginning in 1933, the Tennessee Valley Authority's Mussel Shoals dam provided plentiful and cheap electricity. The completion of the Tennessee-Tombigbee Waterway in 1985 dramatically increased barge traffic by linking the Tennessee River and Mobile Bay. Huntsville has attracted space-related and high-tech businesses since NASA's Marshall Space Flight Center opened in 1960.

Alabama's 4.5 million people have not forgotten their state's past. More than one-fourth of the population is African American, and those who are old enough remember terrible days of violence and racial injustice. But in the 1950s and 1960s gains in voting and other civil rights were achieved across the country.

The economy continues to diversify. An auto assembly plant built in the 1990s has doubled production. Efforts are underway to bolster military bases, increase Mobile's cruise ship and container-port facilities, and expand the state's space industry. While learning from its "old times" Alabama is marching forward to new and better ones.

ALABAMA
Heart of Dixie

STATEHOOD	December 14, 1819; 22nd state
CAPITAL	Montgomery
LARGEST CITY	Birmingham Population 239,416
TOTAL AREA	52,419 sq mi; 135,765 sq km
LAND AREA	50,744 sq mi; 131,426 sq km
POPULATION	4,500,752
POPULATION DENSITY	88.4 people per sq mi
MAJOR RACIAL/ ETHNIC GROUPS	71.1% white; 26.0% African American; .7% Asian; .5% Native American. Hispanic (any race) 1.7%.
INDUSTRY	retail and wholesale trade, services, government, finance, insurance, real estate, transportation, construction, communication
AGRICULTURE	fruits and vegetables, dairy products, cattle, forest products, commercial fishing

NORTHERN FLICKER

CAMELLIA

Did you know?

1. In 1955 Alabama became the first state to have a state-owned television station.
2. Dismals Canyon, a few miles south of Russellville, has natural bridges, waterfalls, and one of the few stands of virgin forest east of the Mississippi River. Aaron Burr used the area as a hideout for several months after killing Alexander Hamilton in a duel in 1804.
3. Twice as much earth was moved to build the Tennessee-Tombigbee Waterway than during the construction of the Panama Canal.
4. George Washington Carver, a freed slave who helped revolutionize the economy of the South through his experiments with peanuts, soybeans, cotton, and sweet potatoes, was the director of agricultural research at the Tuskegee Institute.

ARKANSAS

★ Natural State ★

DIVERSE LANDSCAPES and outdoor activities aplenty earn Arkansas its nickname, the Natural State. On its north and west rise the rugged Ouachita Mountains and the Ozark Plateau. Between them flows the Arkansas River, south and east across the state to the Gulf Coastal Plain. There it joins the Mississippi River, with its many oxbow lakes along Arkansas's eastern border.

Spaniard Hernando de Soto ventured into the region in 1541, and French explorers scouted its resources in the 1670s. The French learned of a native group named for the south wind. The Algonquin called them the *Oo-ka-na-sa,* and French missionary Father Marquette wrote "Arkansas" (pronounced ARK-an-saw). While the French, Spanish, and British each controlled the land for periods of time, Arkansas became part of the U.S. with the Louisiana Purchase in 1803. The Arkansas Territory was formed in 1819, and settlement increased with the forced departure of most Choctaw and Cherokee peoples. Slaveholding Southern planters arrived to grow cotton in the Mississippi bottomlands. The wide valley of the Arkansas River provided fine farmlands, too. Poorer settlers from the southern Appalachians began moving into the Ozarks and Ouachitas, bringing their traditions of music and crafts.

As for the territory's largest city and future state capital, French traders crossed the Arkansas River at a spot where a "petite roche" offered a good landmark. Little Rock was on the map—founded in 1821. Improved river transport was key to early territorial expansion. A steamboat first chugged 300 miles (480 km) up the snag-filled Arkansas River in 1822.

Arkansas entered the Union as the 25th state in 1836. Difficult times followed after the state joined the Confederacy in 1861. The Union

1686

Fur trader Henri de Tonty, the Father of Arkansas, founded the first permanent European settlement on the Arkansas River.

1862

After their victory at Pea Ridge, the largest Civil War battle west of the Mississippi, the Union Army went on to capture Little Rock.

1957

Amid violent protests, this girl and eight other African Americans began attending formerly all-white Little Rock Central High School.

Present day

Arkansas-based Wal-Mart, the world's largest retailer, attracts many suppliers and other businesses to the state.

Natural wonders as diverse as hot springs, a diamond mine open to the public, and miles of scenic trails await visitors to Arkansas. Hikers (opposite) stand atop Hawksbill Crag, or Whitaker Point as the locals call it, overlooking the Buffalo National River.

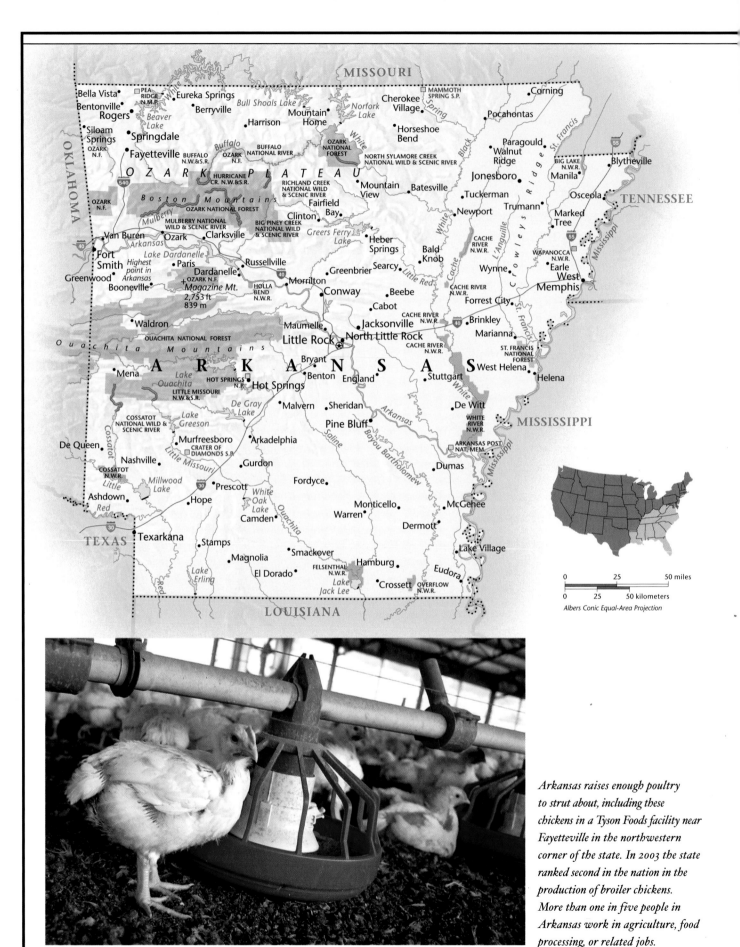

MISSOURI

Bella Vista
PEA RIDGE N.M.P.
Eureka Springs
Corning
MAMMOTH SPRING S.P.
Cherokee Village
Pocahontas
Bentonville
Berryville
Bull Shoals Lake
Norfork Lake
Rogers
Beaver Lake
Harrison
Mountain Home
Horseshoe Bend
Paragould
Walnut Ridge
Siloam Springs
Springdale
OZARK N.F.
Buffalo
BUFFALO NATIONAL RIVER
OZARK NATIONAL FOREST
NORTH SYLAMORE CREEK NATIONAL WILD & SCENIC RIVER
Jonesboro
BIG LAKE N.W.R.
Manila
Blytheville
Fayetteville
BUFFALO N.W.&S.R.
OZARK N.F.
OZARK PLATEAU
Tuckerman
Crowleys Ridge
St. Francis
HURRICANE CR. N.W.&S.R.
RICHLAND CREEK NATIONAL WILD & SCENIC RIVER
Mountain View
Batesville
Newport
Trumann
Osceola
TENNESSEE
OZARK N.F.
Boston Mountains
OZARK NATIONAL FOREST
Fairfield Bay
Clinton
Marked Tree
CACHE RIVER N.W.R.
Van Buren
Mulberry
Ozark
MULBERRY NATIONAL WILD & SCENIC RIVER
BIG PINEY CREEK NATIONAL WILD & SCENIC RIVER
Greers Ferry Lake
Heber Springs
Bald Knob
L'Anguille
WAPANOCCA N.W.R.
Earle
West Memphis
Clarksville
Searcy
Wynne
Arkansas
Lake Dardanelle
Highest point in Arkansas
Paris
Russellville
Greenbrier
Little Red
Cache
CACHE RIVER N.W.R.
Fort Smith
Dardanelle
OZARK N.F.
Morrilton
Conway
Beebe
Forrest City
Greenwood
Magazine Mt. 2,753 ft 839 m
HOLLA BEND N.W.R.
Cabot
CACHE RIVER N.W.R.
Brinkley
Booneville
Maumelle
Jacksonville
Marianna
Waldron
Little Rock
North Little Rock
CACHE RIVER N.W.R.
ST. FRANCIS NATIONAL FOREST
OUACHITA NATIONAL FOREST
Bryant
ARKANSAS
Benton
England
Stuttgart
West Helena
Mena
Lake Ouachita
HOT SPRINGS N.P.
Hot Springs
Helena
Ouachita Mountains
LITTLE MISSOURI N.W.&S.R.
Malvern
Sheridan
White
De Witt
COSSATOT NATIONAL WILD & SCENIC RIVER
De Gray Lake
Lake Greeson
Pine Bluff
Arkansas
WHITE RIVER N.W.R.
MISSISSIPPI
De Queen
Murfreesboro
CRATER OF DIAMONDS S.P.
Arkadelphia
Saline
Bayou Bartholomew
ARKANSAS POST NAT. MEM.
Cossatot
COSSATOT N.W.R.
Nashville
Gurdon
Fordyce
Dumas
Little Missouri
Millwood Lake
Prescott
White Oak Lake
Monticello
McGehee
Ashdown
Little Red
Hope
Camden
Warren
Dermott
Ouachita
Lake Village
Texarkana
Stamps
Smackover
Hamburg
Mississippi
TEXAS
Magnolia
El Dorado
FELSENTHAL N.W.R.
Lake Jack Lee
Crossett
OVERFLOW N.W.R.
Eudora
Lake Erling
LOUISIANA

0   25   50 miles
0   25   50 kilometers
Albers Conic Equal-Area Projection

Arkansas raises enough poultry to strut about, including these chickens in a Tyson Foods facility near Fayetteville in the northwestern corner of the state. In 2003 the state ranked second in the nation in the production of broiler chickens. More than one in five people in Arkansas work in agriculture, food processing, or related jobs.

Army occupied the northern part of the state by early 1863. After the war, the state was not re-admitted to the Union until African Americans were given the right to vote in 1868. While advances came for Arkansas in the decades that followed, many of its people—both white and black—remained poor. Some left for northern industrial cities in the early 20th century, while others migrated west during the Great Depression.

The past few decades have brought better days to Arkansas. State population is now about 2.7 million, with nearly one in six residents of African-American heritage. Agriculture is thriving. Soggy Mississippi River lowlands provide fine rice-growing conditions. Rice fields are flooded to farm fish, too, with nutrients from the fish providing great fertilizer for the next rice crop. The state is second in catfish production, third in turkeys, fourth in cotton, and a leader in raising and processing chickens for sale. Arkansas is the top U.S. producer of bauxite and bromine, and oil and natural gas are also extracted.

Arkansas's economic success is tied to sustainable use of its varied natural resources. Visitors flock to the scenic wooded trails and whitewater routes of the Ozarks and Ouachitas, where forests are managed for recreation, wildlife habitat, and a variety of wood products. Recently, though, a combination of drought, insects, and disease has killed large numbers of red oak trees across these highlands. Wise water management is also critical to the state's economy, since both surface and underground sources provide for drinking, industry, and irrigation. Continued growth—both urban and rural—depends upon adequate and clean water supplies. People of the Natural State know they need to care for the natural environment that nurtures them.

ARKANSAS
Natural State

STATEHOOD	June 15, 1836; 25th state
CAPITAL	Little Rock
LARGEST CITY	Little Rock Population 184,055
TOTAL AREA	53,179 sq mi; 137,732 sq km
LAND AREA	52,068 sq mi; 134,856 sq km
POPULATION	2,725,714
POPULATION DENSITY	52 people per sq mi
MAJOR RACIAL/ ETHNIC GROUPS	80.0% white; 15.7% African American; .8% Asian; .8% Native American. Hispanic (any race) 3.2%.
INDUSTRY	services, food processing, paper products, transportation, metal products, machinery, electronics
AGRICULTURE	poultry and eggs, rice, soybeans, cotton, wheat

MOCKINGBIRD   APPLE BLOSSOM

Did you know?

1. Crater of Diamonds State Park is the only diamond-producing area in the world that allows the public to keep what they find, and near Murfreesboro is the only diamond mine in North America that is open to the public.
2. The average temperature of the waters in the 47 springs that flow out of Hot Springs Mountain is 143°F (62°C).
3. Arkansas has been the country's leading producer of rice since 1973. It produces about 45 percent of the total U.S. crop.
4. In 1932, Arkansas elected the first woman to the U.S. Senate. Her name was Hattie Caraway.
5. Nine million gallons (34, 069 kl) of water flow from Mammoth Spring each hour. The spring forms a scenic 10-acre (4-ha) lake in Mammoth Spring State Park. It is one of the world's largest single springs.

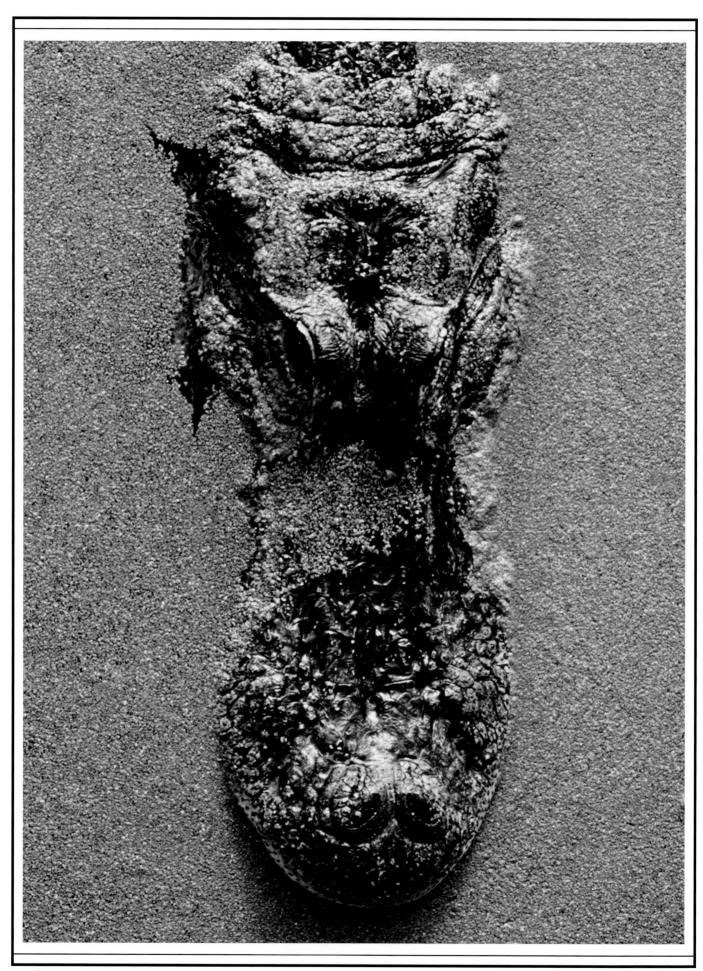

FLORIDA

★ *Sunshine State* ★

COAST TO COAST—to coast! Florida boasts three distinct shores. A long strand of hard-packed sand stretches along 400 miles (640 km) of Atlantic beachfront. Across the giant peninsula are softer, seashell-rich beaches, lining the Gulf of Mexico. To the northwest people play on Panhandle beaches with the color and feel of white sugar. Once a limestone seafloor, the low-relief platform that makes up the state was uncovered as sea level dropped. Florida is the lowest and flattest state.

The Spanish founded St. Augustine in 1565, making it the continent's oldest permanent European settlement. Spain lost the territory to Britain in 1763 but regained it 20 years later. Farmland attracted American settlers in the early 1800s, and a treaty with Spain allowed the U.S. to obtain the territory in 1821. Native Seminoles fought to keep their lands, but most were forced west. When Florida became the 27th state in 1845, Tallahassee was made its capital city.

Florida joined the Confederacy and seceded from the Union just 16 years after statehood. It was readmitted in 1868. Florida's modernization followed the railroads built along its Atlantic and Gulf coasts in the 1890s. Land sales boomed, orange groves were planted, and tourists began to visit from the chilly north. Beachfront hotels and resorts sprang up along the train routes. The Spanish-American War of 1898 and two world wars boosted Florida's growth, with an ever-greater need for military bases and agricultural products. The state soon became a retirement haven for senior citizens, as well as a refuge for immigrants after the Cuban Revolution in 1959. Miami grew to become the nation's major gateway to the Caribbean and much of Latin America.

Since 1950, Florida's population has blossomed from less than 2.8 million to more than

1513

Juan Ponce de León, seeker of the fabled Fountain of Youth, claimed Florida for Spain, naming it Pascua Florida *(Flowery Easter).*

1835

Although the Seminole Wars cost these native people most of their lands, some found refuge and new homes in the Everglades.

1896—1912

By building the Florida East Coast Railway to Miami and then Key West, Henry M. Flagler opened the state to development.

Present day

Cape Canaveral, site of NASA's Kennedy Space Center, is a hub for space-age technology as well as a major tourist attraction.

Looking almost like the long Florida peninsula where it lives, an American alligator (opposite) waits in the duckweed-filled water of the Everglades where it is a key part of the ecosystem. Clean waters and adequate habitat are needed to ensure the reptile's survival.

FLORIDA
Sunshine State

STATEHOOD	March 3, 1845; 27th state
CAPITAL	Tallahassee
LARGEST CITY	Jacksonville Population 762,461
TOTAL AREA	65,755 sq mi; 170,304 sq km
LAND AREA	53,927 sq mi; 139,670 sq km
POPULATION	17,019,068
POPULATION DENSITY	309.9 people per sq mi
MAJOR RACIAL/ ETHNIC GROUPS	78% white; 14.6% African American; 1.7% Asian; .3% Native American. Hispanic (any race) 16.8%.
INDUSTRY	tourism, health services, business services, communications, banking, electronic equipment, insurance
AGRICULTURE	citrus fruits, vegetables, field crops, nursery stock, cattle, dairy products

MOCKINGBIRD

ORANGE BLOSSOM

Did you know?

1. Hurricane Andrew, which struck the Homestead area of South Florida in August 1992, was the most expensive natural disaster to date in U.S. history.
2. Clearwater has the highest rate of per capita lightning strikes of any U.S. city.
3. Citrus fruits originated in Southeast Asia. Ponce de León planted the first citrus in Florida in the mid-1500s.
4. Counting bays and barrier islands along its Atlantic and Gulf coasts, Florida has 8,500 miles (14,000 km) of shoreline. Alaska is the only state with more.
5. The Overseas Highway, which spans 113 miles (182 km) between Key Largo and Key West, has more than 42 bridges and links more than a hundred islands. The longest is the Seven Mile Bridge.
6. Britton Hill, Florida's highest point, is only 345 feet (105 m) above sea level.

17 million. This more than six-fold increase has made Florida the nation's fourth-largest state in population. One in six Floridians is Hispanic, many of them Cuban. A slightly smaller number are African American. Vacationers arrive year-round, but especially in the winter and spring seasons. Spectacular theme parks in Orlando entertain millions annually. Tourists *ooh* and *ah,* watching space launches from NASA's Kennedy Space Center. The Everglades, a unique ecosystem of marsh and swamp fed by waterways linked to Lake Okeechobee, is another major attraction. Alligators and crocodiles live here, as do hundreds of bird species and the endangered Florida panther.

Fertile soils and a warm, wet subtropical climate in the Sunshine State provide farming riches, too. Florida tops the nation in sugarcane and citrus fruit and ranks second in output of tomatoes, strawberries, and greenhouse and nursery products. There are huge harvests of dozens of other fruits and vegetables as well as thousands of beef-cattle operations, especially in the Panhandle. Military bases plus related defense and research companies play a large role in the state's economy and have helped Florida lead the country in job growth in the past two years.

Though Florida continues to prosper, both natural and human-caused difficulties confront the state. Years-long droughts have been damaging in recent years, as have monster storms such as Hurricane Andrew. For decades, abundant water resources have been directed away from the Everglades and other natural needs to those of expanding farms and cities. Efforts are underway to restore this life-giving flow of water. Florida's fast population growth strains all resources. The challenge will be to grow without sacrificing the state's natural treasures.

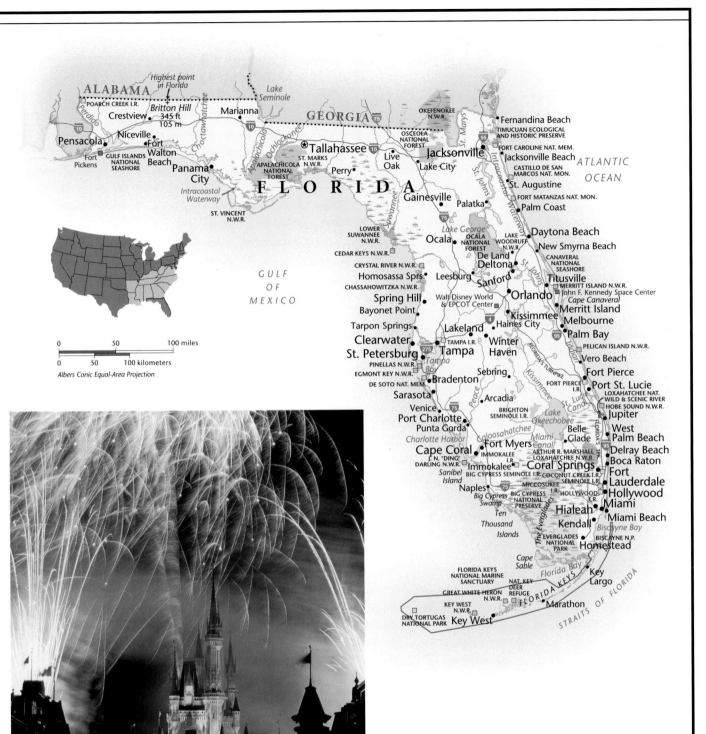

The king of the nation's theme parks, Disney's Magic Kingdom attracts more than three million visitors annually. When it opened in 1971 as the first portion of Walt Disney World, the park transformed Orlando from an agricultural area to a fantasy getaway destination. Florida entertains more than 50 million visitors each year, providing more than 800,000 jobs directly involved in tourism.

GEORGIA
★ Empire State of the South ★

"EMPIRE STATE OF THE SOUTH." A regal-sounding nickname for a U.S. state may seem odd, but it fits Georgia. From majestic, forested highlands to a grand seaport on a palm-fringed coast, Georgia is as landscape-rich as any state. Last established of the 13 British colonies, it's even named for royalty: King George II.

Scouted by one empire and settled by another, the territory was of interest to the Spanish as early as the 1500s, but under English control from 1733. While begun as a place for poor English to start life anew after serving time in debtors' prisons, Georgia soon was like other southern colonies, exporting products such as rice, cotton, lumber, and deerskins to England—with slave labor. After the American Revolution, it ratified the Constitution in 1788, the fourth state to do so. Savannah, a thriving port, was its first capital. Georgia's slave-based plantation economy boomed after the invention

of the cotton gin in 1793. Gold discovered in its northern region in 1828 further speeded settlement and signaled the end of Creek and Cherokee success in resisting the newcomers. These Native Americans were among those forced to walk the Trail of Tears in the 1830s.

Georgia tilts southeastward, from Appalachian heights to a coastline dotted with wildlife refuges that are a birder's paradise. Spanning the Florida border, the Okefenokee National Wildlife Refuge harbors alligators, river otters, and bears in 700 square miles (1,820 sq km) of untamed swamps, bogs, and marshes. Between its low coastal plain and northern wooded heights lies a broad area of rolling forested hills and farmlands—the Piedmont.

It was on the Piedmont, at the foot of the Blue Ridge Mountains, that a settlement named Terminus was founded in 1837 at the endpoint of the promising new rail line. Within a decade

1733

James Oglethorpe founded Savannah as part of a slave-free colony but soon discovered that slave labor brought greater profits.

1793

Eli Whitney helped make cotton king by inventing a gin that could separate cotton seeds from fiber faster than could be done by hand.

1864

After burning Atlanta, Union General Sherman began his march to the sea, destroying property and railroads as he went.

1996

Hosting the Summer Olympics not only brought billions in revenue to Atlanta but also created jobs and world-class facilities.

Atlanta (opposite) has been called the Economic Capital of the Southeast. The city's metro area grew by nearly 40 percent in the 1990s—from 2.9 million to 4.1 million. But growth has its costs: too much pollution and too great a demand on limited resources.

GEORGIA
Empire State of the South

STATEHOOD	January 2, 1788; 4th state
CAPITAL	Atlanta
LARGEST CITY	Atlanta Population 424,868
TOTAL AREA	59,425 sq mi; 153,909 sq km
LAND AREA	57,906 sq mi; 149,976 sq km
POPULATION	8,684,715
POPULATION DENSITY	147.8 people per sq mi
MAJOR RACIAL/ ETHNIC GROUPS	65.1% white; 28.7% African American; 2.1% Asian; .3% Native American. Hispanic (any race) 5.3%.
INDUSTRY	textiles and clothing, transportation equipment, food processing, paper products, chemicals, electrical equipment, tourism
AGRICULTURE	poultry and eggs, cotton, peanuts, vegetables, sweet corn, melons, cattle

BROWN THRASHER   CHEROKEE ROSE

Did you know?

1. The carvings of Confederate leaders Robert E. Lee, Stonewall Jackson, and Jefferson Davis on Stone Mountain near Atlanta make up the world's largest high relief sculpture.
2. Delta Airlines started as a company that dusted crops for boll weevils and developed into one of the country's leading commercial airlines.
3. Martin Luther King, Jr., charismatic African-American civil rights leader and recipient of the Nobel Peace Prize, was born in Atlanta in 1929.
4. The first gold rush in the United States took place in 1828 at Dahlonega.
5. Coca-Cola was invented in 1886 in Atlanta by Dr. John Pemberton and was first sold at the soda fountain in a local pharmacy. First-year sales averaged nine drinks a day for a year-end earning of $50.

Peanuts have been grown in Georgia since colonial times. In 2003 the state grew almost 45 percent of the nation's harvest. Related to beans and alfalfa, peanuts grow on the roots of the plant. Peanuts are eaten roasted, shelled, salted, or as peanut butter or oil. They are even used in livestock feed.

the prospering city took a name invented from the Georgia and Atlantic Railroad: Atlanta. The city and the state supplied food and other resources for the Confederate war effort. Atlanta and Georgia became Civil War targets by 1864. Union forces devastated the state in the fall of that year. Destroying everything in its path, Sherman's Army burned most of Atlanta and left a 50-mile- (80-km) wide swath of ruin to the sea.

Georgia suffered through decades of post-Civil War poverty. Sharecropping, soil erosion, and the boll weevil invasion of the early 20th century hurt farming. Savannah declined in importance, but Atlanta was quickly rebuilt after the war and developed into the transportation, trade, and financial hub of the South.

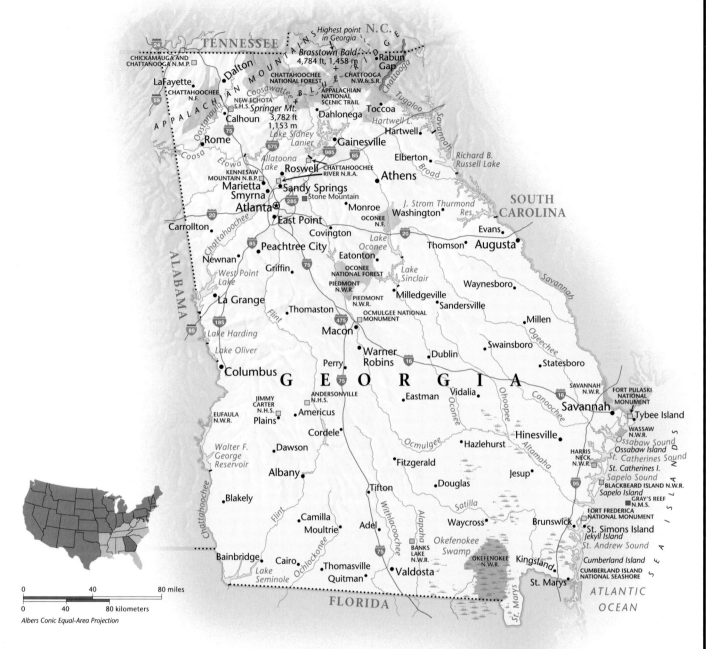

Though still a leader among states in cotton production, Georgia's agriculture has diversified. It is first in egg output and in raising and processing broiler chickens. Georgia is widely known for peanuts, pecans, peaches, and sweet Vidalia onions. Vast pine forests help make it a leader in forest products, and it is number one in paper production. From northeastern quarries, Georgia produces the Greene County granite used to form the plaza of the new National World War II Memorial on the Mall in Washington, D.C.

Georgia has 8.7 million residents. Almost three in ten Georgians have African-American heritage. In 1967, racial violence erupted in Atlanta, which became a center of the civil rights movement. Georgia native Jimmy Carter, who was governor before becoming President in 1976, pushed strongly for equal opportunity. Rapid population gains have caused resource strains on education, healthcare, and highways. Georgians will likely solve these problems and continue to weave prosperity into the future of their southern empire.

KENTUCKY

★ *Bluegrass State* ★

BLUEGRASS STATE. Whether one hears the state's nickname, or hears the refrain from the state song "My Old Kentucky Home," pleasant rural images come to mind. Though Kentucky contains plenty of southern hospitality, it's also a mining and manufacturing state like industrial states to the north.

In the language of the native Iroquois, *kenta-ke* meant "meadow-land," for the open, grassy spaces among its hardwood forests. Kentucky has more than a thousand miles (1,600 km) of navigable waterways, including the Tennessee, Cumberland, Green, Kentucky, and Licking Rivers, which all flow into the Ohio. This broad and deep river, which forms the state's northern border, joins the Mississippi at Kentucky's southwestern tip. High ridges and deep, narrow valleys of the Appalachians and adjoining Cumberland Plateau make up most of eastern Kentucky. Rivers rushing from the heights have carved twisting gorges called gaps through the mountains.

Through these passages pioneers reached central and western Kentucky. When a treaty with the Cherokee opened the region to easterners in 1775, the legendary but real-life Daniel Boone was quick to travel through the Cumberland Gap. The famed pioneer brought his family and others to build Boonesborough. When the American Revolution ended, streams of settlers flowed into what was then a huge, western "county" of Virginia. Kentucky became the 15th state in 1792, with the town of Frankfort as its capital.

After the last Native American claims to Kentucky lands were resolved in 1818, the state developed a booming tobacco-based economy. A pro-slavery/anti-slavery split developed, dividing Kentucky between plantation owners and small-scale farmers and crafts people.

1775

Daniel Boone opened up the Northwest Territory by leading settlers through the Cumberland Gap from Virginia to Kentucky.

1852

A Kentucky slave auction inspired Harriet Beecher Stowe to write her powerful anti-slavery novel Uncle Tom's Cabin.

1930s

The attempt by labor unions to secure better wages and working conditions for coal miners led to violent strikes in Harlan County.

Present day

More than 2.5 million Louisville Sluggers, the official bat of major league baseball, are produced in Kentucky each year.

Kentucky's Thoroughbred horses (opposite), a breed originally from England, are famous for their racing ability. Lexington is the bustling Bluegrass hub of the state's horse-raising operations, where the first racecourse was set up in 1789.

KENTUCKY
Bluegrass State

STATEHOOD	June 1, 1792; 15th state
CAPITAL	Frankfort
LARGEST CITY	Louisville Metro Population 693,604
TOTAL AREA	40,409 sq mi; 104,659 sq km
LAND AREA	39,728 sq mi; 102,896 sq km
POPULATION	4,117,827
POPULATION DENSITY	103 people per sq mi
MAJOR RACIAL/ ETHNIC GROUPS	90.1% white; 7.3% African American; .7% Asian; .2% Native American. Hispanic (any race) 1.5%.
INDUSTRY	manufacturing, services, government, finance, insurance, real estate, retail trade, transportation, wholesale trade, construction, mining
AGRICULTURE	tobacco, horses, cattle, corn, dairy products

CARDINAL   GOLDENROD

Did you know?

1. Mammoth Cave, with its 340 miles (547 km) of mapped passageways, is the longest cave system in the world. Visitors have come to explore it since 1816.
2. Kentucky bluegrass gets its name not from the color of the grass (which is green) but from the bluish buds the grass produces in the spring and that make meadows look blue.
3. Pike County has produced more than 133 billion tons of coal, more than any other county in the country.
4. Abraham Lincoln, President of the United States, and Jefferson Davis, President of the Confederacy, were both born in log houses in Kentucky. Lincoln's birthplace was Sinking Spring Farm, southeast of Elizabethtown (1809); Davis's was in Fairview (1808).

Officially neutral at the outbreak of the Civil War, Kentucky eventually sided with the Union even though about one-third of its soldiers fought for the Confederacy.

First worked in the 1750s, eastern Kentucky's enormous deposits of soft bituminous coal have been mined in great quantities for 150 years. This natural resource provided wealth, fueled labor movements, and caused disastrous environmental problems. Deep-shaft mines and dangerous hand labor were the rule for decades. Eventually, machines did much of the work. Later, shallower western Kentucky coal reserves were strip-mined by huge power shovels and bulldozers. Since the 1970s, federal laws have required that stripped lands be restored to their original condition, but many older mines leave scars on the land.

Kentucky's central Bluegrass region provided green alternatives to the coal economy. A long, warm growing season and calcium-rich soils here yield excellent tobacco and winning horses. At its heart is Lexington. Louisville, home to the famous Kentucky Derby horse race, is a major Ohio River port and highway and air-transport center.

Long a victim of a boom-and-bust mining economy, eastern Kentucky is still the state's poorest region, but it is culturally rich. Its Scotch-Irish heritage is preserved in its distinctive crafts and music. Its forests of oak, walnut, and hickory help make Kentucky a leader among hardwood producing states. Tourism is increasing in this region of pioneer history, state parks, and federal recreation lands.

In a state that combines traits from North and South, Kentuckians retain old customs and activities as they blaze new trails. Long a mostly rural state, most Kentuckians now live in cities. Still a major coal producer, the state explores clean-burning coal technology. Manufacturing remains a force, too, with the fourth-largest production of motor vehicles in the United States. Kentucky seeks to better its standard of living by improving education, by making technology part of everyday life, and by developing strong ties to the national and global economy. People here want to share their ideas and culture with the world as they build their "new" Kentucky homes.

A long tradition of folk music is alive and well in Kentucky. Bluegrass music has roots in the tunes of Scotch-Irish immigrants to the Appalachians, as well as in the music of African-American slaves. The name came from Kentuckian Bill Monroe, who called his 1939 band the Bluegrass Boys, after his home state.

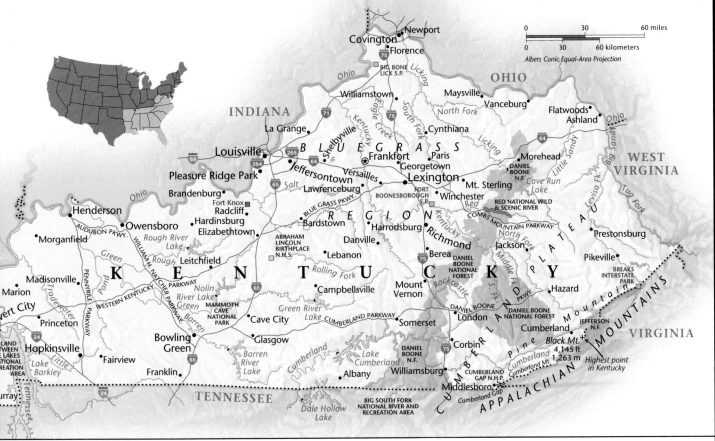

LOUISIANA

★ *Pelican State* ★

THE BAYOU STATE or the Pelican State. Take your pick, both nicknames are about water. Looking like a boot on the Gulf of Mexico shore, Louisiana stands between Texas and Mississippi, with Arkansas to its north. Fresh, salty, or a mix of both called brackish, water is the source of the state's successes—and some of its troubles.

Water was the highway when French explorer La Salle sailed down the Mississippi River in 1682, claiming—and naming—the entire valley for his king, Louis XIV. "Louisiana" was a vast realm then, but the territory eventually was reduced to form the state of today, surrounding the lower reaches of the great river.

With the Louisiana Purchase in 1803, New Orleans, founded almost a century before on a strip of land along a sweeping bend of the Mississippi, was positioned to become the commercial focus for the sprawling river basin.

Steamboats reached Louisiana at about the time it became the 18th state in 1812. The state capital traveled upriver to Baton Rouge in 1849. By that time, New Orleans had become not just a bustling port for cotton and other plantation products, but also the biggest slave-trading market in the South. The state joined the Confederacy, but by 1862 it was in Union hands.

Louisiana's post-Civil War decades brought hard times—corrupt leadership, a declining cotton economy, and continued racial inequalities. Poor African-American farmers struggled to survive in an unfair system. Oil and gas, discovered there in 1901, helped change the state's fortunes. Today, rigs in all sections of the state and in Gulf waters make Louisiana the fourth-largest oil producer in the nation. Refineries and petrochemical plants line the riverbanks from New Orleans to Baton Rouge, turning natural resources into hundreds of products.

1803

The raising of the American flag in New Orleans celebrated the Louisiana Purchase, which doubled the size of the United States.

1862

Confederate sharpshooters failed to keep the Union from capturing New Orleans and gaining control of the mouth of the Mississippi.

1928–1932

Huey Long, a strong advocate of education, the poor, and state's rights, was the most influential politician in Louisiana history.

Present day

Massive oil-and-natural-gas rigs in the Gulf of Mexico help make the state one of the top five U.S. producers of these energy resources.

Fancy floats and feasts mean it's Mardi Gras in New Orleans (opposite). Each year the celebration attracts millions of visitors to this French-founded city. Its picturesque French Quarter, unique foods, and home-grown jazz music make it a popular attraction year-round.

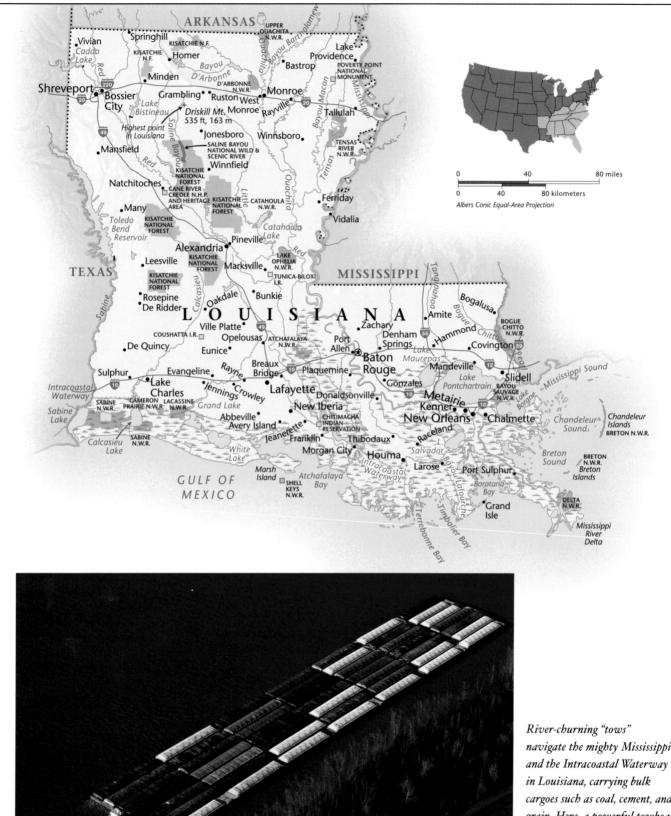

ARKANSAS

UPPER
OUACHITA
N.W.R.

Vivian
Caddo
Lake

Springhill

KISATCHIE N.F.

Homer

KISATCHIE
N.F.

Bayou
D'Arbonne

Lake
Providence

POVERTY POINT
NATIONAL
MONUMENT

Minden

D'ARBONNE
N.W.R.

Bastrop

Monroe

Shreveport

Bossier
City

220

Grambling
Ruston
West
Monroe
Rayville

Tallulah

Driskill Mt.
535 ft, 163 m
Highest point
in Louisiana

Lake
Bistineau

20

Saline Bayou

Jonesboro

Winnsboro

Bayou Macon

Mississippi

49

SALINE BAYOU
NATIONAL WILD &
SCENIC RIVER

Red

Mansfield

Winnfield

TENSAS
RIVER
N.W.R.

Natchitoches

KISATCHIE
NATIONAL
FOREST

CANE RIVER N.H.P.
AND HERITAGE
AREA

Little

KISATCHIE
NATIONAL
FOREST

Ouachita

Catahoula

Ferriday

Tensas

Many

Toledo
Bend
Reservoir

KISATCHIE
NATIONAL
FOREST

Pineville

Catahoula
Lake

Vidalia

CATAHOULA
N.W.R.

Red

TEXAS

Alexandria

Leesville

KISATCHIE
NATIONAL
FOREST

Marksville

LAKE
OPHELIA
N.W.R.

MISSISSIPPI

KISATCHIE
NATIONAL
FOREST

Rosepine
De Ridder

Oakdale

Bunkie

TUNICA-BILOXI
I.R.

L O U I S I A N A

Tangipahoa

Bogalusa

Ville Platte

COUSHATTA I.R.

49

Opelousas

ATCHAFALAYA
N.W.R.

Zachary

Denham
Springs

Amite

Bogue

55

Hammond

Bogue
Chitto

BOGUE
CHITTO
N.W.R.

59

Calcasieu

Sabine

De Quincy

Eunice

Port
Allen

Baton
Rouge

Covington

Sulphur

Evangeline

Rayne

Breaux
Bridge

Plaquemine

10

Gonzales

Lake
Maurepas

Mandeville

Lake
Pontchartrain

12

Slidell

Mississippi Sound

10

Lake Charles

Jennings

Crowley

Lafayette

Donaldsonville

Metairie

Kenner

BAYOU
SAUVAGE
N.W.R.

Lake
Borgne

Intracoastal
Waterway

Sabine
Lake

SABINE
N.W.R.

CAMERON
PRAIRIE N.W.R.

LACASSINE
N.W.R.

Grand Lake

Abbeville

Avery Island

New Iberia

CHITIMACHA
INDIAN
RESERVATION

New Orleans

Chalmette

Chandeleur
Sound

Chandeleur
Islands
BRETON N.W.R.

Calcasieu
Lake

SABINE
N.W.R.

White
Lake

Jeanerette

Franklin

Thibodaux

Raceland

Larose

Breton
Sound

BRETON
N.W.R.
Breton
Islands

Morgan City

Houma

L.
Salvador

Port Sulphur

Marsh
Island

SHELL
KEYS
N.W.R.

Atchafalaya
Bay

Intracoastal
Waterway

Barataria
Bay

GULF OF
MEXICO

Terrebonne Bay

Timbalier Bay

Grand
Isle

Bayou Lafourche

DELTA
N.W.R.

Mississippi
River
Delta

0   40   80 miles

0   40   80 kilometers

Albers Conic Equal-Area Projection

*River-churning "tows"
navigate the mighty Mississippi
and the Intracoastal Waterway
in Louisiana, carrying bulk
cargoes such as coal, cement, and
grain. Here, a powerful towboat
pushes groups of barges, each of
which measures 35 feet (11 m) in
width by 195 feet (59 m) in
length, transporting a typical
load of 1,500 tons (1,350 mt).*

Louisiana owes its very existence to upstream erosion. Borne by the Mississippi and other rivers, sediment has built up the river's lower reaches and shifting delta for millions of years. Well-watered Louisiana lies low, averaging just 100 feet (30 m) above sea level. From hills near Shreveport, the land descends to marshes, swamps, and slow-moving streams called bayous along its Gulf Coast. Here live Cajuns, whose ancestors—the Acadians—were forced from French Canada by the British in the 1700s. Many Cajuns still speak French, and their spicy foods and toe-tapping music combine to make rural Louisiana culture unlike that of any other state.

Louisiana lands the nation's second-biggest commercial fish catch—including shrimp and oysters. The state ranks second among states in sweet potatoes and sugarcane and third in rice production. Fields are flooded to raise catfish and crayfish—a state specialty. Still one of the world's busiest ports for river and ocean-going traffic, New Orleans is also a famous tourist destination.

While the lives and livelihoods of Louisiana's 4.5 million people are rooted in water, threats from water keep them on guard. The enormous and shifting Mississippi has always proven hard to handle, but a disastrous flood in 1927 caused the federal government to try. An extensive system of dams and river embankments called levees are designed to control floods and improve navigation. The state has wetlands rich in wildlife, including alligators, muskrats, and waterfowl. Both urban and rural activities threaten this water-land paradise, as do pollutants from half the country that wash down the Mississippi. Louisiana residents know that water keeps state hopes afloat, so they must work to keep "water woes" from interfering with future success.

LOUISIANA
Pelican State

STATEHOOD	April 30, 1812; 18th state
CAPITAL	Baton Rouge
LARGEST CITY	New Orleans Population 473,681
TOTAL AREA	51,840 sq mi; 134,264 sq km
LAND AREA	43,562 sq mi; 112,825 sq km
POPULATION	4,496,334
POPULATION DENSITY	102.9 people per sq mi
MAJOR RACIAL/ ETHNIC GROUPS	63.9% white; 32.5% African American; 1.2% Asian; .6% Native American. Hispanic (any race) 2.4%.
INDUSTRY	chemicals, petroleum products, food processing, health services, tourism, oil and natural gas extraction, paper products
AGRICULTURE	forest products, poultry, marine fisheries, sugarcane, rice, dairy products, cotton, cattle, aquaculture

BROWN PELICAN

MAGNOLIA

Did you know?

1. Because of its low water table, New Orleans has many cemeteries with above-ground tombs. They are known as Cities of the Dead because the rows of tombs resemble city streets.
2. Louisiana is the only state in the Union that has parishes instead of counties and that refers to the Napoleonic Code in its laws.
3. The 24-mile- (38.6-km-) long Lake Pontchartrain Causeway is the longest bridge completely over water in the world.
4. Louisiana's Creole society is made up of descendants of people of Spanish or French heritage mixed with that of African slaves who gained their freedom before the Civil War.

MISSISSIPPI

★ *Magnolia State* ★

STOP CHANGING CHANNELS! Apparently no one told the loopy Mississippi River that. It has meandered along for ages to form the scalloped western boundary of its namesake state. When the river curls far enough back on itself, it can cut across the narrow neck of land to form what's called an oxbow lake. Dozens of these crescent-shaped water bodies lie along the lower reaches of the Mississippi. Like its great river, the state itself has seen some big changes.

Hernando de Soto scouted the Mississippi for Spain in 1540. The territory was later claimed by the French, who founded their first settlement in 1699 on the Gulf Coast near present-day Ocean Springs. Great Britain controlled the region after the French and Indian War until it passed to the U.S. in 1783. But Spain did not give up its coastal claims. Spanish West Florida, including Mississippi's present shoreline, was officially transferred to the United States in 1819.

Three major native groups were living here when Europeans arrived. The Natchez are remembered for "tracing" a trail—later used by settlers and traders—from their lowland home to hunting grounds in present-day Tennessee. The Chickasaw lived in the north and were great warriors who later helped the British battle the French. The Choctaw were the dominant group—skilled farmers who lived in the central region. Nearly all eventually were forced off their lands by the incoming Americans, and many trekked the Trail of Tears to Oklahoma in the 1830s—or died along the way. The Mississippi Territory was created in 1798, and included for a time present-day Alabama. Mississippi entered the Union as the 20th state in 1817. A small town on the Pearl River, renamed in honor of Andrew Jackson, became the state capital in 1821.

Mississippi was soon ruled by "King Cotton." For more than a century—until the

1806

Using seeds imported from Mexico, planters developed a new variety of cotton that helped make Mississippi a major cotton producer.

1863

The capture of Vicksburg after a 47-day siege gave the Union control of the Mississippi River and hastened the end of the Civil War.

1963

Medgar Evers was killed trying to secure voting rights for African Americans. In 1969 his brother was elected mayor of Fayette.

Present day

The annual shrimp harvest is an important part of Mississippi's seafood industry, along with oysters and red snappers.

The American Queen (opposite), built in 1995, celebrates the 19th-century days of Mississippi River paddle-wheeling. Regular steamboat service for passengers and freight operated between New Orleans and Natchez by 1814.

MISSISSIPPI
Magnolia State

STATEHOOD	December 10, 1817; 20th state
CAPITAL	Jackson
LARGEST CITY	Jackson Population 180,881
TOTAL AREA	48,430 sq mi; 125,434 sq km
LAND AREA	46,907 sq mi; 121,489 sq km
POPULATION	2,881,281
POPULATION DENSITY	61.2 people per sq mi
MAJOR RACIAL/ ETHNIC GROUPS	61.4% white; 36.3% African American; .7% Asian; .4% Native American. Hispanic (any race) 1.4%.
INDUSTRY	petroleum products, health services, electronic equipment, transportation, banking, forest products, communications
AGRICULTURE	poultry and eggs, cotton, catfish, soybeans, cattle, rice, dairy products

MOCKINGBIRD

MAGNOLIA

Did you know?

1. Mississippi is the country's leading supplier of farm-raised catfish. This industry supports other segments of the economy, such as corn, soybeans, and cotton-seed, all of which are used as fish food.
2. The famous crash of the Cannonball Express, which killed folk-song hero Jonathan Luther "Casey" Jones, occurred in Vaughn on April 30, 1900.
3. In 1902 while on a hunting expedition in Mississippi, President Theodore (Teddy) Roosevelt refused to shoot a captured bear. This act resulted in the creation of the world-famous teddy bear.
4. Natchez, settled by the French in 1716, is the oldest permanent European settlement in Mississippi.
5. NASA space shuttle engines are tested at the John C. Stennis Space Center, near Bay St. Louis.

Great Depression of the 1930s—the state's economy and society were dominated by the growing, processing, and selling of the white, fluffy fiber. For much of this time, wealthy white plantation owners lived like royalty while African Americans were enslaved. Poor white, non-slaveholding farmers lived free but like peasants. Mississippi joined the Confederacy and paid dearly for it. Some 770 Civil War battles and skirmishes were fought here, Jackson was burned three times, and at least 25,000 Mississippi soldiers died.

Though slavery was officially abolished after the war, the economic and the social realities did not change much. Both white and black share-croppers were supplied with land to farm, seeds to plant, and tools to use in exchange for a heavy share of the harvest going to the wealthy landowner. Most African-American civil rights were withheld until the protests, violence, and legislation of the 1950s and 1960s finally achieved integration and began to build equal rights.

Mississippi has worked over the past half century both to broaden its farm economy and to balance it with other activities. Long, hot summers, annual rainfall averaging more than 50 inches (127 cm), and rich soils allow diverse agriculture. While cotton farmed in the Delta region, between the Yazoo and Mississippi Rivers, still makes the state a national leader, these flatlands also support huge harvests of rice, soybeans, sorghum, and other crops. Mississippi is the country's largest supplier of pond-raised catfish and a major chicken producer, too.

The state's southern yellow pine forests yield lumber and other forest products. The Gulf Coast, where residents catch and process seafood, pump and refine oil and gas, and build ships, attracts increasing numbers of tourists.

Mississippi is also home to a number of key military facilities.

Not all of Mississippi's problems are solved, and the state still works to correct the impacts of a painful past. The state's per capita income remains among the lowest in the nation. Rural poverty rates are particularly high, especially in places dominated by large groups of the state's more than one million African Americans. But the state strives to improve the lives of all its citizens by pressing for improved education and the creation of more and higher-paying jobs.

Although Mississippi has much greater agricultural diversity today than in the 19th century, the state still ranks among the top three cotton-producing states. The backbreaking method of picking cotton by hand has given way to mechanized cotton harvesters like the one shown here. Field hands traditionally were paid in pennies-per-pound picked; machines that do the job today can cost more than $300,000 each.

NORTH CAROLINA

★ *Tar Heel State* ★

FROM THE MOUNTAINS to the sea, across a broad, hilly piedmont to its wave-dashed Atlantic coastline, North Carolina holds rich and varied landscapes. Mount Mitchell—the highest point east of the Mississippi River—tops out at 6,684 feet (2,037 m) above sea level in the state's Blue Ridge Mountains.

A French expedition sailed along the coast in 1524. Sixty-one years later Sir Walter Raleigh sent a colonizing expedition from England, but the settlers returned after a year. In 1587 more than a hundred people settled on and later vanished from Roanoke Island. In 1629 King Charles I split off a portion of the Virginia Colony and named it after himself (*Carolus* is Latin for Charles). In the 1650s the Indians were forced out when conflicts erupted between settlers and Creeks, Cherokees, and Algonquins. In 1729, the royal colonies of North and South Carolina were formed. The economy centered on naval stores, such as pitch, tar, and turpentine. Soon, tobacco and cotton were grown in the English-settled eastern lowlands, while Scots, Irish, and Germans moved to lands farther west. Opposition to English taxes made North Carolina eager to join the Revolution, and a victory near Wilmington helped win the region for the Americans.

Capes Hatteras, Lookout, and Fear poke seaward from the arc of barrier islands that protect species-rich sounds and bays along the coast. Battered by high winds, Outer Banks waters are hazardous: more than 600 ships have sunk here. Big rivers run swiftly southeast from the uplands, changing to wider, slower waterways the closer they get to the ocean.

North Carolina joined the Union as the 12th state in 1789 and maintained a mostly agricultural economy, which included the use of slaves on cotton and tobacco plantations. Though its citizens were split on the issue of slavery, the state

1591

The word "Croatoan" was the only evidence found of colonists who disappeared from England's first settlement on Roanoke Island.

Early 1900s

Textile mills became the state's chief employer, as farmers left their fields to work in mills, where children often provided cheap labor.

1960

A sit-in at an all-white lunch counter in Greensboro was one of many protests that led to laws banning segregation in public places.

Present day

Fort Bragg and Camp Lejeune are among the military bases that give the armed forces a large presence in North Carolina.

Flashing a powerful warning light across the treacherous Diamond Shoals, Cape Hatteras Lighthouse (opposite) is the tallest and most famous brick lighthouse in the country. Its beacon can be seen for nearly 22 miles (35 km).

North Carolina has extensive forest resources. Large areas of softwood pine forests feed paper and pulp mills. Rich stands of hardwood trees and skilled craftspeople have combined to build a solid reputation for North Carolina furniture makers. Here, a woodworker makes chair legs on a production line. Hickory, High Point, and Thomasville are among the places famous for wooden furniture.

joined the Confederacy in 1861. North Carolina struggled after the war with rural poverty and racial inequalities that persisted well into the 20th century. In 1971 Charlotte was the site of the first major school-busing program to eliminate school segregation.

The tobacco business boomed after the invention of the cigarette-making machine in the 1880s. Textile mills found power in numerous rivers. By the 1920s, oak and maple forests supplied a huge furniture-making industry, which still leads the nation. Rich fisheries and numerous mineral resources were developed, too. Military spending began during World War II and is still strong.

Now, high-tech industries prosper in the famous Research Triangle between Chapel Hill, Durham, and the state capital, Raleigh. Charlotte has grown into one of the top banking cities in the country. Tourists flock to the seashores of the Outer Banks, while Great Smoky Mountains National Park and the Appalachian Trail draw vacationers to the wild western highlands. The state's agriculture is quite diverse. It ranks first in total tobacco harvest and in turkey production, is second only to Iowa in hog raising, and is a major producer of many other farm products.

Both highs and lows seem likely in North Carolina's future. Some businesses, like technology and finance, should continue to shine. But state manufacturing doesn't look so bright. More than 25,000 textile jobs were lost to foreign competition in 2003. State leaders are working to solve these and other problems. They hope that with its rich resources and landscapes from beachfront to rocky top, the state's future will be looking up.

NORTH CAROLINA
Tar Heel State

STATEHOOD	November 21, 1789; 12th state
CAPITAL	Raleigh
LARGEST CITY	Charlotte Population 580,597
TOTAL AREA	53,819 sq mi; 139,389 sq km
LAND AREA	48,711 sq mi; 126,161 sq km
POPULATION	8,407,248
POPULATION DENSITY	170.8 people per sq mi
MAJOR RACIAL/ ETHNIC GROUPS	72.1% white; 21.6% African American; 1.4% Asian; 1.2% Native American. Hispanic (any race) 4.7%.
INDUSTRY	real estate, health services, chemicals, tobacco products, finance, textiles
AGRICULTURE	poultry, hogs, tobacco, nursery stock, cotton, soybeans

CARDINAL

FLOWERING DOGWOOD

Did you know?

1. In 1903 the Wright brothers made the first successful human-powered flight at Kill Devil Hill near Kitty Hawk on the Outer Banks.
2. The state's nickname honors North Carolina's soldiers who refused to turn and run during the Civil War, as if their heels were glued to the ground with tar. Even Confederate General Robert E. Lee recognized the bravery of the "Tar Heel boys."
3. North Carolina has the nation's largest state-maintained highway system, with more than 77,000 miles (124,000 km) of roadway.
4. Edward Teach, also known as the notorious pirate Blackbeard, used Ocracoke Island, part of the Outer Banks, as a hideout. The place off Cape Fear where he was killed is known as Teach's Hole.
5. More than 1,250,000 bricks were used to build the Cape Hatteras Lighthouse.

SOUTH CAROLINA

★ *Palmetto State* ★

SHAPED LIKE A WEDGE or a spreading fan, triangular South Carolina points to the Blue Ridge and waves at the Atlantic. On its ocean edge, warm sea breezes rustle coastal grasses and stately palmetto trees. From the time a Revolutionary War fort built from these tough trees withstood a British attack, South Carolina has been known as the Palmetto State. While smaller than its neighbors, South Carolina has played a major role in the nation's history.

South Carolinians usually divide their state into two broad regions. A small slice of Appalachian highlands and a larger piece of rolling piedmont form the northwestern third of the state called the Up Country. Here, swift streams and rivers roll from the highlands.

The southeastern two-thirds of the state are the Low Country, a South Carolina name for the broad Atlantic Coastal Plain. Here, rivers slow and flow across fine lowland soil and swampy lands. Mild winters and long, hot summers dominate, always with a threat of big storms. Hurricane Hugo tore through Charleston with winds of 135 miles per hour (217 kph) in 1989.

After Spanish and French attempts to colonize the coast failed, the English succeeded at Charles Towne—later renamed Charleston—in 1670. Located a few miles inland on a point between the Ashley and Cooper Rivers, the port prospered as slave-based plantation agriculture took root. Early farming here produced cotton, indigo, and tobacco, but rice soon became the biggest export crop. North and South Carolina were made separate royal colonies in 1729. The ragged shoreline of bays and islands harbored pirates, who raided Carolina shipping and settlements. South Carolina became the eighth state in 1788, and the capital was moved from Charleston to more centrally located Columbia in 1790.

1680

Slaves, shown here unloading rice barges, taught their English masters how to grow rice, which flourished as a plantation crop.

1861

The Civil War began with a Confederate attack on the Union's Fort Sumter, which guarded Charleston harbor.

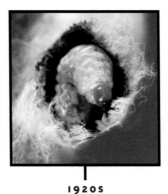

1920S

The damage done to cotton by the boll weevil forced South Carolina and other southern states to plant other crops.

1989

Hurricane Hugo, which piled up boats like toys, eroded beaches, and leveled dunes, had a devastating effect on the tourist industry.

Charleston's historic downtown district (opposite) is considered to be a living museum of early Southern life. Though damaged by Hurricane Hugo in 1989, the city's grand 18th- and 19th-century homes retain their charm and grace.

South Carolina, long home to important U.S. military operations, now honors national defense in another way. Fifty-six pillars of beautiful Kershaw granite, quarried from Lancaster County (left), stand at attention at the National World War II Memorial, on the Mall in Washington, D.C. The pillars represent states and territories—plus the District of Columbia—that were part of the U.S. at the time of the war. The project's architect chose this South Carolina stone for the 17-foot-(5-m-) high columns because it "shone like a diamond."

Highest point in South Carolina

BLUE RIDGE

Sassafras Mt. 3,560 ft 1,085 m

CHATTOOGA N.W.&S.R.
SUMTER N.F.

COWPENS N.B.
Gaffney
KINGS MOUNTAIN N.M.P.
Wylie Lake

Greer
Spartanburg
York
Rock Hill
Fort Mill

NORTH CAROLINA

Greenville
Taylors
Easley
Gantt
Mauldin
Simpsonville
Union

CATAWBA I.R.

Lancaster

Cheraw
Bennettsville

Lake Keowee
Seneca
Clemson

Belton
Laurens
Clinton

Chester

CAROLINA SANDHILLS N.W.R.

Anderson

SUMTER NATIONAL FOREST

Winnsboro

Wateree Lake

Hartsville
Dillon

Hartwell Lake

Newberry
Greenwood
Saluda

Abbeville
NINETY SIX N.H.S.

Lake Murray
Irmo

Camden
Darlington
Florence
Marion
Mullins

Richard B. Russell Lake

SUMTER NATIONAL FOREST

Forest Acres
West Columbia
Cayce
Columbia

SOUTH

Sumter
Lake City

Loris

Batesburg-Leesville

CONGAREE N.P.

CAROLINA

Conway
Socastee
North Myrtle Beach

Edgefield

N. Fork Edisto

Manning
Kingstree

Myrtle Beach
Surfside Beach
Garden City

GEORGIA

Aiken

S. Fork Edisto

SANTEE N.W.R.
Santee
Santee Dam

Lake Marion

Georgetown

North Island

North Augusta
Clearwater
Williston

Orangeburg

Lake Moultrie

FRANCIS MARION NATIONAL FOREST

Barnwell

Bamberg

Moncks Corner
Summerville

Santee

Allendale

Edisto

Goose Creek
Hanahan

CAPE ROMAIN N.W.R.

Cape Island

Hampton
Walterboro

Ladson
North Charleston

CHARLES PINCKNEY N.H.S.

ACE BASIN N.W.R.

Mt. Pleasant
FT. SUMTER NAT. MON.

Charleston

ATLANTIC

Burton
Beaufort
Port Royal
St. Helena Sound

Edisto Island
St. Helena Island

OCEAN

PINCKNEY ISLAND N.W.R.
SAVANNAH N.W.R.

Parris Island
Port Royal Sound

SEA ISLANDS

Hilton Head Island
Hilton Head Island

Daufuskie Island

0 25 50 miles
0 25 50 kilometers
Albers Conic Equal-Area Projection

Invention of the cotton gin in 1793 greatly increased production of the fiber crop. Low Country plantation owners, fearing loss of their wealth if slavery were abolished, led the fateful drive to withdraw from the Union in late 1860. By then, 60 percent of the state's population was African American, almost all slaves. The Civil War's first shot was fired on U.S. Fort Sumter in Charleston harbor on April 12, 1861.

South Carolina's economy suffered through hard times for decades after the war. Small-scale farmers toiled in poverty, and some migrated to Northern cities for work. Soil erosion damaged state farmlands, and cotton output was ruined by the boll weevil in the 1920s. Tobacco then increased in importance and is still a leading state crop. Soybeans now dominate in acreage planted, and the state produces more peaches than Georgia in some years.

First railroads then freeways stitched South Carolina into the nation's industrial fabric along the textile belt between Greenville and Spartanburg. Longleaf and loblolly pine forests support a thriving pulp and paper industry. High-tech businesses, nuclear plants, and military bases also contribute to the economy.

Travelers make South Carolina a top stop. Seaside resorts like Myrtle Beach on the "Grand Strand of Sand" and Hilton Head in the Sea Islands attract millions of visitors annually. Charleston's historic mansions display the lives of South Carolina's early "rich and famous," while the Slave Mart Museum shows the awful conditions of the slave trade. Today, South Carolina works to provide better education, jobs, and quality of life for all its citizens. With its abundant resources and diverse economy, the Palmetto State can look forward to a strong future.

SOUTH CAROLINA
Palmetto State

STATEHOOD	May 23, 1788; 8th state
CAPITAL	Columbia
LARGEST CITY	Columbia Population 117,394
TOTAL AREA	32,020 sq mi; 82,932 sq km
LAND AREA	30,110 sq mi; 77,983 sq km
POPULATION	4,147,152
POPULATION DENSITY	136.4 people per sq mi
MAJOR RACIAL/ ETHNIC GROUPS	67.2% white; 29.5% African American; .9% Asian; .3% Native American. Hispanic (any race) 2.4%.
INDUSTRY	service industries, tourism, chemicals, textiles, machinery, forest products
AGRICULTURE	chickens, tobacco, nursery stock, beef cattle, dairy products, cotton

CAROLINA WREN   YELLOW JESSAMINE

Did you know?

1. Sandhills along the western edge of the coastal plain are the remains of beaches from an ancient sea that once covered the area.
2. Sullivan Island, off the coast of Charleston, is known as the Ellis Island of Slavery. It was here that more than 200,000 enslaved people from West Africa first set foot on American soil.
3. Before it became known as the Palmetto State, South Carolina was known as the Iodine State because of the large quantities of this mineral found in its plants.
4. Francis Marion earned the nickname Swamp Fox for his legendary ability to stage raids against the British and then disappear into the swamps of southern South Carolina during the Revolutionary War.
5. The first French settlement in South Carolina was Parris Island, founded in 1562.

TENNESSEE

★ *Volunteer State* ★

IF YOU THINK Tennessee, think "three." Three stars on Tennessee's flag represent the three physical regions of the state: East, Middle, and West. They may also symbolize that it was the third state to join the Union after the original 13.

East Tennessee is row after row of ridges, topped by the Great Smoky Mountains. Named for the combination of mist and plant vapors that hover in the steep-walled valleys, the Smokies are home to an amazing diversity of plants and animals. This region also includes the deeply eroded Cumberland Plateau. These eastern highlands give way to the gently rolling lands of Middle Tennessee. A large oval basin, the region boasts rich agricultural lands perfect for livestock grazing and crop raising—especially tobacco and corn. West Tennessee is in the flatter and lower expanses of the wide Mississippi River Valley. Its fertile lands are known for growing cotton.

The state's principal river is the Tennessee. Beginning near Knoxville, the river flows southwest past Chattanooga into northern Alabama. But then it loops back into the state, flowing north into Kentucky where it joins the Ohio River. Earthquakes sloshed water from the Mississippi into a low-lying area to form Reelfoot Lake—Tennessee's only large natural lake.

Cherokee people living along rivers of East Tennessee called one of their towns Tanasie, and the region took this name. The French scouted and traded on the rivers by the late 1600s. When Britain gained control after the French and Indian War, Virginians began to migrate to green Tennessee valleys. In 1780 Fort Nashborough was founded on the Cumberland River. This settlement later became Nashville, the state capital. More than 70,000 people lived in the territory when Tennessee was added to the Union in 1796. A series of treaties forced the Chickasaw from

1812

Andrew Jackson became known as a fierce Indian fighter in the War of 1812 and worked for the removal of all Native Americans.

1863

During the Civil War, Union forces captured Chattanooga, which gave them control of an important rail center.

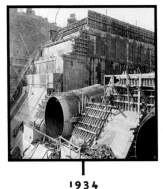

1934

Norris Dam was the first built under the Tennessee Valley Authority, which controlled flooding and provided electricity to rural areas.

Present day

The General Motors Saturn plant at Spring Hill is part of a growing manufacturing region in central Tennessee.

Crested by Clingmans Dome (opposite), Great Smoky Mountains National Park stretches along the border between Tennessee and North Carolina. The park is world-famous for the diversity of its plant and animal species.

their lands in western Tennessee by 1818. After Tennessee native Andrew Jackson became President, he imposed treaties that removed remaining natives from the state in the 1830s.

Immigrants from the eastern states, Ireland, and Scotland set up small farms in the valleys of East Tennessee, while Southern cotton planters moved into western areas near the Mississippi. The Civil War found the state deeply divided. Though Tennessee became the last state to join the Confederacy, thousands of residents fought for the Union. Two bloody days of conflict at Shiloh in April 1862 took the lives of nearly 24,000 men.

Tennessee was first to be readmitted to the Union after the war, but tensions remained between whites and African Americans. The Ku Klux Klan was founded in Pulaski, Tennessee, in 1866. This racist group used threats and violence to keep freed slaves from enjoying the same rights as whites. While the state attempted to rebuild its agricultural economy after the war, there were long decades of poverty for many Tennessee small farmers, both black and white. Disease ravaged its cities, too, as cholera epidemics hit Nashville, and yellow fever killed thousands in Memphis in 1878.

In the depths of the Great Depression, the federal government launched the state into the industrial era. The Tennessee Valley Authority—or TVA—built dozens of dams along the Tennessee River and its tributaries for flood control, navigation, and electric power. The state used this new hydropower to produce aluminum, steel, weapons, chemicals, and textiles. During World War II, the U.S. government built a hidden research facility at Oak Ridge where scientists worked to develop the atomic bomb.

Overall, Tennessee's future looks promising. Great Smoky Mountains National Park tops its tourism successes, attracting at least nine million visitors annually. But pollution from automobiles and distant power plants is threatening the park's health. Middle Tennessee has become a manufacturing hub, including auto assembly plants whose success is dependent on the strength of the nation's economy. And there's music—country in Nashville and blues in Memphis. Like a hard-working musical group, Tennessee's regions seek three-part harmony and prosperity for all.

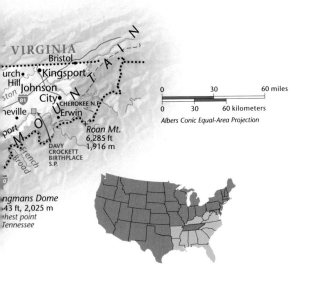

VIRGINIA
Bristol
Kingsport
Hill
Johnson
City
CHEROKEE N.F.
Erwin

Roan Mt.
6,285 ft
1,916 m

DAVY
CROCKETT
BIRTHPLACE
S.P.

ngmans Dome
43 ft, 2,025 m
hest point
Tennessee

0   30   60 miles
0   30   60 kilometers
Albers Conic Equal-Area Projection

TENNESSEE
Volunteer State

STATEHOOD	June 1, 1796; 16th state
CAPITAL	Nashville
LARGEST CITY	Memphis Population 648,882
TOTAL AREA	42,143 sq mi; 109,151 sq km
LAND AREA	41,217 sq mi; 106,752 sq km
POPULATION	5,841,748
POPULATION DENSITY	140.7 people per sq mi
MAJOR RACIAL/ ETHNIC GROUPS	80.2% white; 16.4% African American; 1.0% Asian; .3% Native American. Hispanic (any race) 2.2%.
INDUSTRY	service industries, chemicals, transportation equipment, processed foods, machinery
AGRICULTURE	cattle, cotton, dairy products, hogs, poultry, nursery stock

MOCKINGBIRD

IRIS

Did you know?

1. Many of the lakes in Tennessee are reservoirs created by dams built to control floods and to power turbines that generate electricity.
2. Tennessee shares Great Smoky Mountains National Park with North Carolina. Located within a half-day's drive of nearly half the people in the United States, it is the most visited national park in the country.
3. Graceland, Elvis Presley's mansion in Memphis, is the most visited house in the United States after the White House.
4. The state earned its nickname as the result of the remarkable bravery shown by volunteer soldiers from Tennessee at the Battle of New Orleans during the War of 1812.
5. The National Civil Rights Museum is in Memphis's Lorraine Motel, site of the assassination of Martin Luther King, Jr. in 1968.

Nashville's Grand Ole Opry, first broadcast in 1925 as the "Barn Dance," is the world's longest-running live radio show. Hundreds of thousands of people attend performances of country-and-western music shows each year at the Opry, earning Tennessee's capital city the nickname Music City, USA. Nashville is also the site of the Country Music Hall of Fame and Museum.

VIRGINIA

★ *Old Dominion State* ★

A STATE OF BEGINNINGS—and endings, too. That's Virginia. Jamestown's founding in 1607 marks the beginning of English settlement in America. The American Revolution ended at Yorktown in 1781. Eighty-four years later the Civil War ended at Appomattox Courthouse. Of the first five presidents, four were Virginians.

From ocean-side Virginia Beach, it's more than a 440-mile (708-km) hike to reach the Cumberland Gap at the state's southwestern tip. The low, sandy plain that extends out from the Chesapeake Bay is known as the Tidewater region, because its inlets and rivers feel the pull of ocean tides. Next inland is the Piedmont, which reaches west to the base of the scenic Blue Ridge Mountains. Beyond lie the rich farmlands of the Shenandoah Valley and the rugged Appalachian terrain. A small section of Virginia forms the southern tip of the Delmarva Peninsula, east of the Chesapeake Bay.

In the early 17th century, much of the continent not controlled by the Spanish or French was claimed by England and called Virginia (after Elizabeth I, who was known as the Virgin Queen). In 1607, an expedition sponsored by a merchant group named the Virginia Company established Jamestown along the James River. An attack led by Powhatan in 1622 killed not only a third of the colony's people but also the company, which lost its charter, or legal contract, for the land. Native American resistance was soon put down, and the territory was made a royal colony in 1624—the first in English history.

A plantation society eventually thrived in the Tidewater region, with fields of tobacco tended by thousands of African slaves. Small-scale farmers could not compete, and many moved west and south to pioneer new areas. By the 1760s, Virginians were bitter about increasing

1607

Pocahontas, by saving the life of John Smith, helped ensure the survival of Jamestown, first permanent British colony in America.

1781

The surrender of the British to George Washington at Yorktown ended the Revolutionary War and won independence for America.

1862

The first battle between ironclad ships was fought between the North's Monitor *and the South's* Virginia *at Hampton Roads.*

Present day

Supercomputers at Virginia Tech University are a symbol of the state's growing reputation as the Silicon Valley of the East Coast.

At Colonial Williamsburg (opposite), a craftsman uses the same techniques Virginia bookmakers would have used in the 1700s to bind a book. The city has been restored to give visitors a glimpse of everyday life in Virginia's colonial capital city.

VIRGINIA
Old Dominion State

STATEHOOD	June 25, 1788; 10th state
CAPITAL	Richmond
LARGEST CITY	Virginia Beach Population 433,934
TOTAL AREA	42,774 sq mi; 110,785 sq km
LAND AREA	39,594 sq mi; 102,548 sq km
POPULATION	7,386,330
POPULATION DENSITY	184.2 people per sq mi
MAJOR RACIAL/ ETHNIC GROUPS	72.3% white; 19.6% African American; 3.7% Asian; .3% Native American. Hispanic (any race) 4.7%.
INDUSTRY	food processing, communication and electronic equipment, transportation equipment, printing, shipbuilding, textiles
AGRICULTURE	tobacco, poultry, dairy products, beef cattle, soybeans, hogs

CARDINAL   FLOWERING DOGWOOD

Did you know?

1. King James had high hopes that Jamestown would be suitable for the production of silk. But the silkworms did not take to the native mulberry trees. Tobacco rather than silk saved the colony from financial ruin.
2. Arlington County was a portion of the land surveyed in 1791 to be part of the District of Columbia, but the land was returned to Virginia by the U.S. Congress.
3. Wild ponies have lived on Assateague Island for centuries. The ponies that live on the Virginia end of the island are owned by the Chincoteague Volunteer Fire Department. Each year in a roundup, young ponies swim to Chincoteague where they are auctioned off as a fund-raising event.
4. In 1989 Virginia voters elected the country's first African-American governor, Douglas Wilder.

British control and taxes. Many leaders in the movement for independence, including George Washington and Thomas Jefferson, were Virginians. The British were defeated in 1781. Virginia became the 10th state in 1788, with Richmond as its capital.

The debate over the continued use of slavery divided the country. Richmond was made capital of the Confederacy in 1861, and Virginia was a major battleground in the Civil War. At first, most conflicts fought on state soil were won by the South, but the tide turned by mid-1863. Richmond fell on April 3, 1865, and the South surrendered one week later.

The war left much of the state in ruins, and the end of slavery finished Virginia's plantation system. Virginia agriculture began to diversify. Tobacco was still the chief crop, but dairy farming expanded as did fruit and vegetable growing. The state industrialized, primarily in textiles, food processing, and ship-building. The deep-water harbor of the Hampton Roads area has long been a center of shipyards and naval bases. Virginia is also a major site for military training.

Today, Virginia's population is one of the most diverse in the nation. Proximity to Washington, D.C., and increased federal spending have boosted the state's economy and help keep employment up. Northern Virginia attracts defense and other high-tech research activities. Traffic and other growth-related issues abound, with new housing even springing up near historic battlefields. Although the state is known as the Old Dominion, Virginia is really in a constant state of new beginnings.

KY.

Norton

CUMBERLAND GAP N.H.P.   JEFFERSON N.F.   Big Stor Gap

Powell

TENNESSEE   Holston

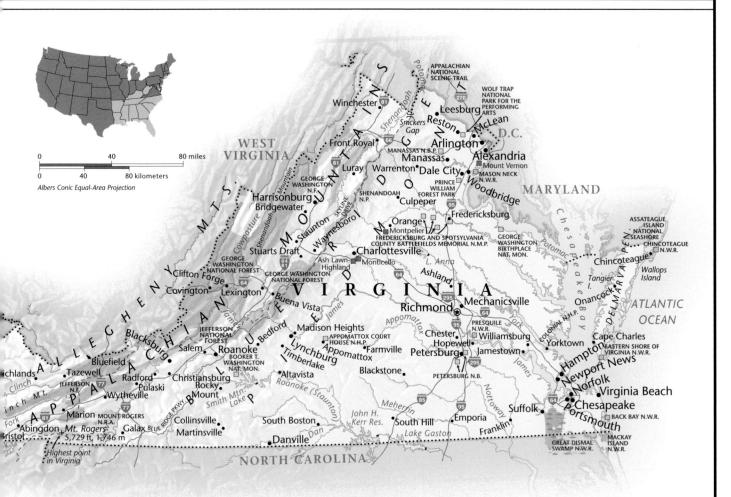

Virginia boasts more than 3,000 caves, mostly in or near the Blue Ridge Mountains. Acidic groundwater dissolves the limestone, leaving great underground chambers. In Luray Caverns (above), narrow passages open to "rooms" from 30 to 140 feet (9–43 m) high. Luray's stalactites (growing downward) and stalagmites (growing upward) add one cubic inch (16.4 cm³) to their length every 120 years as water deposits minerals on them.

WEST VIRGINIA

★ *Mountain State* ★

THE MOUNTAIN STATE is a rough-and-tumble landscape of steep ridges and deep valleys that is sometimes called the Colorado of the East. Enclosed within crooked boundaries that mostly follow winding rivers and uneven mountain tops, West Virginia's rugged isolation has helped shape the state's history and its people.

The thickly forested Appalachians acted as a barrier, keeping people from the east away. Many early German and Scotch-Irish settlers came from Pennsylvania, following long north-south valleys. In 1727 New Mecklenburg (now Shepherdstown) became the first permanent community. Native Americans defended their hunting grounds against the newcomers, but gave up claims to the region after a 1774 defeat.

Having little in common with wealthy, slave-holding Virginia planters who held political power over the region, people looked west to the Kanawha and Ohio Rivers for trade. Most held no slaves and did not want slavery in their region. They voted against secession from the Union in 1861. Outvoted, they decided to secede from Virginia instead. Two years later, West Virginia became the 35th state. Charleston was made its permanent capital in 1885.

The Mountain State's economy has had its highs and lows. Vast forests aboveground and abundant minerals below offered opportunities. Hardwood forests cover more than two-thirds of the state, and it has long produced lumber for the nation. Salt has been mined from the Charleston area since the early 1800s. Natural gas deposits made the state a leader in gas and oil production in the early 20th century.

But it was "Old King Coal" that really heated up state industrial growth. First discovered in the 1740s, vast deposits of soft bituminous coal lie beneath half the state. Coal provided fuel for salt and chemical works, iron and steel mills,

1859

Fiery abolitionist John Brown failed in his attempt to start a slave revolt by raiding the federal arsenal at Harpers Ferry.

1870

Stories about John Henry's skills as a steel-driving man working on the Big Bend Tunnel made him an American folk hero.

Early 1900s

As coal came to dominate the economy, labor union efforts to win better working conditions for men and boys led to mine wars.

Present day

Outdoor recreation seekers, such as these on the Gauley River, now make tourism West Virginia's chief business.

Adventurers of all kinds "dive" into West Virginia's beautiful deep valleys. Here a BASE (Building, Antenna, Span, Earth) jumper skydives off the 876-foot- (265-m-) high New River Gorge Bridge, an activity that is legal only on Bridge Day each October.

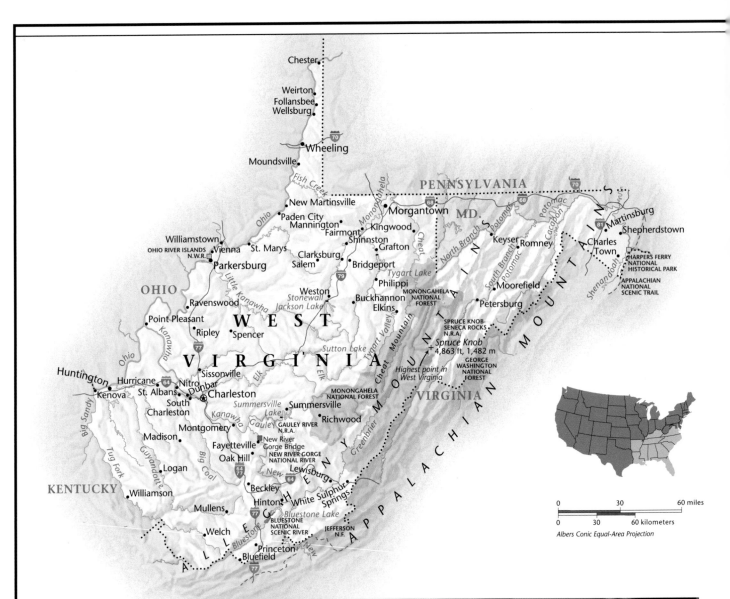

Chester
Weirton
Follansbee
Wellsburg

Wheeling

Moundsville

PENNSYLVANIA

New Martinsville

MD.

Morgantown

Paden City
Mannington
Fairmont
Kingwood
Shinnston

Williamstown
OHIO RIVER ISLANDS
N.W.R.
Vienna
St. Marys
Clarksburg
Grafton

Parkersburg
Salem
Bridgeport
Tygart Lake

OHIO

Philippi

Weston
Stonewall
Jackson Lake
Buckhannon
Elkins

MONONGAHELA
NATIONAL
FOREST

Ravenswood

Keyser
Romney
Charles
Town
Shepherdstown

Martinsburg

HARPERS FERRY
NATIONAL
HISTORICAL PARK

APPALACHIAN
NATIONAL
SCENIC TRAIL

Moorefield

Petersburg

SPRUCE KNOB-
SENECA ROCKS
N.R.A.

Point Pleasant

Ripley
Spencer

Spruce Knob
+ 4,863 ft, 1,482 m
Highest point in
West Virginia

GEORGE
WASHINGTON
NATIONAL
FOREST

W E S T

V I R G I N I A

Sutton Lake

Huntington
Hurricane
Sissonville
Nitro
Dunbar
St. Albans
Charleston
South
Charleston
Kenova

VIRGINIA

Summersville
Lake
Summersville

MONONGAHELA
NATIONAL FOREST

Madison

Kanawha

Richwood

Montgomery

GAULEY RIVER
N.R.A.

New River
Gorge Bridge
NEW RIVER GORGE
NATIONAL RIVER

Greenbrier

Fayetteville
Oak Hill

Lewisburg

Logan

KENTUCKY

Williamson

Beckley

Hinton

White Sulphur
Springs

Mullens

Bluestone Lake

BLUESTONE
NATIONAL
SCENIC RIVER

JEFFERSON
N.F.

Welch

Princeton
Bluefield

Big Sandy

Tug Fork

Guyandotte

Big Coal

New

Bluestone

A L L E G H E N Y   M O U N T A I N S

A P P A L A C H I A N   M O U N T A I N S

0   30   60 miles
0   30   60 kilometers
Albers Conic Equal-Area Projection

Glassmaking has long been a source of income and pride for West Virginia. Fine deposits of silica-rich sandstone provide the raw material, and natural gas furnishes the heat. Here, a glassmaker carefully shapes a fine vase in a glass works east of Huntington.

and glassworks. Steamboats paddled the state's rivers, and then trains, powered by coal, chugged through its mountains. They also transported the fuel—plus lumber and other resources—to homes and businesses across the nation. Immigrants, including whites from the North, blacks from the South, and Southern Europeans, found work in state mines and factories. Both world wars were boom times for West Virginia's economy. The chemical industry expanded and coal production peaked in 1947 with 176 million tons.

But coal mining brought darker times to the state. Years of breathing coal dust brought black lung disease to thousands of miners, and many more died in accidents. Pay was low, with workers too often mistreated and cheated by mining companies. Workers's attempts to get better wages and working conditions by unionizing often ended in violence. The Great Depression brought hard times but also U.S. laws allowing labor unions. By the 1950s, boom times for the nation's steel industry were over, and the market for coal was reduced. Later environmental laws favored cleaner-burning coal from western states. In 1983 unemployment reached a terrible 21 percent. Though West Virginia today trails only Wyoming as a coal producer, the fuel's importance as a job source is declining, and the state has much damage to repair from more than 150 years of mining.

In recent years West Virginia has turned to different resources—especially to its natural beauty—in attempts to strengthen its economy. The state's mostly rural residents work increasingly in service industries. Tourists love to hike the state's mountain trails, raft its rushing rivers, and sample its country crafts and culture. Like state residents, they seek to stay connected to the outside world but find serenity in West Virginia.

WEST VIRGINIA
Mountain State

STATEHOOD	June 20, 1863; 35th state
CAPITAL	Charleston
LARGEST CITY	Charleston Population 51,702
TOTAL AREA	24,230 sq mi; 62,755 sq km
LAND AREA	24,078 sq mi; 62,361 sq km
POPULATION	1,810,354
POPULATION DENSITY	74.8 people per sq mi
MAJOR RACIAL/ ETHNIC GROUPS	95.0% white; 3.2% African American; .5% Asian; .2% Native American. Hispanic (any race) .7%.
INDUSTRY	tourism, coal mining, chemicals, metal manufacturing, forest products, stone, clay, oil, and glass products
AGRICULTURE	poultry and eggs, cattle, dairy products, apples

CARDINAL

RHODODENDRON

Did you know?

1. Moundsville, in the northern panhandle, is one of the nation's oldest and largest Indian burial grounds.
2. The first rural free mail delivery in the United States started in Charles Town on October 6, 1896.
3. West Virginia's mean elevation of 1,500 feet (460 m) makes it the state with the highest average elevation east of the Mississippi.
4. Outdoor advertising began in Wheeling as early as the 1920s when the makers of Mail Pouch tobacco painted bridges and barns with words encouraging people to chew their product.
5. One of the most legendary family feuds in the United States involved the Hatfields, who lived on the West Virginia side of the Tug Fork River, and the McCoys, who lived on the Kentucky side. It lasted from 1863–1891.
6. West Virginia is the only state with two panhandles.

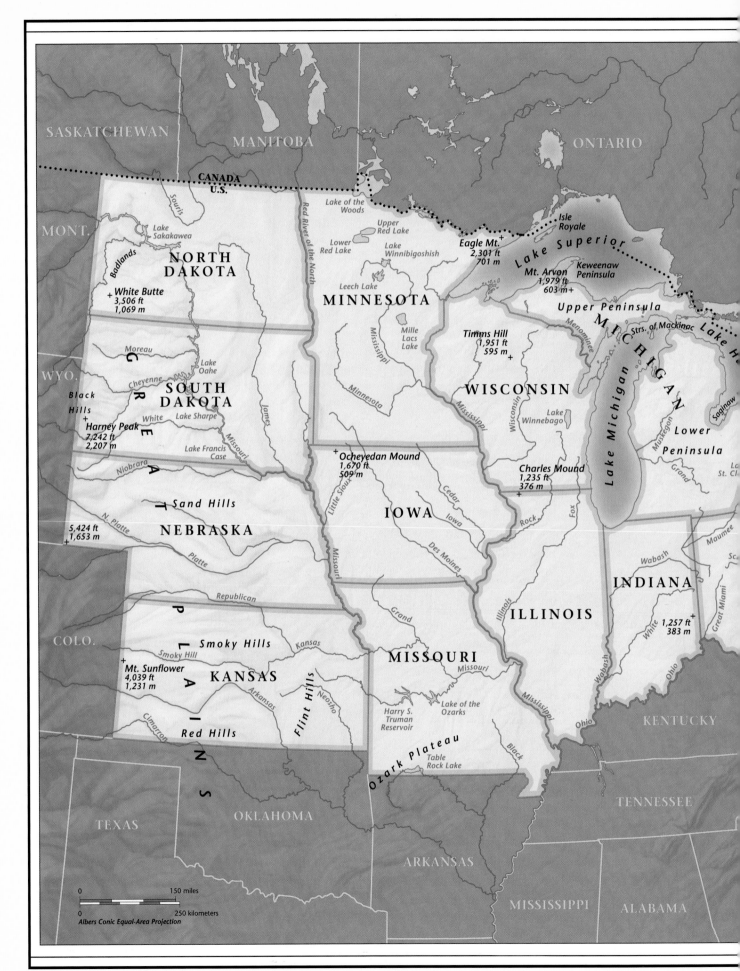

SASKATCHEWAN

MANITOBA

ONTARIO

CANADA
U.S.

Lake of the
Woods

MONT.

Souris

Lake
Sakakawea

Badlands

NORTH
DAKOTA

+ White Butte
3,506 ft
1,069 m

Upper
Red Lake

Lower
Red Lake

Lake
Winnibigoshish

MINNESOTA

Leech Lake

Eagle Mt. +
2,301 ft
701 m

Isle
Royale

Lake Superior

Mt. Arvon
1,979 ft
603 m +

Keweenaw
Peninsula

Upper Peninsula

MICHIGAN

Strs. of Mackinac

Lake H

WYO.

G
R
E
A
T

Moreau

Cheyenne

Lake
Oahe

SOUTH
DAKOTA

Mississippi

Mille
Lacs
Lake

Minnesota

Timms Hill
1,951 ft
595 m +

WISCONSIN

Wisconsin

Lake
Winnebago

Menominee

Lake Michigan

Lower

Peninsula

Muskegon

Saginaw

La
St. Cl

Black
Hills
+
Harney Peak
7,242 ft
2,207 m

White

Lake Sharpe

Lake Francis
Case

Niobrara

Missouri

James

+ Ocheyedan Mound
1,670 ft
509 m

Little Sioux

Cedar

Iowa

IOWA

Charles Mound
1,235 ft
376 m +

Rock

Fox

Grand

N. Platte

5,424 ft
1,653 m

Sand Hills

NEBRASKA

Platte

Republican

P
L
A
I
N
S

Smoky Hills

Smoky Hill

+ Mt. Sunflower
4,039 ft
1,231 m

KANSAS

Arkansas

Cimarron

Red Hills

Flint Hills

Kansas

Neosho

Missouri

MISSOURI

Grand

Des Moines

ILLINOIS

Illinois

Missouri

Mississippi

Lake of the
Ozarks

Harry S.
Truman
Reservoir

Ozark Plateau

Table
Rock Lake

Black

Wabash

INDIANA

1,257 ft +
383 m

White

Wabash

Ohio

Great Miami

Maumee

Sc

KENTUCKY

TENNESSEE

COLO.

TEXAS

OKLAHOMA

ARKANSAS

MISSISSIPPI

ALABAMA

0   150 miles
0   250 kilometers
Albers Conic Equal-Area Projection

The Midwest

THE AMERICAN HEARTLAND stretches across the central United States from Ohio and the Great Lakes almost to the foothills of the Rocky Mountains. Several times in the last Ice Age giant glaciers flowed south from Canada across this gentle land, scooping out thousands of lakes in Minnesota, Wisconsin, and Michigan. Of these, the Great Lakes form the world's largest body of fresh water. Farther south, the ice sheets melted into countless streams that carried crushed rock and fine silt that account for the rolling hills and fertile prairie soils found throughout the lower Midwest.

There are giant rivers, too. The Ohio, Missouri, and a dozen other large rivers join the Mississippi to become the longest and most important river system in North America. Farther west in the Dakotas, sediments from rivers and ancient oceans have eroded into bizarre landforms called badlands. Nearby the Black Hills rise above the Great Plains.

Land of Plenty Under the Prairie Sky

A VAST LANDSCAPE of great forests and endless prairies, this mid-continental heartland adds geographic space and a rural spirit to the United States. Here the bold mark of nature appears in sudden tornadoes, great floods, and thunderstorms that drop hailstones the size of baseballs. Winters can be long and very cold, especially in the far north along the border with Canada. Yet each one ultimately dissolves into humid spring warmth that nurtures new crops, wildflowers, and migrating birds.

For centuries eastern woodland Indians farmed and fished while semi-nomadic prairie tribes hunted bison, elk, coyote, and other mammals on their grassy "American Serengeti." In the early 1600s French fur traders and missionaries arrived in the Great Lakes region and immediately became involved in long-standing Indian wars over territory and resources. In the 1760s France lost eastern portions of their Louisiana Territory to Britain after the French and Indian War and gave control of lands west of the Mississippi to Spain. These western lands were returned to France in 1800. America won the Northwest Territory—the area north of the Ohio River and west to the Mississippi—after the Revolution and then purchased French Louisiana in 1803.

American settlers came mostly from the Northeast. They clung to the densely forested rivers and shores of the Great Lakes and eastern prairie. Later, railroads bridged the Mississippi and steamed westward. The Homestead Act of 1862 made free tracts of land available to people looking for new places to live. Tall grasses grew in the fertile eastern prairie where rainfall was plentiful, but the thick matted roots made the soil difficult to plow until the 1850s when John Deere's steel-bladed plow came into widespread use. Farther west the climate was drier, and the grasses were shorter. Farmers used windmills to pull water from underground storage basins called aquifers. What had been described as the Great American Desert became vast fields of wheat. The Germans, Norwegians, Swedes, and others who came in great numbers cultivated an immense patchwork of fields that largely displaced the Native American way of life.

By 1900 the region had evolved into America's "breadbasket." Corn and soybeans thrive in a well-watered belt from Ohio to Iowa. Dairy farming flourishes in the cool, moist climate of Wisconsin and Minnesota. To the drier west, wheat rules in Kansas, Nebraska, and the Dakotas. Minneapolis grew as a grain-milling center. Cattle, hogs, and poultry are raised on large farms and feedlots across much of this region. By the end of the 19th century Chicago, St. Louis, Kansas City, and Omaha had become meat packing centers. Today, food processing is done in many rural towns. Rich deposits of iron ore and coal turned the Great Lakes region into a manufacturing empire. Steel mills and factories in Chicago, Gary, Detroit, and Cleveland employed a new wave of immigrants from Europe as well as African Americans migrating from the South. The watery highways that attracted Indians and settlers remain the principal routes for transporting grains and ores, while railroads and trucks carry manufactured goods to the rest of the country and beyond.

> "There was nothing but land...the material out of which countries are made."
>
> WILLA CATHER, *The Homesteader's World*

The population and economy of the Midwest is on the move once again. Corporate agribusiness is swallowing up traditional family farms. Computer and biotechnology firms are slowly replacing steel mills and automobile assembly plants, and expanding suburbs are causing farms to disappear. Commerce still centers on Chicago, one of the busiest air, rail, and shipping crossroads on the continent. New immigrants from Asia and Latin America arrive daily in search of jobs and a good life under the prairie sky.

Slaughtered almost to extinction, the bison (above) is still a symbol of the great rolling grasslands that cover much of the Midwest, where pigs, poultry, cattle, and dairy cows now reign. Most of the prairie has been planted in corn, soybeans, and wheat.

ILLINOIS
★ *Land of Lincoln* ★

PANCAKE FLAT—that's what most of Illinois is except for some northwest uplands and a strip of southwest hills. Until less than two centuries ago it was covered by tall, waving prairie grasses. Thousands of years ago, invading ice sheets ended their southward campaign in Illinois, grinding down landforms on their advance and leaving rich, dark soils during their retreat. Hundreds of south-flowing rivers drain to the Wabash, Ohio, and Mississippi—rivers that form most of the state's boundaries.

When French explorers Marquette and Joliet canoed down the Mississippi in 1673, they met people who called themselves the "Illini"—an Algonquin word for "men" or "warriors." The European newcomers founded Cahokia along the big river as the first Illinois settlement in 1699. British military forces and traders followed, and for a time they lived in harmony with the French and various Native American groups. Peace turned to conflict with the French and Indian War. In 1763 the victorious British took over the Illinois Territory.

The U.S. gained control two decades later, following independence. Illinois formed part of the Northwest Territory of 1787, and settlers swarmed to the region. Illinois became the 21st state in 1818, with its capital first in Kaskaskia and then Vandalia—both in the south. Abraham Lincoln, then an Illinois legislator, worked hard to get the capital moved in 1837 to Springfield, a more central location. Today, that city celebrates the 16th President's many accomplishments, and Illinois is often called the Land of Lincoln.

Where nature once raised grasses, settlers planted wheat. At first, the gummy soils proved tough to plow with wooden or iron blades. But that was before 1838, when a blacksmith named John Deere perfected his steel plow. The prairie

1673

French explorers Father Jacques Marquette and Louis Joliet were likely the first Europeans to enter the Illinois area.

1858

Views on slavery expressed by Abraham Lincoln in his debates with Stephen A. Douglas led to his election as President in 1860.

1908–1919

Rioting caused by racial tensions between blacks and whites in Chicago and other cities forced some people to move to safer places.

1955

The Fermi National Accelerator Laboratory near Batavia is one of the world's leading centers for the study of the atom.

Buildings of the "Loop," Chicago's main shopping district (opposite), are evidence of the decades when Chicago and New York City competed in raising ever-higher skyscrapers. The Sears Tower thrusts 1,454 feet (443 m) upward—the tallest building in the U.S.

Highest point in Illinois
+ Charles Mound 1,235 ft, 376 m

WISCONSIN

Galena

UPPER MISSISSIPPI RIVER NATIONAL WILDLIFE AND FISH REFUGE

Freeport
Pecatonica
Harvard
Waukegan

LAKE MICHIGAN

IOWA

MISSISSIPPI PALISADES S.P.
Savanna
Rockford
Belvidere
Schaumburg
Arlington Heights
Evanston
Chicago
Cicero

Grand Detour
Sycamore
Elgin
De Kalb
Sterling
Dixon
Naperville
Aurora
Sandwich

Moline
Geneseo
Tampico
Mendota
Joliet

Rock Island
Ottawa
Morris
La Salle
Peru

MARK TWAIN N.W.R.
Kewanee
Streator
Kankakee

Galesburg
Chillicothe
Pontiac

Monmouth
Iroquois
Watseka

Peoria
Morton
Hoopeston

Nauvoo
Canton
Pekin
Normal
Bloomington
Rantoul

Macomb
EMIQUON N.W.R.
CHAUTAUQUA N.W.R.
VERMILION NATIONAL WILD & SCENIC RIVER
Danville

Carthage
Clinton
Champaign
Urbana

ILLINOIS

MARK TWAIN N.W.R.
Beardstown
LINCOLN'S NEW SALEM S.H.S.
Lincoln
Salt Creek

Quincy
MEREDOSIA N.W.R.
McKee Cr.
Springfield
Decatur
Tuscola

Pittsfield
Jacksonville
Sangamon
Paris

MARK TWAIN N.W.R.
White Hall
Taylorville
Lake Shelbyville
Mattoon
Charleston

Carlinville
Pana

INDIANA

MARK TWAIN N.W.R.
Jerseyville
Litchfield
Kaskaskia
Effingham
Robinson

MARK TWAIN N.W.R.
Olney

Alton
Vandalia
Carlyle Lake
Lawrenceville

Edwardsville
Salem
Flora

Granite City
CAHOKIA MOUNDS S.H.S.
Centralia
Mt. Carmel

East St. Louis
Mt. Vernon
Fairfield

Belleville

MISSOURI
Red Bud
Nashville
Rend Lake
Carmi

Du Quoin
Benton
Saline

Kaskaskia Island
Chester
West Frankfort

Murphysboro
CRAB ORCHARD N.W.R.
Harrisburg
Shawneetown

Carbondale
Marion

Anna
SHAWNEE N.F.
CYPRESS CREEK N.W.R.
SHAWNEE NATIONAL FOREST
Ohio

KENTUCKY

Metropolis
Cairo

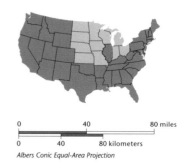

0   40   80 miles
0   40   80 kilometers
Albers Conic Equal-Area Projection

Illinois produces enormous crops of corn and soybeans on some of the most fertile farmland on the planet. Here a crew applies herbicide to soybeans, knowing they must be careful to select a chemical that will kill the weeds without damaging the crop or the soil. Some farmers have gone organic, which means they don't use chemicals on their fields.

had finally met its match. Farm machinery is still a top Illinois export, and the state usually ranks second in both corn and soybean production.

Beginning in the 1860s, Illinois grew into an industrial as well as an agricultural giant—with Chicago leading the way. Its fiery steel mills boomed, with iron ore shipped in from the Lake Superior region and coal hauled in by rail from downstate deposits. Immigrants from all across Europe plus African Americans from southern states came to work in huge and often dangerous slaughterhouses, foundries, and other factories. Protests and strikes erupted between management and workers, and unions were eventually organized to improve working conditions.

Chicago is one of the world's great cities. With almost 2.8 million people and a greater metropolitan area triple that, it's bigger than any other city between New York City and Los Angeles. With a great location at the southern end of Lake Michigan, Chicago has long been the top transportation center in the country—by water, rail, truck, and air. Though Chicagoland factories still churn out everything from steel and machinery to candy and gum, the industrial "city of the broad shoulders" increasingly processes ideas and information, too.

As they look forward, Illinois leaders tackle tough issues. The state has recently lost more than 160,000 manufacturing jobs, so keeping high-wage employment is a challenge. While four of five Illinois residents live in its cities, four of five state acres are farmed. But urban areas are sprawling out and taking over some of the world's best cropland. Some worry that Illinois should use that land to grow food. These and other struggles will test the minds of Illinois people as they face the future across their Prairie State.

ILLINOIS
Land of Lincoln

STATEHOOD	December 3, 1818; 21st state
CAPITAL	Springfield
LARGEST CITY	Chicago Population 2,886,251
TOTAL AREA	57,914 sq mi; 149,998 sq km
LAND AREA	55,584 sq mi; 143,961 sq km
POPULATION	12,653,544
POPULATION DENSITY	226.7 people per sq mi
MAJOR RACIAL/ ETHNIC GROUPS	73.5% white; 15.1% African American; 3.4% Asian; .2% Native American. Hispanic (any race) 12.3%.
INDUSTRY	industrial machinery, electronic equipment, food processing, chemicals, metals, printing and publishing, rubber and plastics, motor vehicles
AGRICULTURE	corn, soybeans, hogs, cattle, dairy products, nursery stock

CARDINAL   VIOLET

Did you know?

1. Illinois was the first state to ratify the 13th Amendment to the U.S. Constitution, which made slavery illegal.
2. Between 1910 and 1930 Chicago's African-American population grew to nearly a quarter million, as the Great Migration brought black workers from the agricultural South to industrial cities in the North. The city also became a mecca for blues musicians, such as B.B. King, Memphis Minnie, and Muddy Waters.
3. On St. Patrick's Day the Chicago River is dyed green.
4. Chicago's nickname "Windy City" came from Charles Dana, editor of the New York *Sun,* who grew tired of hearing Chicagoans boast about the Columbian Exposition—the Chicago World's Fair of 1893.
5. The first controlled atomic chain reaction took place on a squash court at the University of Chicago in 1942 under the direction of physicist Enrico Fermi.

INDIANA
★ *Hoosier State* ★

"HOOSIER?" If someone knocked on the door of an early Indiana cabin, the pioneer inside might have called out "Who's here?" So goes one idea about how the state's nickname originated. Another is that a hardworking group of Indiana canal laborers were called Hoosier's Men, after their foreman. No one is certain, but Indiana's friendly, reliable people have been known by the name since the 1830s.

Indiana wears the results of ancient continental ice sheets across five-sixths of its land. Kettle lakes and huge piles of glacial gravel lie sprinkled across northern sections. A mixture of clay, sand, rocks, and other sediments called glacial till provides central Indiana's gentle landscape with fertile prairie soils. The state's southern reaches escaped these giant icy bulldozers and are more ruggedly landscaped with tree-covered hills and lowlands. Most of the state slopes gently to the southwest—draining to the Wabash River and from there to the Ohio River, which forms the southern border.

Early mound-building peoples left traces of their presence, but Algonquin peoples lived here when the French arrived in the 1670s. To protect their water route between the Great Lakes and the Mississippi River, the French constructed forts along Indiana rivers, including Vincennes on the lower Wabash. The earliest European settlement in the region, this became British property with the end of the French and Indian War in 1763. But in 1779, during the American Revolution, rebels from Kentucky seized Vincennes. Settlers poured in via this southern connection in the years that followed, leading to conflicts with Native Americans. The Battle of Tippecanoe in 1811 signaled the end of Native American control of the region. Most were forced to leave the land that the U.S. Congress named for them. The Indiana

1779
George Rogers Clark's capture of Vincennes from the British helped Americans gain control of the Northwest Territory.

1850s
The Underground Railroad, a network of escape routes that helped slaves find freedom, was very active in Indiana.

Early 1900s
Enormous mills built by U.S. Steel in Gary attracted migrant workers and laid the foundation for Indiana's steel industry.

Present day
The Indianapolis 500 auto race, held each Memorial Day weekend, attracts huge crowds and celebrates Indiana's auto heritage.

This covered bridge (opposite) is one of about 90 that are still preserved in Indiana. Built in the 19th century, these bridges were often the largest roofed area in a community, which made them good sites for weddings and political rallies.

LAKE MICHIGAN

MICHIGAN

Michigan
City
INDIANA DUNES
NATIONAL
LAKESHORE
East Chicago
Gary
Hammond
Portage
Merrillville
Crown
Point
Lowell

South Bend
Mishawaka
LaPorte

Elkhart
Goshen

Angola

Pigeon

Valparaiso
Plymouth

Nappanee
Lake
Wawasee

Kendallville
Auburn

Warsaw
Columbia
City

Cedar Cr.

St. Joseph

Tippecanoe

Rochester

North
Manchester

Eel

Fort Wayne

Rensselaer

Lake
Shafer

Wabash

Huntington
Lake

Huntington

Decatur

St. Marys

Maumee

OHIO

Iroquois

Monticello
Lake
Freeman

Logansport

Peru

Mississinewa
Lake

Salamonie
Lake

Wabash

Lafayette

Wildcat Creek

Kokomo

Marion

Gas City

Hartford
City

Portland

Mississinewa

Salamonie

469

69

Frankfort

Elwood

Alexandria

I N D I A N A

White

Winchester

Crawfordsville

Lebanon

Noblesville
Carmel

Anderson

Muncie

1,257 ft
383 m
Highest point
in Indiana

New Castle

465

Sugar Cr.

Cecil M.
Harden
Lake

Big Raccoon Cr.

Sugar Creek

74

Lawrence

70

Richmond

Indianapolis

Beech
Grove

Greenfield

Plainfield

Clinton

Greencastle

Connersville

Big Blue

Terre
Haute

Brazil

Greenwood

Franklin

Mill Cr.

Rushville

Brookville
Lake

White

Martinsville

Shelbyville

Eel

Cagles
Mill
Lake

Lake
Lemon

Flatrock

Greensburg

Whitewater

74

Wabash

Columbus

65

Sand Creek

Lawrenceburg

Bloomington

BROWN
COUNTY
S.P.

Monroe
Lake

HOOSIER
NATIONAL
FOREST

North Vernon

Linton

Salt Creek

MUSCATATUCK N.W.R.

White

Seymour

East Fork White

Muscatatuck

Bedford

Madison

Vincennes

Washington

Salem

Blue

Scottsburg

65

Ohio

KENTUCKY

HOOSIER
NATIONAL
FOREST

Charlestown

East Fork White

Patoka

Jasper

Patoka
Lake

265

Jeffersonville

Princeton

Huntingburg

Santa
Claus

HOOSIER
NATIONAL
FOREST

New Albany

Corydon

Wyandotte
Cave

NEW
HARMONY
S.H.S.

64

LINCOLN BOYHOOD
NATIONAL MEMORIAL

64

Evansville

164

Boonville

Tell
City

Ohio

Mount
Vernon

MILES
0   50   100 miles
0   50   100 kilometers
Albers Conic Equal-Area Projection

This craftsman is sculpting a block of Indiana limestone, which formed more than 300 million years ago
when the area was an inland sea. This handsome and
durable stone can be seen in many landmark buildings
across the nation, including New York's Empire State
Building, the Pentagon, near Washington, D.C., and
many state capitol buildings.

Territory was separated from the larger Northwest Territory at the turn of the 19th century, and statehood was welcomed in 1816.

Abundant rains and warm summers made the state a farming leader. Indiana industry sprouted with the arrival of the railroads at mid-century. Manufactured goods were joined by a giant steel-making effort at the beginning of the 20th century. Labor movements got an early start in Indiana. By 1920, the state had almost three million people. Indiana's economy "bottomed out" during the Great Depression but boomed both during and after World War II, producing automobile parts, electrical goods, and communications equipment.

Indiana's central location gave rise to the nickname Crossroads of America. Indianapolis became an early hub of farm product shipping and processing. An early auto-making center that lost its lead to Detroit, the city celebrates each Memorial Day weekend with the famous Indianapolis 500 race. From bike racing to basketball, other sports also draw attention to the Hoosier State. College and university athletes from across the country are honored in the new NCAA Hall of Champions in Indianapolis.

Indiana's economy, like others in the region, is shifting from an emphasis on heavy industry to a more technology-oriented job market. As factories close, workers who were accustomed to high union wages often have to settle for lower paying jobs. But there are bright spots. The opening of automobile assembly plants has brought thousands of new jobs over the past two decades. Indiana continues to be a top-ranking agricultural state, and jobs in service industries, such as tourism, insurance, and pharmaceuticals, are increasing. Overall the future looks promising for Indiana's 6.2 million residents.

INDIANA
Hoosier State

STATEHOOD	December 11, 1816; 19th state
CAPITAL	Indianapolis
LARGEST CITY	Indianapolis Population 783,612
TOTAL AREA	36,418 sq mi; 94,321 sq km
LAND AREA	35,867 sq mi; 92,895 sq km
POPULATION	6,195,643
POPULATION DENSITY	171.7 people per sq mi
MAJOR RACIAL/ ETHNIC GROUPS	87.5% white; 8.4% African American; 1% Asian; .3% Native American. Hispanic (any race) 3.5%.
INDUSTRY	transportation equipment, steel, pharmaceutical and chemical products, machinery, petroleum, and coal
AGRICULTURE	corn, soybeans, hogs, poultry and eggs, cattle, dairy products

CARDINAL

PEONY

Did you know?

1. Indiana has more miles of interstate highway for each square mile of territory than any other state, and more major interstate highways intersect in Indiana than anywhere else in the country.
2. Between 1900 and 1920, more than 200 different kinds of cars, including Duesenburgs, Auburns, Stutzes, and Maxwells, were manufactured in Indiana.
3. John Chapman, better known as Johnny Appleseed, is buried in Archer Park in Fort Wayne. Every year Fort Wayne hosts the Johnny Appleseed Festival to commemorate the man who planted apple orchards from Pennsylvania to Illinois.
4. In 1880 Wabash became the first city in the country to be lighted by electric lights.
5. The first Raggedy Ann doll was created by Marcella Gruelle in Indianapolis in 1914.

IOWA
★ *Hawkeye State* ★

IOWA IS RICH from the ground up. Its soils are legendary—some layered hundreds of feet deep. More than nine of every ten acres of the state are used for agriculture. Long, warm summer days, plenty of rainfall, and winters that preserve plant nutrients combine to make Iowa croplands the envy of other farm states. The state produces more corn, soybeans, hogs, and eggs than any other. Iowa's treasure lies not in silver or gold but in abundant and fertile soil.

Iowa is held in the arms of two great rivers, the Mississippi to the east and Missouri to the west. Thousands of years ago massive sheets of ice from the north formed most of Iowa's gently-rolling landscape. Iowa's other streams flow in southerly paths to meet up with one of the two river giants. In some years, spring snowmelt or summer downpours cause flooding and damage along some or all of Iowa's rivers.

In the summer of 1673, French explorers Marquette and Joliet canoed down the Mississippi, meeting natives on its western shore who called themselves "the people." That word, translated and changed by French and later English speakers, is "Iowa." The region was not settled by large numbers of whites until the 1830s. Its prairie soils, which supported grasses as high as riders on horseback, were difficult to plow until the invention of the steel plow. The federal government fought the Sauk and Fox peoples for Iowa lands in the Black Hawk War in 1832. Within 20 years, the last of the Native American groups was forced out to the west.

At first part of the Michigan and then the Wisconsin Territory, Iowa became the 29th state in late 1846. The state's population grew as immigrants from northern Europe arrived. Steamboats moved settlers in and goods out. The completion of a bridge over the Mississippi River at Davenport paved the way for the railroad.

1832

The defeat of the Sauk Indians at the Battle of Bad Axe along the Mississippi River helped open Iowa to white settlers.

1867

The arrival of the railroad at Council Bluffs opened a new and faster way to get goods to market. It also brought more settlers.

1930S

During the Depression, farmers seeking more money for their products tried to decrease supply by blocking roads to market.

1993

The Great Flood of 1993 was one of the worst in Iowa's history, causing more than two billion dollars in property damage.

Today, Iowa's farmers produce more than any previous generation. This bounty is due in part to the use of multipurpose agricultural machines (opposite), satellite weather data, and careful soil testing. Seed companies contribute by offering high-yield crop types.

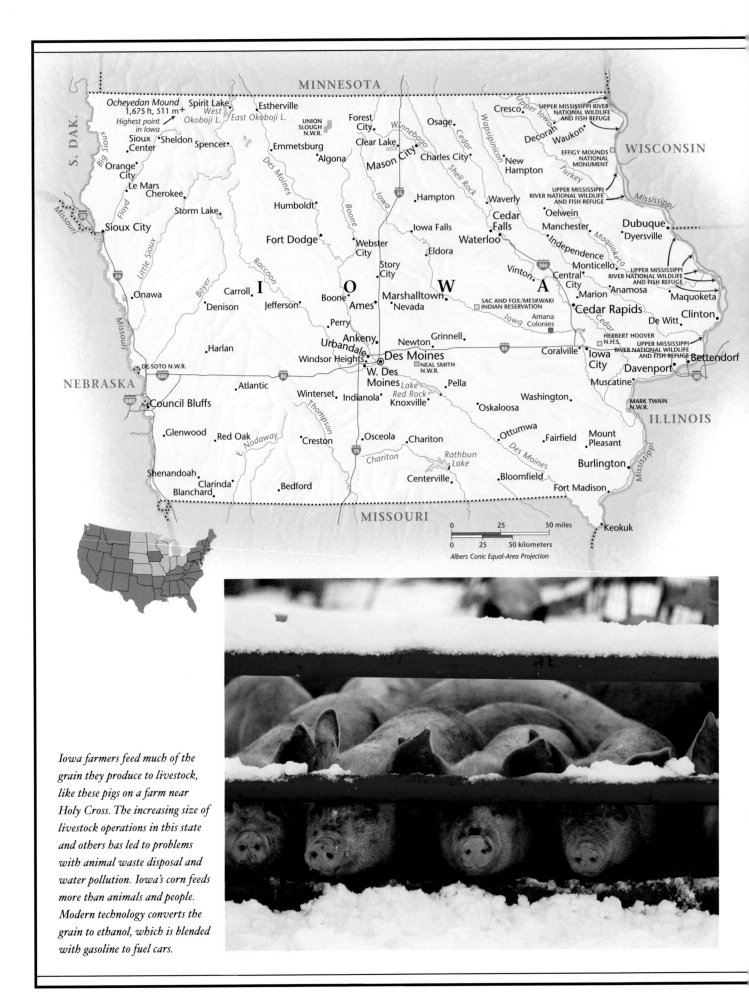

MINNESOTA

S. DAK.

Ocheyedan Mound
1,675 ft, 511 m +
Highest point
in Iowa

Spirit Lake
West
Okoboji L.   East Okoboji L.

Estherville

Cresco

Upper Iowa

UPPER MISSISSIPPI RIVER
NATIONAL WILDLIFE
AND FISH REFUGE

Sioux
Center   Sheldon   Spencer

Orange
City

Le Mars

Cherokee

Storm Lake

Sioux City

Emmetsburg

Algona

Forest
City

Clear Lake

Mason City

Winnebago

Osage

Charles City

Shell Rock

New
Hampton

Cedar

Wapsipinicon

Decorah

Waukon

EFFIGY MOUNDS
NATIONAL
MONUMENT

WISCONSIN

Turkey

UPPER MISSISSIPPI
RIVER NATIONAL WILDLIFE
AND FISH REFUGE

Mississippi

Humboldt

Des Moines

Boone

Iowa

Hampton

Iowa Falls

Waverly

Cedar
Falls

Oelwein

Manchester

Independence

Maquoketa

Dubuque

Dyersville

Fort Dodge

Webster
City

Story
City

Eldora

Waterloo

Vinton

Central
City

Monticello

Anamosa

Marion

UPPER MISSISSIPPI
RIVER NATIONAL WILDLIFE
AND FISH REFUGE

Maquoketa

Clinton

Onawa

Carroll

Denison

Jefferson

Perry

Boone

Ames

Marshalltown

Nevada

SAC AND FOX/MESKWAKI
INDIAN RESERVATION

Iowa

Amana
Colonies

Cedar Rapids

Cedar

De Witt

Little Sioux

Boyer

Raccoon

Harlan

Ankeny

Urbandale

Windsor Heights

Grinnell

Newton

Des Moines

HERBERT HOOVER
N.H.S.

Coralville

Iowa
City

UPPER MISSISSIPPI
RIVER NATIONAL WILDLIFE
AND FISH REFUGE

Bettendorf

DE SOTO N.W.R.

NEBRASKA

Atlantic

Winterset

Indianola

Knoxville

Pella

W. Des
Moines   Lake
Red Rock

NEAL SMITH
N.W.R.

Washington

Muscatine

Davenport

MARK TWAIN
N.W.R.

ILLINOIS

Council Bluffs

Glenwood

Red Oak

E. Nodaway

Thompson

Creston

Osceola

Chariton

Oskaloosa

Ottumwa

Fairfield

Mount
Pleasant

Des Moines

Burlington

Mississippi

Shenandoah

Clarinda
Blanchard

Bedford

Chariton

Rathbun
Lake

Centerville

Bloomfield

Fort Madison

Missouri

Floyd

Big Sioux

I

O

W

A

MISSOURI

Keokuk

0   25   50 miles
0   25   50 kilometers
Albers Conic Equal-Area Projection

Iowa farmers feed much of the grain they produce to livestock, like these pigs on a farm near Holy Cross. The increasing size of livestock operations in this state and others has led to problems with animal waste disposal and water pollution. Iowa's corn feeds more than animals and people. Modern technology converts the grain to ethanol, which is blended with gasoline to fuel cars.

When men boarded trains to fight in the Civil War, women kept the farms going.

The completion of a railroad across the state after the war helped bring growth and prosperity. But good times were mixed with hard times in the late 1800s. Organizations like the Grange were formed to help insure farmers fair prices for their crops. With the development of cars and trucks in the early 20th century, Iowans built better roads to bring their crops to market, and in the 1930s rural electric cooperatives made power available to every house and farm. The Great Depression hit Iowa farmers hard, but World War II helped restore prosperity by boosting demand for farm products. Tough times returned in the 1980s, forcing thousands of farmers to go out of business. The state population fell by nearly 140,000 between 1980 and 1990.

Efforts to diversify the economy helped the population rebound to a slow-growing 2.9 million. But Iowa is still tied to its soil. Recent years have seen bigger farms but fewer farmers, who use huge machinery and satellite technology to precisely plant, weed, and harvest their sprawling fields. On average, one Iowa farm grows enough food to feed 280 people. Agriculture has long fed the state's chief industry—food processing— which includes cereal milling, meat packing, and even popcorn bagging. The manufacture of farm machinery, the sale of ethanol for fuel, and the use of wind farms to generate electricity are all sources of income for Iowa's farmers. Its cities are known for insurance, banking, and printing and publishing.

To ensure the future health of its agriculture and its citizens, Iowa plans to improve water quality by curbing farm run-off and to fight erosion by continuing conservation efforts to keep its rich soil right where it belongs.

IOWA
Hawkeye State

STATEHOOD	December 28, 1846; 29th state
CAPITAL	Des Moines
LARGEST CITY	Des Moines Population 198,076
TOTAL AREA	56,272 sq mi; 145,743 sq km
LAND AREA	55,869 sq mi; 144,701 sq km
POPULATION	2,944,062
POPULATION DENSITY	52.6 people per sq mi
MAJOR RACIAL/ ETHNIC GROUPS	93.9% white; 2.1% African American; 1.3% Asian; .3% Native American. Hispanic (any race) 2.8%.
INDUSTRY	real estate, health services, industrial machinery, food processing, construction
AGRICULTURE	hogs, corn, soybeans, oats, cattle, dairy products

AMERICAN GOLDFINCH   WILD ROSE

Did you know?

1. Iowa ranks as the nation's second largest agricultural producer after California, which has almost three times its area.
2. In the 1800s Iowa's topsoil was as much as five feet (1.5 m) deep. Today, decades of farming have reduced it to an average depth of two feet (.6 m).
3. Iowa's nickname comes from Chief Black Hawk, a Sauk Indian chief who started what became known as the Black Hawk War in 1832.
4. The Amana Colonies, established in 1855 by people of German heritage who belonged to a religious group called the Community of True Inspiration, strived to achieve an ideal society that promoted equality, humility, and a simple way of life. In 1931 the community formed a corporation that became famous for making refrigerators, freezers, and air conditioners.
5. The world's largest popcorn factory is in Sioux City.

KANSAS

★ *Sunflower State* ★

"HOME ON THE RANGE." Every American has heard—and sung—the song in school, but it was a Kansas doctor, Brewster Higley, who wrote the famous lyrics. His song describes an ideal 19th-century farming life of happy homesteads where "the skies are not cloudy all day." Most Kansans would probably still agree with him about their prairie state.

The landscape of Kansas is mostly low, rolling hills, with wooded river valleys in its eastern half. Its surface slopes gently upward from Missouri to Colorado. In the east, the rocky Flint Hills preserve a 50-mile- (80-km-) long swath of prairie. The iron-colored Red Hills in the southwest and the fossil-rich Smoky Hills in the state's north-central section reveal that much of Kansas was the bottom of a vast shallow sea millions of years ago. Fossil hunters once competed for the best examples of prehistoric specimens for museums and collectors.

The state takes its name from the Kansa— "people of the south wind"—but winds are not always kind to Kansas. Storms produce hail that can ruin crops and property. Tornadoes twist their way across the Sunflower State, and blizzards howl in winter. Precipitation levels are higher in the east. The rain and snow, combined with fine soil conditions, were perfect for growing eye-high bluestem grass that covered the region before settlers arrived. Rainfall declines to the west, where shorter grasses dominate.

In 1541, the Spanish explorer Francisco Vásquez Coronado searched here in vain for a city of gold. Wichita, Cheyenne, Osage, and Kiowa peoples—among others—called the region home. U.S. control came in 1803 with the Louisiana Purchase, and the Santa Fe Trail brought settlers and traders in the 1820s. But most considered the land here unfit to settle, so eastern Kansas was set up to be used as land for

1855

The violence caused when Border Ruffians from Missouri tried to get Kansas to vote for slavery led to the nickname Bleeding Kansas.

1870s

Railroad expansion and a movement to drive Native Americans out of Kansas led to the slaughter of millions of bison.

1862

Carry A. Nation, who smashed saloons with her hatchet, was part of the reform movement that was given voice by the Populist Party.

Present day

The aviation industry, which developed after World War II, now contributes more to the state's economy than wheat does.

No other state grows wheat like Kansas (opposite). While drought and storms cause output to vary from year to year, the state produced 480 million bushels in 2003—28 percent of the U.S. total!

KANSAS
Sunflower State

KANSAS

STATEHOOD	January 29, 1861; 34th state
CAPITAL	Topeka
LARGEST CITY	Wichita Population 355,126
TOTAL AREA	82,277 sq mi; 213,096 sq km
LAND AREA	81,815 sq mi; 211,900 sq km
POPULATION	2,723,507
POPULATION DENSITY	33.2 people per sq mi
MAJOR RACIAL/ ETHNIC GROUPS	86.1% white; 5.7% African American; 1.7% Asian; .9% Native American. Hispanic (any race) 7%.
INDUSTRY	aircraft manufacturing, transportation equipment, construction, food processing, printing and publishing, health care
AGRICULTURE	cattle, wheat, sorghum, soybeans, hogs, corn

WESTERN MEADOWLARK

SUNFLOWER

Did you know?

1. So many fossils were found in Kansas in the late 1800s that competing paleontologists launched the "Kansas Fossil Wars," resorting to bribes and trickery to get the best specimens.
2. Dry air and a constant temperature of 68.5°F (20.3°C) in the underground chambers of an old salt mine near Hutchinson make them ideal for storing valuables, including thousands of original Hollywood movies.
3. Barton County is named for Clara Barton, famed Civil War nurse and founder of the American Red Cross.
4. Pizza Hut, the world's largest pizza company, opened its first restaurant in Wichita in 1958.
5. Samuel Perry Dinsmoor used 113 tons (102 metric tons) of concrete to create the Garden of Eden, in Lucas, Kansas. Visitors can still see Dinsmoor, who died in 1932. He lies in a concrete tomb with a glass top.

Rail towns like Dodge City and Abilene were once destinations for cattle drives from Texas. Kansas is still cattle country, producing 6.6 million cattle and calves in 2004—enough for every Kansan to herd two or three. But crowded feedlots, not open range, are where many cattle spend their time these days. The chance, however unlikely, of mad cow disease finding a route to its feedlots keeps Kansas on its guard.

the relocation of Native Americans in the 1830s. But within two decades, Congress decided that the land was needed for white settlement after all.

The Kansas-Nebraska Act of 1854 brought waves of immigrant settlers and allowed them to vote whether or not they wanted slavery. Newcomers began pushing Native Americans out, and groups for and against slavery battled each other. Pro-slavery "Border Ruffians" attacked Lawrence and other cities in 1856, and famous anti-slavery fighter John Brown led a raid in return. Kansas finally joined the Union as a free state in 1861, just before the Civil War.

Kansas boomed after the war. Within a few decades, enormous herds of bison that once roamed free were wiped out, and beef cattle took their place. Cowboys drove longhorns north from Texas to the railroad at Dodge City and

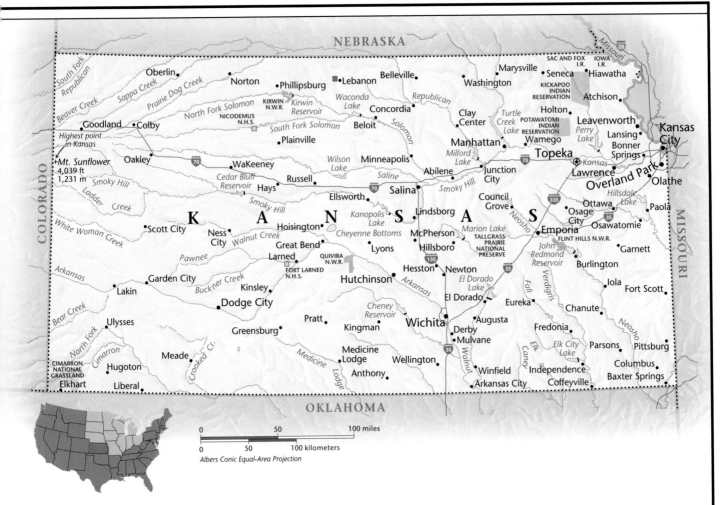

Abilene. While cattle were bought, gunfights were fought. Storybook lawmen like Bat Masterson, Wild Bill Hickok, and Wyatt Earp really did battle outlaws here in the Wild West. Another famous Kansas battler, hatchet-carrying Carry Nation, helped lead the Prohibition movement to ban alcohol in the late 19th century.

Two world wars sparked food demand, and Kansas reaped farming benefits. Then drought hit with the terrible Dust Bowl of the 1930s. Thousands left the state, but Kansas fought back with groundwater irrigation in the west and better conservation methods overall. Soon known as the breadbasket of America, Kansas still produces more wheat than any other state. Kansas is also a leader in sorghum, a grain used for livestock feed.

The state's industrial economy soared in the 20th century with airplane manufacturing based in Wichita. Meat-packing facilities have long prepared state beef for market. Huge military bases add thousands of jobs to the economy. Oil and natural gas wells dot the Kansas plains, and it is one of the few sources of helium, a gas used to float blimps and balloons.

Today, the majority of the 2.7 million Kansans live in its eastern cities. Hispanics make up the largest minority, followed by African Americans and Asians. The country recently marked the anniversary of the famous Brown v. Board of Education of Topeka court case that helped integrate the nation's schools. Looking to the future, the state seeks to expand an emerging medical sciences business, while keeping its industry, military bases, and agriculture intact. Yes, most Kansans would seldom say a "discouraging word" about their "Home on the Range."

MICHIGAN

★ *Great Lake State* ★

GREAT LAKE STATE is the perfect nickname for Michigan, with its two huge peninsulas surrounded by the country's four largest lakes: Superior, Huron, Michigan, and Erie. The name is from the Chippewa word *"mici-gama,"* meaning "great lake."

Michigan's Upper Peninsula extends east from Wisconsin, and its Lower Peninsula juts north from Ohio and Indiana. The "Big Mac" bridge links the two at the four-mile- (6.4-km-) wide Straits of Mackinac. The lakes provided easy transport routes for the French in the 17th century, when they met and traded furs with Ojibwa, Ottawa, and Potawatomi peoples. Father Marquette established the first European settlement at Sault Sainte Marie in 1668.

The British defeated the French here during the French and Indian War then abandoned the region to the United States by 1796. The Michigan Territory was formed in 1805, and New Englanders moved in, farming and building towns. By 1837, Michigan had gained the resource-rich Upper Peninsula and statehood.

For decades, Upper Peninsula mines led the U.S. in iron and copper output. Michigan also produced salt, gypsum, and oil. Loggers cut white pines on both peninsulas. Railroads and steamships hauled cargo to market, a task made easier by the completion of locks on the Soo Canals that linked Lakes Superior and Huron.

By the late 1800s, the iron and steel industry had grown strong here, ignited by several "horseless carriage" pioneers in the 1890s, including Henry Ford with his mass production of automobiles. Assembly-line jobs gave rise to labor unions and attracted immigrants. Huge numbers of African Americans from southern states plus Germans, Hungarians, Poles, Irish, Ukrainians, and Italians. During World War II, auto factories were converted to military uses, and

1762–1763

Chief Pontiac's efforts to drive the British from the region ended in defeat for the Ottawa, who were forced to sign a peace treaty.

1855

The completion of the Soo Canal provided a means of shipping iron ore mined on the Upper Peninsula to steel centers on the Great Lakes.

1913

The introduction of the auto assembly line at the Highland Park Ford Plant revolutionized mass production in industry.

Present day

Battle Creek, headquarters of cereal giants Post and Kelloggs, has long been a center for nutrition research.

Though Detroit's wheels have slowed in recent decades with changes in the auto industry (opposite), it is still known as the Motor City. Michigan produced more than one out of every five of the nation's motor vehicles in 2003.

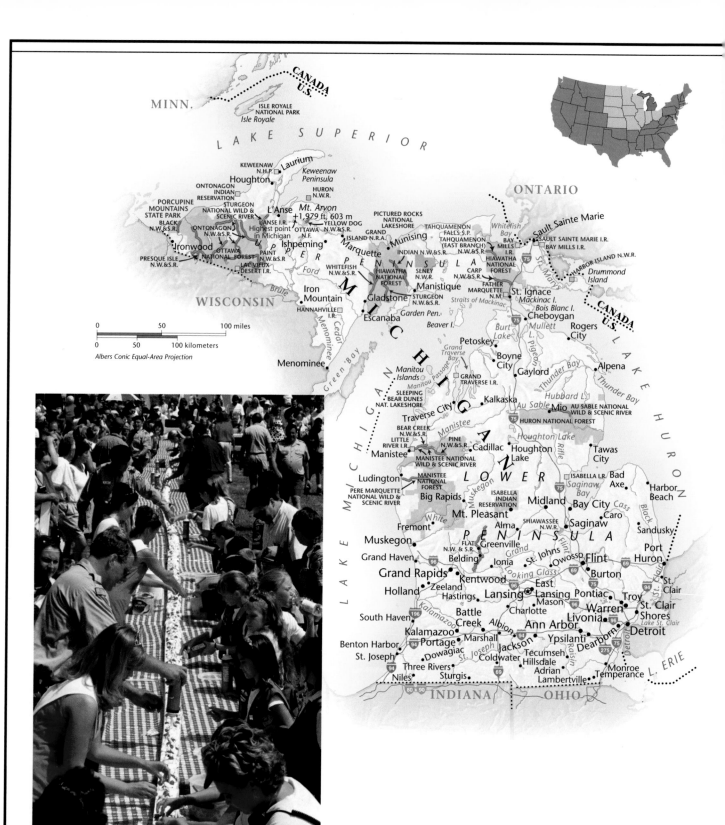

Michigan is a giant among cherry growers—number one in tart cherry output in 2003 and a major producer of sweet cherries, too. At Traverse City's annual National Cherry Festival, 160 pounds (73 kg) of ice cream and 300 pounds (136 kg) of fresh cherries went into the making of this 320-foot-(98-m) long cherry sundae. It fed 3,000 happy people.

the state earned the name Arsenal of Democracy.

The state's auto-making methods spread abroad, and by the 1970s, foreign competition had slowed Detroit's momentum. The city declined along with its top industry. It has lost jobs and fully half its population in the past few decades. Racial tensions, which had flared violently during the 1940s, erupted again into riots in 1967. The city has worked hard since to address racial concerns and to restart its economy.

Low rolling hills spread across the Lower Peninsula's southern half, while a higher plateau of birches, aspens, and oaks covers the northern half. Towering along Lake Michigan's shore are rows of sand dunes, which attract hordes of tourists. Here also is a climate perfect for fruit, and Michigan ranks as the top producer of cherries and blueberries. Pine forests dominate the wild "U.P." Black bear and white-tailed deer abound, while moose and wolves still live on Isle Royale in Lake Superior. Winter brings snow-sports enthusiasts to ski resorts, and summer vacationers enjoy water activities on more than ten thousand inland lakes.

Today, nearly 90 percent of the state's 10.1 million people live south of a line stretching from Muskegon to Bay City. This ethnically diverse state includes the largest group of Arab peoples in the country. Detroit ("Motown") is a national hub of African-American entertainment and culture.

Michigan still ranks as the U.S. leader in automobile and parts production but is also known for a variety of other products, ranging from chemicals to breakfast food. Michigan is working hard to diversify its economy, focusing on service and high-technology businesses. This will be a long, difficult process, but Michigan people are fortunate to be able to count on the resources of their two big peninsulas and four Great Lakes.

MICHIGAN
Great Lake State

STATEHOOD	January 26, 1837; 26th state
CAPITAL	Lansing
LARGEST CITY	Detroit Population 925,051
TOTAL AREA	96,716 sq mi; 250,494 sq km
LAND AREA	56,804 sq mi; 147,121 sq km
POPULATION	10,079,985
POPULATION DENSITY	176.9 people per sq mi
MAJOR RACIAL/ ETHNIC GROUPS	80.2% white; 14.2% African American; 1.8% Asian; .6% Native American. Hispanic (any race) 3.3%.
INDUSTRY	motor vehicles and parts, machinery, metal products, office furniture, tourism, chemicals
AGRICULTURE	dairy products, cattle, vegetables, hogs, corn, nursery stock, soybeans, hay, fruit

ROBIN   APPLE BLOSSOM

Did you know?

1. Michigan's unique location on the Great Lakes gives it a range of climates for growing a variety of farm products. It is second only to California in crop diversity.
2. The largest registered Holstein herd of dairy cows lives in a town called Elsie.
3. The first tunnel that allowed motor vehicles to travel between two countries connects Detroit and Windsor, Ontario, in Canada.
4. Although Michigan is sometimes known as the Wolverine State because of the many wolverine pelts traded by early trappers, none of these animals are left in the state.
5. Isle Royale was designated an International Biosphere Reserve in 1980. The wolf/moose predator-prey study conducted there is the longest running such study in the world.

MINNESOTA
★ *Gopher State* ★

AWASH IN WATER—falling, flowing, still, and marshy—that's Minnesota. The state borders the greatest of the Great Lakes—Superior—and is the source of the country's mightiest river—the Mississippi. State license plates read "Land of 10,000 Lakes." Minnesotans might mention that there are actually twice that many or more. "Minnesota" comes from a Dakota term meaning "cloudy water," describing the light-colored clay suspended in the Minnesota River.

While thick woods and lakes cover Minnesota's gravelly northern third, its central and southwest areas are nearly treeless plains with soils perfect for farming. Its many rivers flow in three directions. The Mississippi drains south to the Gulf of Mexico. Northern rivers flow east to Lake Superior or north into Canada.

When French fur traders scouted Minnesota lands and waters in the late 17th century, they met eastern Dakota peoples. Within decades, rival Ojibwas armed with French guns pushed the Dakota southwest into the prairies. The territory came under American control by 1818. The U.S. Army established Fort Snelling as a key frontier outpost in 1820. Most of the Minnesota Territory was opened for settlement by 1851, and the 32nd state joined the Union in 1858. Fierce conflict soon arose between the settlers and the Dakota, and the Indians were largely driven north to Canada and west to the Dakota Territory. For the next half-century, Minnesota's tall timber, fertile soils, and mineral resources attracted waves of newcomers, especially from Norway, Sweden, and Germany.

Over several decades, Minnesota's vast pine forests were largely clear-cut for lumber. Eventually, many cut-over areas were reforested and are today national, state, and private forests. The use of smaller trees for pulpwood and paper has helped to keep timber an impor-

1680

Father Louis Hennepin, while held captive by the Dakota, was the first white person to see the site that is now Minneapolis.

1862

The Battle of New Ulm marked the last effort by the Dakota to take back their lands. Their defeat opened the area to new settlement.

1880s–1950s

Workers like these mined hematite iron ore from rich deposits in the Mesabi Range. Today, lower grade taconite iron ore is mined.

Present day

Each year 42 million people visit Bloomington's Mall of America, largest enclosed retail/ family entertainment complex in the U.S.

Minnesotans and visitors alike treasure great scenery, peace, and terrific fishing on the state's amazing number and variety of lakes. A lone boater (opposite) motors across a misty Lake Winnibigoshish—called Lake Win-nee by locals—near Grand Rapids.

MANITOBA
RED LAKE
INDIAN RESERVATION
CANADA
U.S.

Hallock
Roseau
Baudette
International Falls
ONTARIO

Lake of the Woods
Rainy Lake
Namakan Lake

RED LAKE I.R.
RED LAKE I.R.

Warren
Mud Lake
AGASSIZ N.W.R.
Thief River Falls
East Grand Forks
Crookston
Red Lake

RED LAKE INDIAN RESERVATION

Upper Red Lake
Lower Red Lake

BOIS FORTE I.R.
Vermilion Lake
BOIS FORTE (DEER CREEK) I.R.
BOIS FORTE (VERMILION LAKE) I.R.

VOYAGEURS NATIONAL PARK

Highest point in Minnesota
Boundary Waters Canoe Area Wilderness
Eagle Mt. 2,301 ft 701 m
Ely
GRAND PORTAGE I.R.
GRAND PORTAGE NAT. MON.
Pigeon
Grand Marais

SUPERIOR N.F.
SUPERIOR NATIONAL FOREST

Bemidji
CHIPPEWA NATIONAL FOREST
Lake Winnibigoshish
Mesabi Range
Virginia
Chisholm
Hibbing
Grand Rapids

WHITE EARTH INDIAN RESERVATION
Lake Itasca
LEECH LAKE I.R.
Leech Lake
Walker

NORTH DAKOTA
Red River of the North
Red Lake
Wild Rice
Mississippi

Moorhead
Detroit Lakes
Perham
Park Rapids
Menahga
TAMARAC N.W.R.
HAMDEN SLOUGH N.W.R.

SANDY LAKE I.R.
FOND DU LAC INDIAN RESERVATION
St. Louis
Duluth
Proctor
Cloquet

Two Harbors

LAKE SUPERIOR

WIS.

Pelican Rapids
Fergus Falls
Wadena
Aitkin
Brainerd
RICE LAKE N.W.R.
Mille Lacs Lake

Otter Tail Lake
Otter Tail

MINNESOTA

Long Prairie
Little Falls
MILLE LACS I.R.
Sandstone
MILLE LACS I.R.

Wheaton
Alexandria
Morris
Sauk Centre
Milaca
Mora
Pine City
Rum
St. Croix
ST. CROIX NATIONAL SCENIC RIVERWAY

Lake Traverse
Big Stone Lake
Ortonville
Benson
St. Cloud
Cold Spring
SHERBURNE N.W.R.
MISSISSIPPI NATIONAL RIVER & N.R.A.

BIG STONE N.W.R.
Madison
Willmar
Litchfield
Brooklyn Park
Plymouth
Coon Rapids
Stillwater

Montevideo
Hutchinson
Olivia
Minneapolis
Bloomington
St. Paul
Eagan
Lakeville
Red Wing
PRAIRIE ISLAND I.R.
Lake Pepin

SOUTH DAKOTA
Bois de Sioux
Minnesota
UPPER SIOUX INDIAN RESERVATION
LOWER SIOUX INDIAN RESERVATION
SHAKOPEE I.R.
MINNESOTA VALLEY N.W.R.

Redwood Falls
Marshall
New Ulm
St. Peter
Faribault
Mankato
Northfield
ST. CROIX N.W.&S.R.

PIPESTONE NAT. MON.
Slayton
St. James
Waseca
Owatonna
Rochester
Winona
UPPER MISSISSIPPI RIVER NATIONAL WILDLIFE AND FISH REFUGE

Pipestone
Windom
Des Moines
Blue Earth
La Crescent
Root
Mississippi

Luverne
Worthington
Fairmont
Albert Lea
Austin
Preston
Caledonia
UPPER MISSISSIPPI RIVER NATIONAL WILDLIFE AND FISH REFUGE

IOWA

3   83   433 Pilohv

3   83   433 Nlorp hwhuv

Dehu Frqlf t xdo Dhd Surth wl q

Why wait for summer? People in Minnesota don't let snow and ice get them down. The first signs of winter find cross-country skiers packing, snowboarders waxing, and diehard ice fishers grabbing their down parkas, tackle, and trusty augers for drilling holes in the ice. Minnesota winters can be frigid. The record low for the state is -60°F (-51°C), set on February 2, 1996, at Tower, in the northeastern part of the state.

tant Minnesota business. While wheat had grown to be the top crop by 1870, other grains and dairy farming gained importance later on. It is still a bountiful farm state, where farmers grow oats, corn, and soybeans, raise pigs and cows, and produce milk and cheese.

In 1865, rich deposits of iron ore were found in northeastern Minnesota's Mesabi Range. Mining boomed, with more than a hundred open pits by 1900. Transported to Duluth then shipped to blast furnaces along Lakes Erie and Michigan, Minnesota iron ore became U.S. steel. The state has led the nation in iron ore production ever since.

Minneapolis grew up around the Falls of St. Anthony, where the Mississippi's power was used to grind grains of wheat and cut miles of timber. Just ten miles downstream, St. Paul became Minnesota's capital. Water highways and railroad empires helped make the "Twin Cities" a premier trading and market center, serving areas all the way to the Pacific. Innovative manufacturing of plastics and other products followed. Nearly half of Minnesota's people now live in cities big and small, producing processed foods, machinery, paper, printed materials, and chemical products.

Minnesota today is an exciting mix of "cold and new." Rather than letting chilly winters keep them indoors, Minnesotans celebrate the frigid season with snowy sports such as ice fishing, hockey, and snowmobiling. Summers bring great north woods swimming, fishing, and canoeing.

The state's 5.1 million residents are protecting their water resources while they plunge into new industries. A pioneer in computers and other high-tech manufacturing, Minnesota intends to lead the coming biotechnology industry. In these and other ways, Minnesota's future seems—like its sky-blue waters—limitless!

MINNESOTA
Gopher State

STATEHOOD	May 11, 1858; 32nd state
CAPITAL	St. Paul
LARGEST CITY	Minneapolis Population 375,635
TOTAL AREA	86,939 sq mi; 225,171 sq km
LAND AREA	79,610 sq mi; 206,189 sq km
POPULATION	5,059,375
POPULATION DENSITY	63.1 people per sq mi
MAJOR RACIAL/ ETHNIC GROUPS	89.4% white; 3.5% African American; 2.9% Asian; 1.1% Native American. Hispanic (any race) 2.9%.
INDUSTRY	health services, tourism, real estate, banking and insurance, industrial machinery, printing and publishing, food processing, scientific equipment
AGRICULTURE	corn, soybeans, dairy products, hogs, cattle, turkeys, wheat

COMMON LOON   SHOWY LADY'S SLIPPER

Did you know?

1. The first cellophane tape was produced by Minnesota Mining and Manufacturing (3M) Company in 1932.
2. The nickname Gopher State comes from an 1859 cartoon in which men who wanted to build a railroad through the state were pictured as gophers wearing top hats and pulling a train.
3. The opening of the St. Lawrence Seaway in 1959 connected the Port of Duluth and the Atlantic Ocean.
4. The world's first open-heart operation was performed at the University of Minnesota in 1952, and Rochester is home to the world-famous Mayo Clinic.
5. In-line skates were invented by two Minnesota students. Looking for a way to practice hockey in the summer, they replaced the blades on their skates with wheels.

MISSOURI
★ *Show Me State* ★

"GATEWAY TO THE WEST." With its mid-continent location and the country's two longest rivers embracing the state, it was natural that Missouri would be described this way. The broad and swift Missouri River sweeps across the state from the west to join the mighty Mississippi on its eastern edge—linking its two biggest cities.

Missouri's name comes from a native group whose name meant "wooden canoe people," or the "town of large canoes." When French settlers arrived in 1680, they found Osage and Algonquin peoples—and valuable deposits of lead. Trappers and traders peacefully paddled the region's rivers, at least until the U.S. bought the vast Louisiana Territory from France in 1803. Lewis and Clark set out the next year up the muddy Missouri to open the American West.

Missouri was made a territory in 1812. Broken treaties with Native Americans caused violence until a pact was signed with most native groups in 1815. Settlement was stoked by the arrival of the first bellowing riverboats, which reached Missouri in 1816. The fur-trading center of St. Louis soon grew to be a major transport hub. The Missouri Compromise of 1820 allowed Missouri to join the Union as a slave state in 1821. Tent cities sprang up around the state as pioneers headed west from Independence—the jumping-off point for the Santa Fe and Oregon Trails. Pony Express riders high-tailed it west with their mailbags from St. Joseph for fast-and-furious ten-day rides to California.

But tensions grew between residents who were for slavery and those who were against it. While Missouri officially sided with the Union during the Civil War, thousands of its soldiers fought for the Confederacy. Post-war Missouri healed slowly but was prospering in both agriculture and industry by the end of the century. It celebrated its success in 1904 with two events:

1735

French settlers established Missouri's first permanent white settlement along the Mississippi at Ste. Genevieve.

1860

The route used by the Pony Express to carry mail from Missouri to California paved the way for the transcontinental railroad.

1904

The St. Louis World's Fair marked the centennial of the Louisiana Purchase and showcased electricity and early automobiles.

Present day

Branson has become a major country music center, helping to make tourism a multi-billion-dollar industry for Missouri.

Twin symbols of Missouri's central role in the nation's westward growth can be seen together today on the St. Louis waterfront (opposite): the massive Gateway Arch and a steamboat's paddle wheel churning the waters of the Mississippi River.

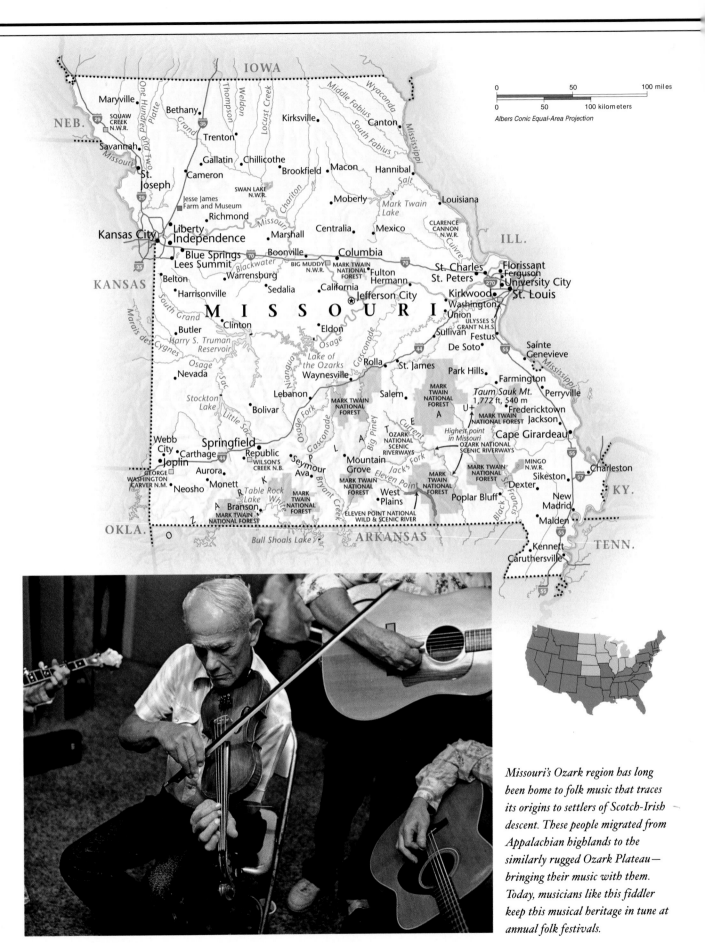

Missouri's Ozark region has long been home to folk music that traces its origins to settlers of Scotch-Irish descent. These people migrated from Appalachian highlands to the similarly rugged Ozark Plateau— bringing their music with them. Today, musicians like this fiddler keep this musical heritage in tune at annual folk festivals.

the Olympics and World's Fair, both in St. Louis.

The rugged Ozark Plateau, coated with oak, hickory, and pine forests shared with Arkansas and Oklahoma, covers much of Missouri's south. North of the Missouri River lie hills, valleys, and glacially-formed fertile croplands of corn and soybeans, much like in neighboring Iowa and Illinois. Cotton and rice carpet the Mississippi River bottomlands as in the nearby southern states.

Missouri's economy is amazingly diverse. More than 100,000 farms, a greater number than in any other state but Texas, make Missouri a major producer of soybeans, corn, cattle, and hogs. More than three centuries after lead was first mined, Missouri still leads the nation in lead production, and barge traffic makes St. Louis one of the busiest inland ports in the nation.

Long a center of metal and chemical manufacturing, St. Louis has lost many jobs and residents in the past few decades. Giant stockyards in Kansas City closed in the 1990s, but the urban area—linked to its Kansas twin—is still a major farm supplier and a center of auto making. Springfield, in the southwest, is a fast-growing trade and manufacturing city. Nearby, the scenic Ozarks boast numerous reservoirs lined with vacation cabins and boat docks. Besides trail trekkers and river rafters, country music lovers flock to this region. Branson's dozens of theaters host famous country-western singers for national crowds.

As Missouri strengthens its traditional economic bases, it also strives to be included in a "Bio-Belt" of life-science research by encouraging the growth of high-tech industries. The spectacular Gateway Arch is more than a symbol of the state's historic role in the nation's settlement. It is also the symbol of an open doorway to Missouri's future success.

MISSOURI
Show Me State

STATEHOOD	August 10, 1821; 24th state
CAPITAL	Jefferson City
LARGEST CITY	Kansas City Population 443,471
TOTAL AREA	69,704 sq mi; 180,533 sq mi
LAND AREA	68,886 sq mi; 178,414 sq km
POPULATION	5,704,484
POPULATION DENSITY	82.3 people per sq mi
MAJOR RACIAL/ ETHNIC GROUPS	84.9% white; 11.2% African American; 1.1% Asian; .4% Native American. Hispanic (any race) 2.1%.
INDUSTRY	transportation equipment, food processing, chemicals, electrical equipment, metal products
AGRICULTURE	cattle, soybeans, hogs, corn, poultry and eggs, dairy products

EASTERN BLUEBIRD

HAWTHORN

Did you know?

1. Kansas City has a second level of roads, offices, and storage areas built into natural caves below the streets of the city.
2. Samuel Clemens (Mark Twain) used his hometown of Hannibal as the model for settings in his novels *Tom Sawyer* and *Huckleberry Finn*.
3. In late 1811 and early 1812, three of the strongest earthquakes in U.S. history rocked Missouri near New Madrid. The quakes, which scientists believe measured 8 on the Richter scale, caused the Mississippi River to flow backward temporarily.
4. According to one account, the state's nickname comes from a speech by Missouri's U.S. Congressman Willard Duncan Vandiver in 1899. He said, "...frothy eloquence neither convinces nor satisfies me. I am from Missouri. You have got to show me."

NEBRASKA
★ *Cornhusker State* ★

"THE GREAT AMERICAN DESERT." So wrote Major Stephen Long after he mapped the Nebraska plains for the U.S. government in 1820. Seeing the rolling and mostly tree-free prairies during a bad drought, his expedition found it "almost wholly unfit for cultivation." Nebraskans might chuckle today if they could show the explorer a map showing 95 percent of their state covered with farms and ranches.

Based upon Long's report, the area that included Nebraska was set up as Indian Territory—but not for long. In the 1840s, Omaha, with its fine location along the Missouri and near the Platte River, was the starting point for the long journey west for many Oregon and Mormon Trail trekkers. A natural east-west travel corridor, the broad and shallow Platte gave Nebraska its name, from an Oto Indian term meaning "flat water." Thousands of wagon trains rumbled west along-side the Platte. Some people also put down roots in the area, especially in the tall-grass eastern prairies.

Both precipitation and population decline as one travels west in Nebraska. Corn and soybeans thrive in the usually well-watered eastern sections along the Missouri River border, where corn-fed pigs and poultry are raised, too. "Dry farming" is practiced in the west, where one crop year is followed by a year or two with no planting. Water from reservoirs on the Platte and other streams provides irrigation for agriculture. Catching rainfall like a sponge, the grass-covered Sand Hills help refresh the Ogalalla Aquifer, a source of groundwater tapped by thousands of wells.

Two acts of the U.S. Congress had great impacts on Nebraska in the mid-19th century. The Kansas-Nebraska Act in 1854 made the two neighbor territories part of the U.S. The

Pre 1854

Native Americans gave up their lands in eastern Nebraska to the U.S. by 1854, but tribes in the west did not surrender theirs until 1877.

1862

The Homestead Act brought a rush of settlers, many building homes of sod because so few trees grew on the Nebraska prairie.

1890

Farmers seeking relief from low prices and overuse of credit, supported Populist Party candidate William Jennings Bryan.

Present day

The Strategic Air Command, based near Omaha, gathers military information and plays a key role in the state's economy.

Hundreds of thousands of westbound Oregon, California, and Mormon Trail riders welcomed the sight of Chimney Rock (opposite), near Nebraska's western border. The limestone landmark rises above the prairie 325 feet (99 m) from base to tip.

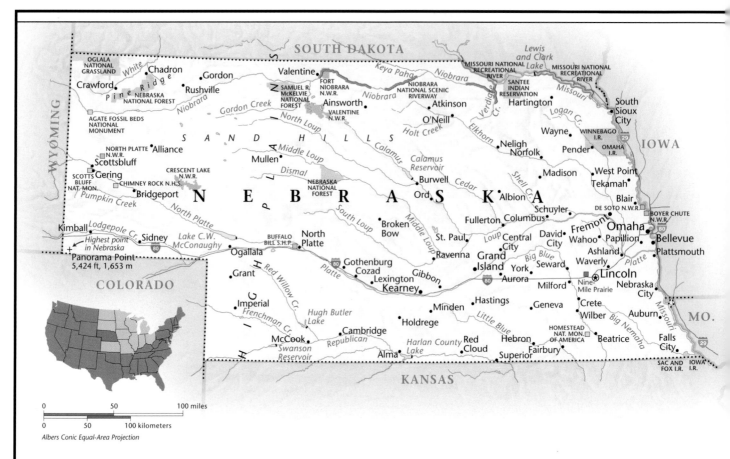

Nebraska harvested 1.25 billion bushels of corn in 2003, ranking third behind Iowa and Illinois in corn harvest. Much of the corn is fed to livestock—especially cattle—which are then processed in state meat-packing plants. Twenty-two percent of the people in the Cornhusker State are employed in agriculture or related jobs.

Homestead Act of 1862 allowed white settlers to claim—and keep—a "section" of 160 acres (65 ha) of land, if they worked for five years to develop it. As immigrants swarmed to Nebraska to obtain their land, the Sioux and Cheyenne of Nebraska lost more and more of theirs. Nebraska became the 37th state in 1867. The tiny town of Lancaster was renamed Lincoln—after the 16th President—and was made the state capital.

In 1869, the Union Pacific Railroad steamed its way across the new state, bringing more immigrants both through and to Nebraska. Families fought the loneliness of a hard life on their scattered homesteads by sometimes meeting with neighbors. The state's nickname may have come from such gatherings, where people would visit and husk their corn crop. In most areas, wood was scarce, so many farm families built homes using prairie sod. Cut into blocks held together by strong root systems, this "Nebraska marble" proved to be a durable building material. A Nebraska newspaperman started Arbor Day in 1872—planting trees to help hold soil in place.

Nebraska's population has not grown much since 1900. The state's farmers have ridden an economic "roller coaster" of good followed by bad times over the past century. As elsewhere in the country, the size of farms has increased while the number of farmers has decreased. Some rural counties struggle to keep their people from leaving. Overall, irrigation has expanded, causing concern that overuse of groundwater may leave little for the future. Other activities are helping the state to prosper—meat packing, insurance, banking, telecommunications, health care, and the U.S. military. Nebraska's slow-growing population will continue to have its roots in the prairies and its eyes on the future.

NEBRASKA
Cornhusker State

STATEHOOD	March 1, 1867; 37th state
CAPITAL	Lincoln
LARGEST CITY	Omaha Population 399,357
TOTAL AREA	77,354 sq mi; 200,345 sq km
LAND AREA	76,872 sq mi; 199,099 sq km
POPULATION	1,739,291
POPULATION DENSITY	22.5 people per sq mi
MAJOR RACIAL/ ETHNIC GROUPS	89.6% white; 4.0% African American; 1.3% Asian; .9% Native American. Hispanic (any race) 5.5%
INDUSTRY	food processing, machinery, electrical equipment, printing and publishing
AGRICULTURE	cattle, corn, hogs, soybeans, wheat, sorghum

WESTERN MEADOWLARK   GOLDENROD

Did you know?

1. Fossils of prehistoric elephants called mammoths have been found in almost every county in Nebraska. The largest is on display at the University of Nebraska State Museum in Lincoln.
2. Nebraska was known as the Tree Planter's State until 1945 when the name Cornhusker State was adopted. The state has the only national forest that was planted by people.
3. Nebraska has more miles of river within its boundaries than any other state.
4. The largest expanse of original native prairie in the United States is in the Sand Hills region. It is an important stopover for migrating sandhill cranes.
5. The system of center pivot irrigation, which opens more land to crop production, originated in Nebraska. It is estimated that by 2010 this method of irrigation will water 70 percent of the state's cropland.

NORTH DAKOTA

★ *Flickertail State* ★

"LOOK AT THE FLICKERTAILS!" North Dakota's little ground squirrels emerge from their burrows to watch the prairies as they flick their tails in expectation. The lives and livelihoods of people in the Flickertail State are also rooted in these rolling lands.

Huge Ice Age glaciers scoured the eastern two-thirds of the land, changing and blocking river courses. Several streams combined to form today's mighty Missouri, which cuts its channel across the state from west to south. West of the river, lands not smoothed by ice sheets have been eroded into rugged hills and "badlands." North and east of the Missouri Valley, thousands of pan-shaped lakes and ponds left by glaciers dot the state's Drift Prairie. These kettle holes make temporary homes for migrating waterfowl. The terrain slopes gradually downward to the state's eastern border, which is marked by the Red River of the North. This flat valley, once the bottom of a vast glacial lake, contains some of the world's best farmland—and is often subject to flooding.

Although French explorers moved through in the 1730s, it was the Corps of Discovery led by Lewis and Clark that put the area on the map. Staying with Mandan people along the Missouri River in what is now central North Dakota, they met a Shoshone woman named Sakakawea during the winter of 1804–05. As a guide and interpreter, she was indispensible to the expedition. Lake Sakakawea, formed by a dam on the Missouri River, is named in her honor.

Permanent settlement was slow, even after the Dakota Territory was formed in 1861—in part because of later conflicts with Native Americans. It took the coming of the railroad in the 1870s for farmers and ranchers to arrive in greater numbers. North Dakota entered the Union as the 39th state in 1889.

1804

Lewis and Clark met Sakakawea, who guided them across plains and mountains to the Pacific Ocean, at Fort Mandan.

1874–1890

Wheat farms as large as 65,000 acres (26,000 ha) earned such huge profits that they became known as "bonanza farms."

1951

Oil discovered near Tioga became the state's most valuable mineral. The area currently supplies much of North Dakota's propane gas.

Present day

Garrison Dam provides electricity, flood control, irrigation, and, by creating Lake Sakakawea, supports a rising recreation industry.

Rich soils, long days of summer sunshine, and plentiful rainfall grow head-high sunflowers in the Red River Valley (opposite). Used for cooking oil, birdseed, and snacks, more than half the U.S. sunflower harvest comes from North Dakota farmland.

Located in the middle of the continent, North Dakota chills deeply in winter. Norwegian and other European immigrants who arrived in the late 18th and early 19th centuries, found summers too short for some crops to mature. But quick-ripening grains like oats, barley (shown here), and wheat varieties planted in spring can be sown and reaped. North Dakota leads the nation in the production of each of these grains.

0   50   100 miles
0   50   100 kilometers
Albers Conic Equal-Area Projection

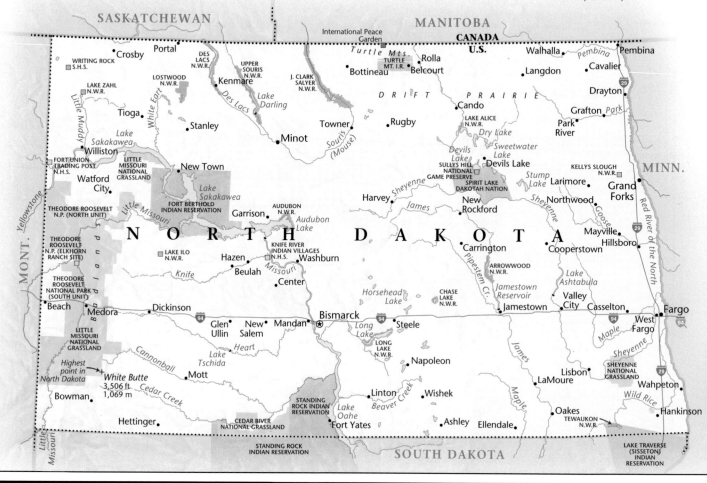

SASKATCHEWAN

MANITOBA

International Peace Garden

CANADA
U.S.

• Crosby • Portal

WRITING ROCK
S.H.S.

DES LACS N.W.R.

UPPER SOURIS N.W.R.

J. CLARK SALYER N.W.R.

Turtle Mts.

• Rolla

TURTLE MT. I.R.

• Bottineau • Belcourt

• Walhalla

Pembina

• Pembina

• Cavalier

• Langdon

LOSTWOOD N.W.R.

• Kenmare

D R I F T

P R A I R I E

• Drayton

LAKE ZAHL N.W.R.

Des Lacs

Lake Darling

• Cando

LAKE ALICE N.W.R.

• Grafton Park

• Tioga

White Earth

Souris (Mouse)

• Towner

• Rugby

Dry Lake

• Park River

Little Muddy

• Stanley

• Minot

Sweetwater Lake

KELLYS SLOUGH N.W.R.

MINN.

Lake Sakakawea

• Williston

• New Town

Devils Lake

SULLYS HILL NATIONAL GAME PRESERVE

• Devils Lake

Stump Lake

• Larimore

• Grand Forks

FORT UNION TRADING POST N.H.S.

LITTLE MISSOURI NATIONAL GRASSLAND

SPIRIT LAKE DAKOTAH NATION

• Watford City

Little Missouri

FORT BERTHOLD INDIAN RESERVATION

• Garrison

AUDUBON N.W.R.

Sheyenne

• Harvey

• New Rockford

• Northwood

Yellowstone

THEODORE ROOSEVELT N.P. (NORTH UNIT)

N O R T H

Audubon Lake

James

Sheyenne

• Mayville

• Cooperstown

• Hillsboro

Badlands

THEODORE ROOSEVELT N.P. (ELKHORN RANCH SITE)

LAKE ILO N.W.R.

• Hazen

KNIFE RIVER INDIAN VILLAGES N.H.S.

• Washburn

D A K O T A

• Carrington

Red River of the North

THEODORE ROOSEVELT NATIONAL PARK (SOUTH UNIT)

• Beulah

Knife

• Center

Missouri

ARROWWOOD N.W.R.

Lake Ashtabula

• Beach

• Medora

• Dickinson

Horsehead Lake

CHASE LAKE N.W.R.

Jamestown Reservoir

Pipestem Cr.

• Valley City

• Casselton

• Jamestown

• Fargo

Highest point in North Dakota

• Glen Ullin

• New Salem

• Mandan

• Bismarck

• Steele

Long Lake

• West Fargo

Cannonball

Heart

Lake Tschida

LONG LAKE N.W.R.

Maple

White Butte 3,506 ft. 1,069 m

• Mott

Cedar Creek

• Napoleon

James

• Lisbon

SHEYENNE NATIONAL GRASSLAND

• Wahpeton

• Bowman

• Linton

• Wishek

• LaMoure

Wild Rice

• Hettinger

STANDING ROCK INDIAN RESERVATION

Lake Oahe

Beaver Creek

• Fort Yates

• Ashley

• Ellendale

• Oakes

TEWAUKON N.W.R.

• Hankinson

CEDAR RIVER NATIONAL GRASSLAND

Maple

Little Missouri

STANDING ROCK INDIAN RESERVATION

SOUTH DAKOTA

LAKE TRAVERSE (SISSETON) INDIAN RESERVATION

MONT.

Farming became and is still the major economic activity in the state even though it has not always been easy. North Dakota farmers have endured drought, dust storms, invasions of grasshoppers, terrible economic times, and of course, the cold. Blizzards can reduce visibility from miles to feet in minutes. But North Dakota's summer days are long, warm—even hot. Many hours of sunshine at the state's high latitude allow the short growing season to produce fine crops.

Wheat is the top crop here, and North Dakota farms produce lots of it. A typical year's harvest is about 300 million bushels, which is more than enough to provide a bushel for every person in the country. The state leads the country in producing sunflowers, oats, barley, canola, flax seed, and dry beans.

North Dakotans look both below and above their rolling prairies for future vitality—and energy. Since the 1970s, oil and natural gas reserves have been tapped in the western half of the state. Closer to the surface lie huge deposits of a kind of coal called lignite, which is burned in nearby power plants to produce electricity. Above ground, strong winds turn towering wind turbines that generate electricity. This rich variety of energy resources makes North Dakota an exporter of energy to neighboring states and holds continued promise for its economic future.

There is concern over the recent decline in the state's population. Only two states have fewer people than the 633,837 who call North Dakota home. Building on North Dakota's fine education system, state officials work to keep young people from leaving the state to find jobs in other places. Keeping home-grown talent in the state will help ensure a future full of energy and hope.

NORTH DAKOTA
Flickertail State

STATEHOOD	November 2, 1889; 39th state
CAPITAL	Bismarck
LARGEST CITY	Fargo Population 91,204
TOTAL AREA	70,700 sq mi; 183,112 sq km
LAND AREA	68,976 sq mi; 178,647 sq km
POPULATION	633,837
POPULATION DENSITY	9.2 people per sq mi
MAJOR RACIAL/ ETHNIC GROUPS	92.4% white; 4.9% Native American; .6% African American; .6% Asian. Hispanic (any race) 1.2%.
INDUSTRY	services, government, finance, construction, transportation, oil and gas
AGRICULTURE	wheat, cattle, sunflowers, barley, soybeans

WESTERN MEADOWLARK

WILD PRAIRIE ROSE

Did you know?

1. Theodore Roosevelt National Park is the only such park named for a U.S. President.
2. Sunflowers grow as tall as 13 feet (4 m) in North Dakota.
3. Each year a demolition derby using farm combines is held at the State Fair in Minot.
4. A bronze statue of Sakakawea and her baby son Jean Baptiste stands at the entrance to the North Dakota Heritage Center on the grounds of the state capitol in Bismarck.
5. More waterfowl hatch in the many prairie kettle holes and sloughs of North Dakota than in any other state.
6. The International Peace Garden straddles the boundary between North Dakota and Manitoba, in Canada.
7. Devils Lake, the largest natural body of water in North Dakota, is known among fishermen as the Perch Capital of the World.

OHIO

★ Buckeye State ★

THREE BIG *C*s—and so much more! Shaped a bit like a deep bowl on the map, Ohio brims with natural resources, rich farmlands, lots of people, and three big *C* cities: Cleveland lies in the north on the shore of Lake Erie, Columbus anchors the middle, and in the southwest stands Cincinnati—alongside the great river that gives Ohio its name.

Long before the Iroquois named the big west-flowing river, the Adena, Hopewell, and Mississippian cultures built huge burial mounds on southern Ohio hilltops. While the French and British struggled to control the Ohio Country in the mid-1700s, the first permanent white settlement was established at Marietta—on the banks of the Ohio—in 1788. The first of many successful Ohio River ports, it was soon surpassed in importance by down-river Cincinnati. The battle of Fallen Timbers, a total victory for the U.S. Army in 1794, forced the

Indians of the Northwest Territory to sign a treaty that opened much of the Ohio Valley to settlers. In 1796, New Englanders arrived on Lake Erie's shores and founded Cleveland. Ohio became the 17th state in 1803, with its capital first at Chillicothe and then Zanesville. In 1816, Ohio established Columbus as its seat of government.

Ohio prospered with its key waterways linking regions east and west. Its Lake Erie rim bustled with business, especially after the Erie Canal was finished in 1825. This provided a route for East Coast water traffic to reach the frontier. Flatboats and then steamboats navigated the Ohio River. The state grew quickly. The growing of corn, wheat, oats, and potatoes—plus the raising of cattle and hogs—made it an agricultural powerhouse by 1850. Industry soon followed, led by meat packing. By that time, rails connected most major state cities.

1794

General "Mad" Anthony Wayne's defeat of Native Americans at the Battle of Fallen Timbers helped open the Ohio Valley to settlers.

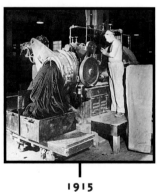

1915

Akron's first rubber products were made in the 1870s, and by 1915 it had become known as the Rubber Capital of the World.

1969

When the Cuyahoga River caught fire in 1969, it became a symbol of a polluted America and led to environmental legislation.

Present day

The Rock and Roll Hall of Fame, a centerpiece of Cleveland's cleaned-up waterfront, attracts thousands of visitors each year.

Ohio's Serpent Mound (opposite) is among the best preserved of the prehistoric effigy mounds—earthworks created in the shape of animals—that appear in several areas of the Midwest. It is 450 yards (415 m) long, with an average elevation of about 4 feet (1.2 m).

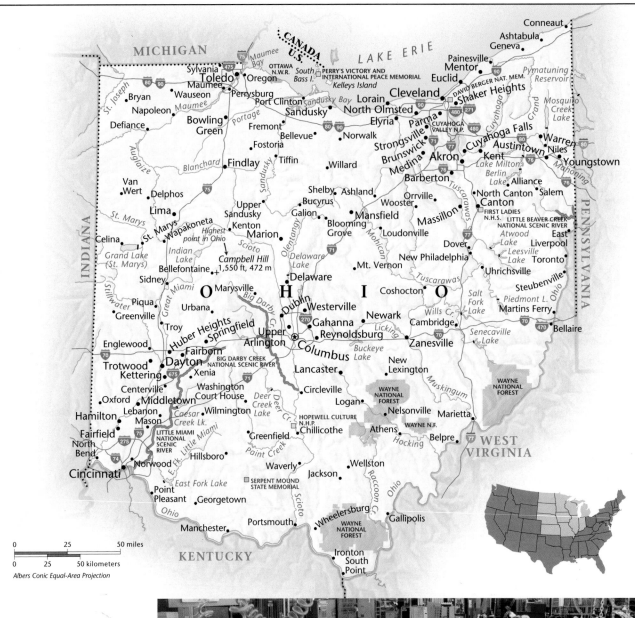

MICHIGAN

CANADA
U.S.

LAKE ERIE

Conneaut
Ashtabula
Geneva

Painesville
Mentor
Euclid

DAVID BERGER NAT. MEM.

Pymatuning
Reservoir

Sylvania
Toledo
Maumee
Oregon
Perrysburg
Port Clinton
Sandusky
Bryan
Wauseon
Napoleon
Defiance
Bowling
Green
Fostoria
Fremont
Bellevue
Norwalk

OTTAWA
N.W.R.

South
Bass I.

Kelleys Island

PERRY'S VICTORY AND
INTERNATIONAL PEACE MEMORIAL

Cleveland
Shaker Heights
Lorain
North Olmsted
Elyria
Parma
Strongsville
Brunswick
Medina

CUYAHOGA
VALLEY N.P.

Cuyahoga Falls
Akron
Kent
Austintown
Niles
Warren
Youngstown

Mosquito
Creek
Lake

PENNSYLVANIA

Van
Wert
Delphos
Lima

St. Marys
Wapakoneta
Kenton
Marion

Findlay
Tiffin
Willard

Shelby
Bucyrus
Galion
Blooming
Grove

Ashland
Wooster
Orrville
Loudonville

Mansfield

Massillon

Barberton
North Canton
Canton

FIRST LADIES
N.H.S.

Salem
Alliance

Berlin
Lake

Lake Milton

LITTLE BEAVER CREEK
NATIONAL SCENIC RIVER

Celina

Grand Lake
(St. Marys)

Indian
Lake

Highest
point in Ohio

Campbell Hill
1,550 ft, 472 m

Bellefontaine

Sidney

Marysville

Delaware
Lake

Mt. Vernon

Delaware

Coshocton

New Philadelphia

Dover

Atwood
Lake

Leesville
Lake

East
Liverpool
Toronto

Uhrichsville

Steubenville

Salt
Fork
Lake

Piedmont L.

Martins Ferry

Bellaire

O H I O

Piqua
Greenville
Troy
Urbana

Huber Heights
Springfield

Englewood

Trotwood
Dayton
Kettering
Xenia
Fairborn

Centerville
Middletown
Oxford
Lebanon
Mason

Hamilton

Fairfield
North
Bend

Norwood

Cincinnati

Point
Pleasant

Washington
Court House
Wilmington

Hillsboro

Georgetown

Manchester

Dublin
Westerville
Gahanna
Reynoldsburg

Upper
Arlington
Columbus

Newark
Cambridge
Zanesville

Licking

Senecaville
Lake

Buckeye
Lake

Lancaster

Circleville

Logan

New
Lexington

Nelsonville

Greenfield
Chillicothe

HOPEWELL CULTURE
N.H.P.

Waverly

Jackson

SERPENT MOUND
STATE MEMORIAL

Wellston

Wheelersburg

Portsmouth

Ironton
South
Point

Gallipolis

WAYNE
NATIONAL
FOREST

Marietta

Athens

Belpre

WEST
VIRGINIA

WAYNE
NATIONAL
FOREST

BIG DARBY CREEK
NATIONAL SCENIC RIVER

LITTLE MIAMI
NATIONAL
SCENIC
RIVER

Deer
Creek
Lake

Caesar
Creek Lk.

East Fork Lake

KENTUCKY

0   25   50 miles
0   25   50 kilometers

Albers Conic Equal-Area Projection

*Ohio has long been a manufac-
turing giant. The list of Buckeye
State products is impressive:
food, soap, iron and steel,
aluminum, rubber, plastics, glass,
appliances, chemicals, and more.
Greater than one-fourth of the
state's manufacturing is related to
the production of motor vehicles.
Recent annual production of cars
and light trucks stands at more
than 1.8 million.*

The so-called Underground Railroad—a loose network of people who helped escaped slaves move north to freedom—maintained many "stations," or safehouses, in Ohio. After the Civil War, the iron and steel industry fired the state's economy. Rich deposits of coal and oil from outside and inside the state fueled this growth.

European immigrants arrived in huge numbers through the second half of the 19th century, finding work in Ohio's thriving factories. Organized labor groups were formed to promote workers' rights.

Ohio suffered huge job losses during the Great Depression, but its economy rebounded during and after World War II. Ohio became a major manufacturer of rubber and plastics. Lake Erie ports handled bulk mineral cargoes as well as finished products. The Ohio River carried huge volumes of oil and steel in multi-barge tows. By the 1960s pollution problems darkened Ohio's skies and discolored its waterways, especially Lake Erie. Decades of clean-up efforts have paid off, and the state's environment has rebounded well.

Today, the Buckeye State is prospering. With just under 11.5 million people, Ohio is the seventh most populous state and still a leading farm state. Ohio agriculture supports more than a thousand food-processing operations, making everything from jellies to sausages. Huge, efficient auto assembly and parts plants have been built recently, making the state second only to Michigan in car manufacturing. The state seeks to attract information technology and other emerging industries, while striving to make its cities and towns more livable for residents. Boding well for Ohio's future is the state's continued emphasis on education. It has more than 130 colleges and universities, graduating more than 50,000 students each year.

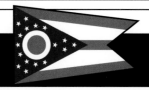

OHIO
Buckeye State

STATEHOOD	March 1, 1803; 17th state
CAPITAL	Columbus
LARGEST CITY	Columbus Population 725,228
TOTAL AREA	44,825 sq mi; 116,096 sq km
LAND AREA	40,948 sq mi; 106,056 sq km
POPULATION	11,435,798
POPULATION DENSITY	278.9 people per sq mi
MAJOR RACIAL/ ETHNIC GROUPS	85.0% white; 11.5% African American; 1.2% Asian; .2% Native American. Hispanic (any race) 1.9%.
INDUSTRY	transportation equipment, metal products, machinery, food processing, electrical equipment
AGRICULTURE	soybeans, dairy products, corn, hogs, cattle, poultry and eggs

CARDINAL

SCARLET CARNATION

Did you know?

1. Fires set by anti-union workers in 1884 in coal mines around New Straitsville, southeast of Columbus, are still burning. The underground fires have reached Wayne National Forest, where smoke has been seen coming up through the forest floor.
2. Ohio has the largest Amish-Mennonite community in the world. The Amish and Mennonite Heritage Center is located in Berlin, near New Philadelphia.
3. Twinsburg, located just south of Cleveland, has been hosting the Twins Days Festival every August since 1976. It is attended by more than 3,000 sets of twins from around the world.
4. Marietta, Ohio's first permanent European settlement, was named for the French Queen Marie Antoinette.
5. The Cincinnati Reds were the first professional baseball team.

SOUTH DAKOTA

★ *Mount Rushmore State* ★

WHAT'S IN A WORD? "Dakota" means "allies" or "friends" to people of the Sioux nations. When French explorers moved through the area in the 1740s, they met people of the Sioux federation who treated them well, and in 1804 Lewis and Clark were allowed to pass through Indian territory as they moved up the Missouri River. But fur traders and settlers who followed in the decades after had clashes with these Native Americans.

In 1868 the Dakota Territory included both North and South Dakota. Within a few years, immigrants, especially from Central Europe and Scandinavia, began arriving by rail. Most made their homesteads in the fertile eastern half of the state. They found rich prairie-grass soils and enough precipitation there to grow wheat and other crops. To the west of the Missouri the newcomers encountered drier conditions, better suited for grazing cattle and sheep. The Dakota Territory was split in half when both North and South Dakota were admitted to the Union on the same day in 1889. Pierre (pronounced "peer") was made the capital of the southern state.

South Dakota has only one large area of forest, the Black Hills. Named for the dark color of their stately ponderosa pines, the Black Hills are the highest peaks east of the Rocky Mountains. More important, they are sacred to the Lakota people, who see them as "the heart of everything that is." An 1868 treaty had promised to let the Lakota keep their rich hunting grounds forever, but all this changed when the U.S. Army, led by George Armstrong Custer, reported gold in the Black Hills. Although the Lakota, led by Sitting Bull and Crazy Horse, wiped out Custer's troops in neighboring Montana in 1876, they could not win against the bitter campaign launched by the Army. The last

1830s

The arrival of steamboats on the upper Missouri River stimulated the fur trade and helped open the region to development.

1874–2002

The discovery of gold in the Black Hills led to the opening of the Homestake Mine, richest and longest-producing mine in the U.S.

1930s

Dust storms called black blizzards and plagues of grasshoppers accompanied a 10-year drought, worst in the state's history.

Present day

The completion of a monument to Lakota chief Crazy Horse is part of a new drive to attract visitors and build the tourist industry.

The Badlands (opposite), strange shapes etched into layers of volcanic ash and soft sediments, frustrated early white settlers. Today, they enchant visitors to Badlands National Park, where wind, rain, snow, and ice erode an average of one inch (2.5 cm) per year.

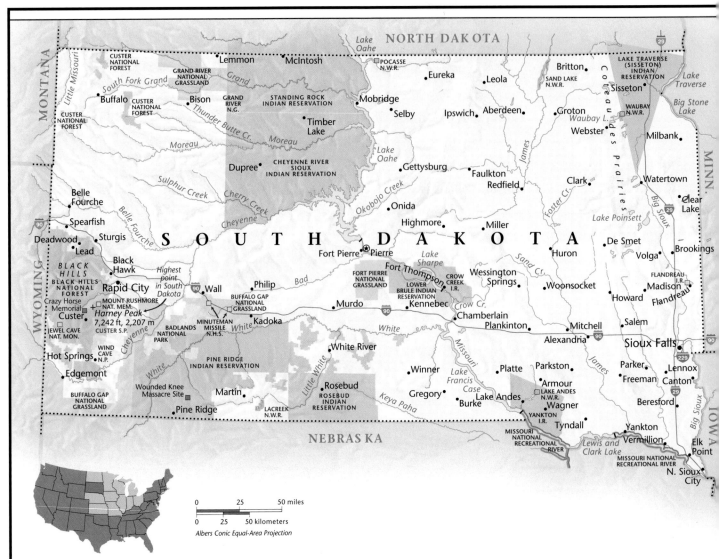

NORTH DAKOTA

MONTANA

CUSTER NATIONAL FOREST

Lemmon   McIntosh

Little Missouri

South Fork Grand

GRAND RIVER NATIONAL GRASSLAND

Buffalo   CUSTER NATIONAL FOREST   Bison

Grand

GRAND RIVER N.G.

STANDING ROCK INDIAN RESERVATION

CUSTER NATIONAL FOREST

Thunder Butte Cr.

Timber Lake

POCASSE N.W.R.

Eureka   Leola

Mobridge

Selby

Britton   LAKE TRAVERSE (SISSETON) INDIAN RESERVATION

SAND LAKE N.W.R.

Sisseton

Lake Traverse

Moreau   *Moreau*

Dupree   CHEYENNE RIVER SIOUX INDIAN RESERVATION

Lake Oahe

Ipswich   Aberdeen

Gettysburg

James

Groton

WAUBAY N.W.R.

Webster   *Waubay L.*

Milbank

Big Stone Lake

MINN.

Sulphur Creek

Cherry Creek

Cheyenne

Faulkton   Redfield

Clark

Watertown

Foster Cr.

Lake Poinsett

Clear Lake

Belle Fourche

Belle Fourche

Spearfish

Deadwood   Sturgis   Lead

BLACK HILLS

BLACK HILLS NATIONAL FOREST

Black Hawk

Rapid City

Crazy Horse Memorial

Custer

JEWEL CAVE NAT. MON.

Highest point in South Dakota

MOUNT RUSHMORE NAT. MEM.

Harney Peak 7,242 ft, 2,207 m

CUSTER S.P.

WIND CAVE N.P.

Hot Springs

Edgemont

BUFFALO GAP NATIONAL GRASSLAND

S O U T H   D A K O T A

Onida

Highmore

Miller

De Smet

Volga

Brookings

Fort Pierre   Pierre

Lake Sharpe

Huron

Sand Cr.

Wall

Cheyenne

Philip

Bad

Murdo

Kadoka

BADLANDS NATIONAL PARK

MINUTEMAN MISSILE N.H.S.

White

FORT PIERRE NATIONAL GRASSLAND

Fort Thompson

LOWER BRULE INDIAN RESERVATION

CROW CREEK I.R.

Wessington Springs

Kennebec

White

Crow Cr.

Chamberlain

Plankinton

Woonsocket

Howard

FLANDREAU I.R.

Madison

Flandreau

Salem

Mitchell

Alexandria

Sioux Falls

BUFFALO GAP NATIONAL GRASSLAND

WYOMING

Cheyenne

White

PINE RIDGE INDIAN RESERVATION

White River

Winner

Little White

Martin

Wounded Knee Massacre Site

Pine Ridge

LACREEK N.W.R.

Rosebud

ROSEBUD INDIAN RESERVATION

Gregory

Keya Paha

Missouri

Lake Francis Case

Platte

Lake Andes

Burke

Parkston

Armour

LAKE ANDES N.W.R.

Wagner

YANKTON I.R.

Tyndall

James

Parker

Freeman

Beresford

Canton

Lennox

Yankton

MISSOURI NATIONAL RECREATIONAL RIVER

Lewis and Clark Lake

Vermillion

MISSOURI NATIONAL RECREATIONAL RIVER

Elk Point

N. Sioux City

IOWA

NEBRASKA

Albers Conic Equal-Area Projection

0   25   50 miles
0   25   50 kilometers

Four Presidents who played key roles in the first 150 years of the nation—(left to right) George Washington, Thomas Jefferson, Theodore Roosevelt, and Abraham Lincoln—are commemorated in the Mount Rushmore National Memorial. The sculpture represents the vision of Gutzon Borglum, who began work on his Shrine of Democracy in 1927. Gazing from a granite mountainside in the Black Hills, these 60-foot- (18-m-) high figures inspire people from around the world.

major battle in the Indian Wars took place along Wounded Knee Creek on the Pine Ridge Reservation. There, U.S. troops massacred 300 Native American men, women, and children.

Today, one in twelve of South Dakota's people is American Indian. Most live on the nine reservations scattered across the state. Many battle poverty on these poor lands. Some fight through the courts for lands that were once theirs. In the Black Hills, the Lakota are honoring Chief Crazy Horse with a gigantic memorial that is being carved out of solid granite.

Another monumental structure in the Black Hills—Mount Rushmore—attracts nearly three million people each year, making the region a major source of income for the state. Vacationers find a bit of the past in herds of bison and in the "Wild West" town of Deadwood, where Wild Bill Hickok and Calamity Jane lived.

Farming and ranching still form key parts of the state's economy. South Dakota is a top producer of millet, soybeans, sunflowers, rye, sheep, and cattle. Special facilities convert corn to a motor fuel called ethanol. Meat packing and other food processing also add value to state farm products. In recent years, the manufacture of computers and the processing of credit card information have brought jobs to many workers, especially in the Sioux Falls area. A pioneering effort is also underway to turn the remains of an old industry into a brand-new one. The Homestake Mine, which closed in 2002, will work again for South Dakota. The State government has plans to turn the 8,000-foot- (2,400-m-) deep gold mine into a world-class, high-tech underground research laboratory. As they look ahead, the people of South Dakota know that the past is with them as they scout the future.

SOUTH DAKOTA
Mount Rushmore State

STATEHOOD	November 2, 1889; 40th state
CAPITAL	Pierre
LARGEST CITY	Sioux Falls Population 130,491
TOTAL AREA	77,117 sq mi; 199,731 sq km
LAND AREA	75,885 sq mi; 196,540 sq km
POPULATION	764,309
POPULATION DENSITY	10 people per sq mi
MAJOR RACIAL/ ETHNIC GROUPS	88.7% white; 8.3% Native American; .6% African American; .6% Asian. Hispanic (any race) 1.4%.
INDUSTRY	finance, services, manufacturing, government, retail trade, transportation and utilities, wholesale trade, construction, mining
AGRICULTURE	cattle, corn, soybeans, wheat, hogs, hay, dairy products

RING-NECKED PHEASANT

PASQUEFLOWER

Did you know?

1. The world's largest, most complete, and best preserved specimen of *Tyrannosaurus rex* discovered to date was unearthed on the Cheyenne River Indian Reservation in 1990. It was named Sue after the fossil hunter who found it.
2. Petrified Wood Park in Lemmon is the largest park of its kind in the world. Fossils and petrified wood are arranged in unusual shapes, including a castle and pyramids.
3. South Dakota is the home of the Dakota, Lakota, and Nakota tribes, which together make up the Sioux Nation.
4. In 1959, with the addition of Alaska and Hawaii to the Union, the geographic center of the United States moved from Lebanon, Kansas, to a point near Belle Fourche, South Dakota.

WISCONSIN

★ *Badger State* ★

BADGER STATE, a name that refers to lead miners who lived like burrowing animals in caves during the 1820s, is one state nickname. Another—America's Dairyland—comes from the state's cheese-making and milk-producing traditions. Wisconsinites would say that while both of these names refer to particular resources, neither captures the state's wide-ranging landscapes and activities.

Jean Nicolet, a Frenchman searching for a Northwest Passage to Asia, stepped ashore from "La Baye" (Green Bay) to meet not Chinese but Winnebago natives in 1634. Marquette and Joliet found Ojibwa and Menominee peoples as they paddled and portaged their way across the territory in 1673 to reach the Mississippi River. The explorers found waterways everywhere— lakes, streams, and wetlands of all sizes in this region the Ojibwa called "gathering of the waters," or the French called "Ouisconsin."

Gigantic fingers of continental glaciers formed much of Wisconsin's present landscape, gouging out Lake Superior and Lake Michigan. As they retreated, the glaciers left looping mounds of glacial rocks called morraines across northern uplands and eastern lowlands. Expansive central wetlands that produce the nation's top cranberry crop were once a glacial lake bed. Ridges blocked the glaciers' paths into southwestern Wisconsin, leaving tall bluffs and steep-sided valleys untouched.

The British took control of all French lands east of the Mississippi in 1763. Green Bay became Wisconsin's first permanent European settlement the next year. The region passed to American control after the Revolutionary War, becoming part of the sprawling Northwest Territory. Native American resistance ended with the Black Hawk War in 1832, and the Wisconsin Territory was formed in 1836.

1634

French explorer Jean Nicolet, who was seeking a water route to China, was the first European to set foot on Wisconsin soil.

1820s

The mining of lead for use in paint and in shot for guns rose sharply, causing miners to pour into southwestern Wisconsin.

1890—1925

Wisconsin's Progressive Movement, led by "Fighting Bob" La Follette, initiated key political, social, and economic reforms.

Present day

Hundred-year-old Harley David-son Motor Company is a symbol of the state's tradition as a center of small engine manufacturing.

Two dairy farms share a bluff top in southwestern Wisconsin (opposite), a region that continental ice sheets largely missed. To prevent erosion, these steep-sided valleys that the French called "coulees" must be planted in rows parallel to the contour.

APOSTLE ISLANDS
NATIONAL LAKESHORE

Apostle Islands

LAKE SUPERIOR

RED CLIFF
INDIAN
RESERVATION

BAD RIVER
I.R.

*Madeline
Island*

Superior

Washburn

Ashland

BAD RIVER
INDIAN
RESERVATION

Hurley

MICHIGAN

MINNESOTA

ST. CROIX NATIONAL
SCENIC RIVERWAY

St. Croix

Bois Brule

CHEQUAMEGON
NATIONAL
FOREST

*Turtle-
Flambeau
Flowage*

Land O'Lakes

LAC DU FLAMBEAU
INDIAN
RESERVATION

Eagle
River

Pine

Brule

Menominee

Namekagon

Hayward

LAC COURTE
OREILLES
I.R.

*Lake
Chippewa*

Park
Falls

CHEQUAMEGON
NATIONAL
FOREST

NICOLET
NATIONAL
FOREST

Popple

Niagara

*Washington
Island*

Spooner

Rhinelander

SOKAOGON
CHIPPEWA
INDIAN
RESERVATION

FOREST COUNTY
POTAWATOMI
INDIAN
RESERVATION

Rice Lake

St. Croix Falls

Chippewa

Flambeau

Ladysmith

Jump

Highest
point in
Wisconsin

Tomahawk
+
Timms Hill
1,951ft
595 m

Wisconsin

Wolf

NICOLET
NATIONAL
FOREST

WOLF NATIONAL
WILD & SCENIC RIVER

Peshtigo

Marinette

ST. CROIX
I.R.

New
Richmond

ST. CROIX NATIONAL
SCENIC RIVERWAY

Red Cedar

Chippewa
Falls

CHEQUAMEGON
NATIONAL
FOREST

Merrill

Antigo

Oconto

Marinette

Green Bay

DOOR PENINSULA

Sturgeon Bay

Hudson

ST. CROIX
N.W.&S.R.

River Falls

Menomonie

Altoona

Eau Claire

Yellow

Medford

*Big
Eau Pleine
Res.*

Wausau

STOCKBRIDGE
INDIAN
RESERVATION

MENOMINEE
I.R.

Oconto

Shawano

Algoma

Mississippi

Chippewa

Lake Wissota

Marshfield

Lake Du Bay

WISCONSIN

Wolf

Ashwaubenon

ONEIDA INDIAN
RESERVATION

Green Bay

De Pere

*Lake
Pepin*

Pepin

WISCONSIN
WINNEBAGO
I.R.

Black River Falls

Stevens Point

Plover

New London

Waupaca

Appleton

Kaukauna

Two Rivers

UPPER MISSISSIPPI
RIVER NATIONAL
WILDLIFE AND
FISH REFUGE

TREMPEALEAU
N.W.R.

Black

NECEDAH
NATIONAL
WILDLIFE
REFUGE

*Petenwell
Lake*

Wisconsin
Rapids

Wisconsin

*Lake
Poygan*

Neenah

Menasha

*Lake
Winnebago*

Manitowoc

Onalaska

Tomah

Sparta

*Castle Rock
Lake*

Oshkosh

Ripon

Fond
du Lac

Fox

Sheboygan

La Crosse

Viroqua

Kickapoo

Reedsburg

Wisconsin
Dells

Waupun

HORICON
NATIONAL
WILDLIFE
REFUGE

Fox

Milwaukee

LAKE
MICHIGAN

Richland
Center

Baraboo

*Lake
Wisconsin*

Portage

Beaver Dam

West
Bend

Port Washington

UPPER MISSISSIPPI
RIVER NATIONAL
WILDLIFE AND
FISH REFUGE

Wisconsin

Sun Prairie

Menomonee
Falls

Mequon

Prairie du Chien

Middleton

Taliesin

*Lake
Mendota*

Madison

Watertown

Brookfield

Wauwatosa

Rock

Milwaukee

Dodgeville

Lancaster

Monona

Waukesha

West
Allis

S. Milwaukee

Platteville

Stoughton

Fort Atkinson

Fox

Racine

Pecatonica

Janesville

Whitewater

Lake
Geneva

Burlington

Monroe

Sugar

Rock

Beloit

Pleasant Prairie

Kenosha

IOWA

ILLINOIS

IGHLAND

0   50   100 miles
0   50   100 kilometers
Albers Conic Equal-Area Projection

Swiss, German, and other European
settlers brought their skills in raising
dairy cows for milk, butter, and
especially cheese to Wisconsin. Soon
large milking barns appeared across
the state. In Monroe, a master
cheesemaker (left) racks 18-lb (8-kg)
wheels of Grand Cru Gruyere cheese
for drying—one of hundreds of types
made in the Dairy State. In 2003
Wisconsin produced 26 percent of
the country's total cheese output.

Wisconsin joined the Union in 1848 as the 30th state, with Madison as its capital. German immigrants arrived in great numbers and settled in Milwaukee. The city became a center of German culture, with its meat packing and beer brewing.

Rural settlers found soils across southern Wisconsin fertile enough to grow wheat and other crops. Loggers cut down immense stands of white pines across the northern half of the state. Wisconsin owes its trademark dairy farming to Swiss settlers. For most of the 20th century, Wisconsin was the country's largest producer of dairy products.

The 20th century also saw industrial Wisconsin reach high gear. Cities large and small built factories, turning out everything from bathroom fixtures to cooking pots. "Machine Shop to the World," Milwaukee rumbled with the manufacture of railroad cars, heavy machinery, and then small engines. Large numbers of Polish and African-American laborers arrived to fill factory jobs there. Wisconsin grew to be one of the world's top paper-making centers as sawmills and pulp mills harnessed hydropower. Wisconsin's water resources also made it a haven for hunters, fishers, and sport enthusiasts.

Today, Wisconsin is facing the decline of manufacturing and family-owned farms as well as an urgent need to protect natural resources. The state works to keep existing factories successful and sponsors research to expand biotechnology and other new businesses. It has also launched a major program to clean up industrial pollutants in the Fox River. Farmers are looking to new markets as they grow both profitable and earth-friendly organic crops. Long a leader in social and environmental action, the state is working hard to protect the future of its 5.5 million people.

WISCONSIN
Badger State

1848

STATEHOOD	May 29, 1848; 30th state
CAPITAL	Madison
LARGEST CITY	Milwaukee Population 590,895
TOTAL AREA	65,498 sq mi; 169,639 sq km
LAND AREA	54,310 sq mi; 140,663 sq km
POPULATION	5,472,299
POPULATION DENSITY	100.2 people per sq mi
MAJOR RACIAL/ ETHNIC GROUPS	88.9% white; 5.7% African American; 1.7% Asian; .9% Native American. Hispanic (any race) 3.6%.
INDUSTRY	industrial machinery, paper products, food processing, metal products, electronic equipment, transportation
AGRICULTURE	dairy products, cattle, corn, poultry and eggs, soybeans

ROBIN

WOOD VIOLET

Did you know?

1. The first hydroelectric plant in the country was built on the Fox River in Appleton in 1882.
2. The first snowmachine patent was issued to Carl Eliason of Sayner, Wisconsin. Today the state has more than 25,000 miles (40,000 km) of groomed snowmobile trails.
3. In 1856 a German immigrant named Margarethe Schurz opened the first kindergarten in the United States in Watertown. Her concept of teaching young children through play quickly spread across the U.S.
4. Door County, which includes Door Peninsula, has more than 250 miles (400 km) of shoreline, more than any other county in the United States.
5. Laura Ingalls Wilder was born in Pepin in 1867. Her famous "Little House" books are based on her childhood life in the forests and prairies of the Midwest.
6. Baraboo is the birthplace of the Ringling Bros. Circus.

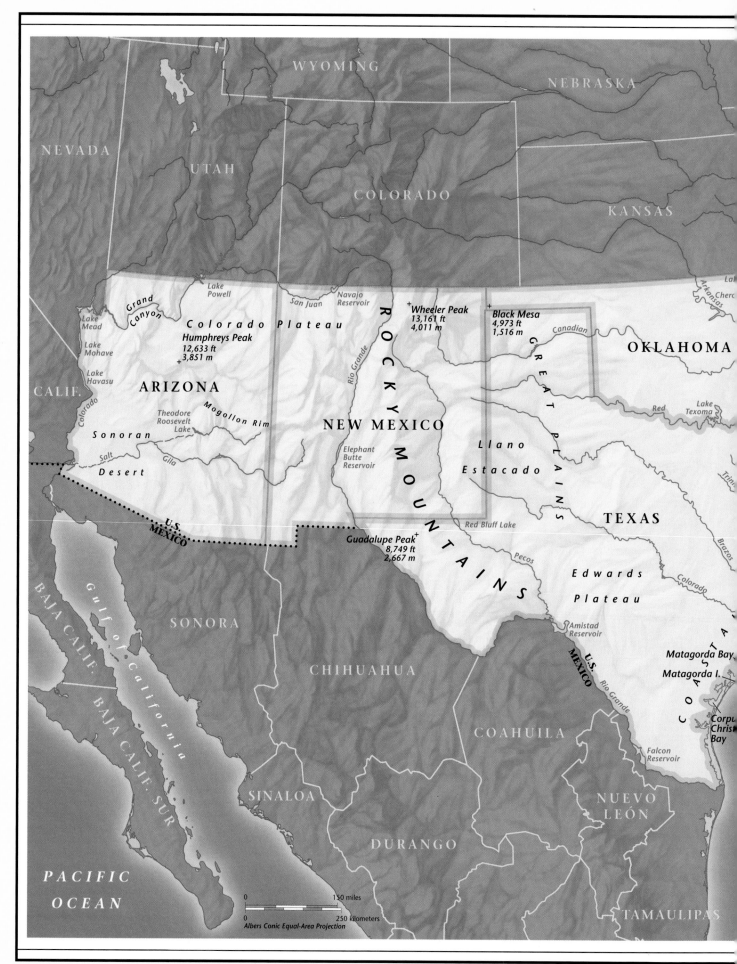

NEVADA

UTAH

WYOMING

NEBRASKA

COLORADO

KANSAS

CALIF.

Lake
Mead

Lake
Mohave

Lake
Havasu

*Grand
Canyon*

Lake
Powell

Colorado   Plateau

San Juan

Navajo
Reservoir

Wheeler Peak
13,161 ft
4,011 m

Black Mesa
4,973 ft
1,516 m

Canadian

Arkansas

Lak

Cher

OKLAHOMA

Humphreys Peak
12,633 ft
3,851 m

ARIZONA

Colorado

Sonoran

Salt

Gila

Theodore
Roosevelt
Lake

Mogollon Rim

Rio Grande

R O C K Y

NEW MEXICO

Elephant
Butte
Reservoir

Red Bluff Lake

G R E A T   P L A I N S

Llano

Estacado

Red

Lake
Texoma

Desert

U.S.
MEXICO

Guadalupe Peak
8,749 ft
2,667 m

M O U N T A I N S

Pecos

TEXAS

Edwards

Plateau

Colorado

Brazos

Trini

BAJA CALIF.

Gulf   of   California

SONORA

CHIHUAHUA

Rio Grande

U.S.
MEXICO

Amistad
Reservoir

C O A S T A

Matagorda Bay

Matagorda I.

BAJA CALIF. SUR

COAHUILA

Corpu
Chris
Bay

SINALOA

NUEVO
LEÓN

Falcon
Reservoir

PACIFIC

OCEAN

DURANGO

0   150 miles

0   250 kilometers

Albers Conic Equal-Area Projection

TAMAULIPAS

The Southwest

DIVERSE LANDSCAPES and sunny weather characterize the American Southwest. Deep canyons dominate the Colorado Plateau west of the Rockies, where the Colorado River winds through Arizona's Grand Canyon. Dams and reservoirs now tame this once mighty waterway, which provides water and power to cities and farms. South of the plateau the Sonoran Desert stretches into Mexico. The silt-laden Rio Grande flows out of the Rocky Mountains, carrying snowmelt to thirsty lands along the Texas-Mexico border. The windswept Great Plains stretch east of the Rockies across mostly level Texas and Oklahoma. Rivers move southeast through this short-grass prairie to the coastal plain, then empty into the Gulf of Mexico. Like the land, the climate changes with location. Precipitation is scarce except in the eastern part of the region. Southwestern winters can be cold and snowy, but summers are hot and sunny.

Enchanted Places and Multicultural Faces

LONG BEFORE COLUMBUS reached the New World resourceful Indians farmed the landscapes of the Southwest. Near rivers and springs, ancestral Puebloans, Zuni, and Hopi peoples planted fields of corn, beans, and squash. To these staples they added piñon nuts, venison, rabbit, and chili peppers. High atop mesas, the Hopi built villages with sun-baked adobe bricks. In contrast, the Puebloans wedged homes and granaries within the vertical walls of sheltered canyons. East of the Rocky Mountains, the Comanche and Apache adapted to life on the southern Great Plains by hunting buffalo and gathering plants.

In 1540 the Spanish conquistador Francisco Vásquez de Coronado rode north from Mexico to claim this "Kingdom of New Mexico." By 1610, just ten years before *Mayflower* pilgrims settled Massachusetts, Spain's cluster of buildings near Santa Fe became America's first capital city. During the next century European guns and diseases overwhelmed the Indians.

In 1821, the Santa Fe Trail broadened American trade and settlement. The next year Stephen F. Austin led the first band of American farmers into the hill country of central Texas. Farms and cattle ranches began to blanket the countryside. Although by 1824 Mexico had gained control of the Southwest from Spain, *Los Americanos* were now firmly established in this dry region. Soon they were driving herds of Texas longhorns north along the Shawnee and Chisholm Trails to railroad yards in the Midwest. In 1835 rebellious Americans in Texas revolted against Mexican rule. Ten years later Texas joined the Union. In 1848 after war with Mexico, Arizona and New Mexico became part of the United States.

Under American control, the region's economy began to change. The cattle drives ended in the 1870s as barbed wire and railroads stretched into Texas. Land-hungry settlers in Oklahoma encouraged the U.S. government to either purchase or take land promised to the Indians. Elsewhere a series of broken treaties forced Native Americans from their remaining homelands. Oil discoveries in the early 1900s attracted new settlers to Texas and Oklahoma.

Also at this time, water and electricity provided by dams built on the Colorado River and the Rio Grande, as well as dozens of smaller water projects, led to the growth of modern cities and huge farming operations. Today, the Southwest is a major exporter of grain, fruit, cotton, and vegetables, much of it harvested by workers from nearby Mexico. Sheep, goats, as well as cattle ranching and feeding operations remain important to the region.

In recent decades new industries have emerged. The cities of Dallas, Oklahoma City, Phoenix, and Albuquerque are important centers of technology and business. New Mexico is a key player in solar energy and weapons research, while Texas hosts the command post for U.S. astronauts. Since 1914 the Houston Ship channel has linked the city's oil refineries with the Gulf Coast and the rest of the world. Abundant sunshine and a slower lifestyle attract newcomers. While growth fuels the economy, it depletes the water in huge natural reservoirs called aquifers that lie beneath much of the region.

The Southwest is a fast-growing region with a dynamic modern economy that retains much of its Native American, Hispanic, and Wild West heritage. Indian traditions of fine pottery, weavings, and architecture are abundantly evident throughout New Mexico and Arizona. Each year millions of tourists explore its canyons, mountains, and deserts. These landscapes, combined with the region's unique settlement history, contribute to its reputation as an enchanted and multicultural place.

> "Wilderness so godful, cosmic, primeval, bestows a new sense of Earth's beauty and size."
>
> —JOHN MUIR, *STEEP TRAILS*

The famous Mitten Buttes create a magical desert landscape against a Southwestern sky. The red sandstone formations, which rise 900 feet (275 m) above the floor of Monument Valley, are part of a Navajo tribal park on the Utah-Arizona border.

ARIZONA

★ Grand Canyon State ★

"LITTLE SPRING"—that's the meaning of the Native American term for Arizona. Knowing this, you'd expect water to be a big deal here, and you'd be right. Very little rain falls on much of the state, and most rivers and streams flow for only part of the year. Conserving water is key to Arizona's future success.

Millions of years of tug-of-war between uplift in Earth's crust and erosion by rivers has created the spectacular scenery of the Colorado Plateau in the north. The mile- (1.6-km-) deep Grand Canyon is the plateau's crown jewel, but Monument Valley and the Painted Desert are among its other treasures. Forests of ponderosa pine grow on the Mogollon Rim, a long line of steep cliffs that provide a 2,000-foot (600-m) step-down to the Basin and Range region. Major dams have been built to harness rivers here. To the south and west, ranges are lower and basins are broader—and bone dry. The

Sonoran Desert stretches across more than 25,000 square miles (65,000 sq km) of the state into Mexico. Some areas of the desert average less than two inches (5 cm) of rain per year. Summer sun bakes the saguaro and other cacti, with daily summer temperatures averaging above 100°F (37°C).

Native peoples have succeeded in this challenging land for more than 2,500 years. The ancestral Puebloans inhabited cliff dwellings in Canyon de Chelly, and the Hohokam built dams and dug ditches to bring water from the Gila and Salt Rivers to fields of corn, beans, and squash. The Hopi were living in Oraibi when the Navajo and Apache peoples arrived more than 500 years ago. First Spain then Mexico ruled the region, and settlers fought the Indians for control of the land. Arizona became a U.S. territory after the Mexican-American War in 1848.

Silver and copper attracted settlers from the

1690

San Xavier del Bac, near Tucson, was the first of many Spanish missions built to teach Native Americans Christianity.

1896

Arizona's Indian Wars ended when a lack of food forced Apache chief Geronimo (3rd from left) to surrender to the U.S. Army.

1911

The Roosevelt Dam, first of several in the Salt River Project, brings water and electricity to fast-growing Phoenix.

Present day

The Kitt Peak National Observatory's 20-some telescopes earn Tucson the title Astronomy Capital of the World.

The Colorado River has been carving the Grand Canyon (opposite) for millions of years, creating what President Theodore Roosevelt called "the most impressive piece of scenery I have ever looked at." Each year it attracts five million tourists.

UTAH
Lake Powell
Monument Valley
Four Corners
COLO.

NEVADA

COLORADO CITY
Virgin
KAIBAB I.R.
PIPE SPRING NAT. MON.
VERMILION CLIFFS NAT. MON.
GLEN CANYON N.R.A.
Paria Canyon
Page
Glen Canyon Dam
NAVAJO NAT. MON. (KEET SEEL RUIN)
NAVAJO NAT. MON. (INSCRIPTION HOUSE RUIN)
Kayenta
NAVAJO NAT. MON. (BETATAKIN RUIN)
Chinle Wash
CANYON DE CHELLY N.M.

GRAND CANYON-PARASHANT NAT. MON.
KAIBAB NATIONAL FOREST
GRAND CANYON NATIONAL PARK
Kaibab Plateau
Marble Canyon
Black Mesa
NAVAJO NATION RESERVATION
Chinle

Lake Mead
Hoover Dam
LAKE MEAD NAT'L RECREATION AREA
Black Mountains
Red Lake
GRAND CANYON NATIONAL PARK
HAVASUPAI I.R.
Grand Canyon
KAIBAB NATIONAL FOREST
Coconino Plateau
Tuba City
HOPI I.R.
Little Colorado
Painted Desert
Old Oraibi
HOPI INDIAN RESERVATION
Polacca
Fort Defiance
HUBBELL TRADING POST N.H.S.
Window Rock

Lake Mohave
HUALAPAI INDIAN RESERVATION
Colorado
Aubrey Cliffs
Highest point in Arizona
Humphreys Peak 12,633 ft 3,851 m
WUPATKI NAT. MON.
SUNSET CRATER VOLCANO NAT. MON.

Dolan Springs
Bullhead City
FT. MOJAVE I.R.
Kingman
Big Sandy
Seligman
Williams
KAIBAB N.F.
Flagstaff
WALNUT CANYON NAT. MON.
Winslow
PETRIFIED FOREST N.P.
Puerco
NEW MEXICO

Lake Havasu
Lake Havasu City
PRESCOTT NATIONAL FOREST
Verde
Sedona
COCONINO N.F.
Meteor Crater
Clear Creek
Holbrook
ZUNI I.R.
Zuni

BILL WILLIAMS RIVER N.W.R.
Chino Valley
TUZIGOOT NAT. MON.
Cottonwood
CAMP VERDE I.R.
MONTEZUMA CASTLE N.M.
Chevelon Cr.
St. Johns
Snowflake
Little Colorado

CALIFORNIA
Bill Williams
Prescott Valley
YAVAPAI I.R.
Prescott
PRESCOTT N.F.
Camp Verde
APACHE-SITGREAVES NATIONAL FOREST
Show Low
Eagar
APACHE-SITGREAVES NATIONAL FORESTS
San Francisco

Parker
COLORADO RIVER INDIAN RESERVATION
A R I Z O N A
VERDE N.W.&S.R.
Mogollon Rim
Pinetop-Lakeside
Whiteriver

Colorado
Wickenburg
AGUA FRIA NAT. MON.
Verde
Payson
TONTO NATIONAL FOREST
WHITE MOUNTAIN APACHE RESERVATION
White

Quartzsite
Agua Fria
Theodore Roosevelt Lake
TONTO NAT. MON.
Salt
Black

CIBOLA N.W.R.
KOFA NATIONAL WILDLIFE REFUGE
Sun City
Glendale
FT. McDOWELL I.R.
SALT RIVER I.R.
Scottsdale
Phoenix
Mesa
Tempe
Chandler
Globe
SAN CARLOS APACHE RESERVATION
San Carlos
SAN CARLOS Reservoir
Clifton
APACHE-SITGREAVES NATIONAL FORESTS

IMPERIAL N.W.R.
S O N O R A N
GILA RIVER I.R.
Gila
CASA GRANDE RUINS NAT. MON.
CORONADO N.F.
Safford

MARICOPA (AK-CHIN) I.R.
Florence
San Manuel
CORONADO N.F.
San Pedro

GILA BEND I.R.
Casa Grande
Coolidge
Eloy
Catalina
Oro Valley
CORONADO N.F.
Gila
Willcox
FORT BOWIE N.H.S.

Gila
Wellton
D E S E R T
Santa Cruz
SAGUARO N.P.
CORONADO N.F.
Yuma
COCOPAH I.R.
IRONWOOD FOREST NAT. MON.
Tucson
SAGUARO N.P.

San Luis
CABEZA PRIETA NATIONAL WILDLIFE REFUGE
Ajo
TOHONO O'ODHAM INDIAN RESERVATION
PASCUA YAQUI I.R.
Benson
CHIRICAHUA NAT. MON.
CORONADO N.F.

BAJA CALIF.
ORGAN PIPE CACTUS NAT. MON.
Kitt Peak National Observatory
Sells
SAN XAVIER I.R.
Green Valley
CORONADO N.F.
Tombstone
CORONADO N.F.
SAN BERNARDINO N.W.R.

U.S.
MEXICO
BUENOS AIRES N.W.R.
TUMACACORI N.H.P.
CORONADO N.F.
Sierra Vista
Bisbee
Douglas
Nogales
CORONADO NAT. MEM.
SONORA

0   50   100 miles
0   50   100 kilometers
Albers Conic Equal-Area Projection

The Navajo became sheep and goat herders early in the 19th century. Herding provided the Navajo with a steady supply of food and also with wool for the production of trade goods. Their population prospered and grew, doubling by the mid-1800s. In the past century overgrazing and erosion have resulted in loss of grazing land and reduction in the size of their herds.

East, as did cheap land for sheep and cattle ranching. But settlement didn't really begin to grow until after the fighting with the Apache ended in 1886. By the time statehood was granted in 1912, huge irrigation projects were underway. Farming of cotton and citrus fruits boomed. Year-round water meant opportunities for industries, too.

Arizona is now home to 5.6 million people, with most of this growth occurring after World War II. Before the war the population was mainly rural, but now most people live in and around Phoenix and Tucson. The state's climate and scenic beauties have attracted residents, tourists, and businesses alike. People come just to breathe its clean, dry air. The introduction of air-conditioning brought even more people. Cloud-free skies and wide-open spaces attracted the military, especially for air bases and desert warfare research. Related industries, such as aircraft and weapons manufacture, followed. Recently, electronics and other high-tech businesses have thrived.

All this growth brings challenges. For decades, Arizona's "Five Cs"—copper, cattle, cotton, citrus, and climate—were the basis for the state's prosperity. Arizona still produces more copper than all other states combined, but its importance has declined. The three agricultural Cs are still farmed but face problems with markets and water supply. Water "wars" between farmers, Native Americans, and city dwellers are ongoing. In addition, the Central Arizona Project, a massive effort to bring Colorado River water to the growing cities of Phoenix and Tucson, puts Arizona at odds with neighboring California and Nevada. If questions of water use are addressed, the state will continue to prosper, and its fifth C—climate—will always encourage people to "follow the sun" to Arizona.

ARIZONA
Grand Canyon State

STATEHOOD	February 14, 1912; 48th state
CAPITAL	Phoenix
LARGEST CITY	Phoenix Population 1,371,960
TOTAL AREA	113,998 sq mi; 295,254 sq km
LAND AREA	113,635 sq mi; 294,312
POPULATION	5,580,811
POPULATION DENSITY	48 people per sq mi
MAJOR RACIAL/ ETHNIC GROUPS	75.5% white; 5% Native American; 3.1% African American; 1.8% Asian. Hispanic (any race) 25.3%.
INDUSTRY	real estate, manufactured goods, retail, state and local government, transportation and public utilities, wholesale trade, health services, tourism, electronics
AGRICULTURE	vegetables, cattle, dairy products, cotton, fruit, nursery stock, nuts

CACTUS WREN   SAGUARO

Did you know?

1. The federal government owns 88 percent of Arizona's land, including 21 Indian reservations. Of these, the Navajo Nation Reservation is the largest.
2. The planet Pluto was discovered from the Lowell Observatory in Flagstaff in 1930.
3. Arizona's largest lizard, the Gila monster, is the only poisonous lizard in the United States.
4. Lake Powell, the nation's second largest reservoir, is named for John Wesley Powell, the one-armed Civil War veteran who was the first white person to successfully navigate and map the Grand Canyon.
5. London Bridge, which once spanned England's River Thames, was purchased for Lake Havasu City in the 1960s. The bridge was shipped across the Atlantic and reconstructed in the Arizona desert.

NEW MEXICO

★ *Land of Enchantment* ★

THE YEAR WAS 1610. Ten years before the *Mayflower* landed, the governor of New Spain sent soldiers, priests, and settlers from Mexico City to Santa Fe. Nearly four centuries later, the handsome Palace of the Governors still stands in what is now the state capital. Spanish, Mexican, and Native American influences blend across rugged and scenic New Mexico.

The state's landscape was shaped by forces much older—the uplift of ancient seafloors, massive volcanic eruptions, and millions of years of erosion. The northwest corner contains the Colorado Plateau's deeply-cut valleys and mesas. Ship Rock, the hardened neck of an eroded volcano, stands there as a lonely reminder of a fiery past. Rolling lands of the Great Plains cover the eastern third of the state, while the rugged spine of the Rockies reaches into central New Mexico. The Rio Grande flows through its middle from Colorado south to Texas and Mexico, and deserts cover much of the southern portion.

Immigrants have long ventured to New Mexico. The first may have been Ice-Age hunters 12,000 years ago. Evidence of their presence has been found near the town of Clovis, and tips from their spears are known worldwide as Clovis points. When the Spanish first explored here in the 1500s, they found Zuni, Hopi, and Tewa peoples living in clusters of apartment-like structures. They named these adobe (stone-and-mud-brick) buildings pueblos after the Spanish word for towns. Some of these centuries-old dwellings are still occupied. The newcomers settled across the region, building missions, setting up ranches, and trading with the native people.

After Mexico gained independence from Spain in 1821, it began trading with the United States. As the Santa Fe Trail brought more and

1610

Santa Fe, the oldest capital city in the nation, has been the seat of government in New Mexico since Spanish territorial days.

1863–1868

Thousands of Navajo were rounded up by the U.S. Army and forced to march to a reservation called Bosque Redondo.

1945

The first test of a U.S.-made atomic bomb was at Trinity Site in the desert near Alamogordo on July 16, 1945.

Present day

Forest fires are a yearly spring-summer threat in New Mexico. The state averages the most acres destroyed by fire in the Southwest.

Almost one in ten residents of New Mexico is Native American. The state hosts powwows—celebrations of Native American dancing and singing—that attract participants from all across the United States.

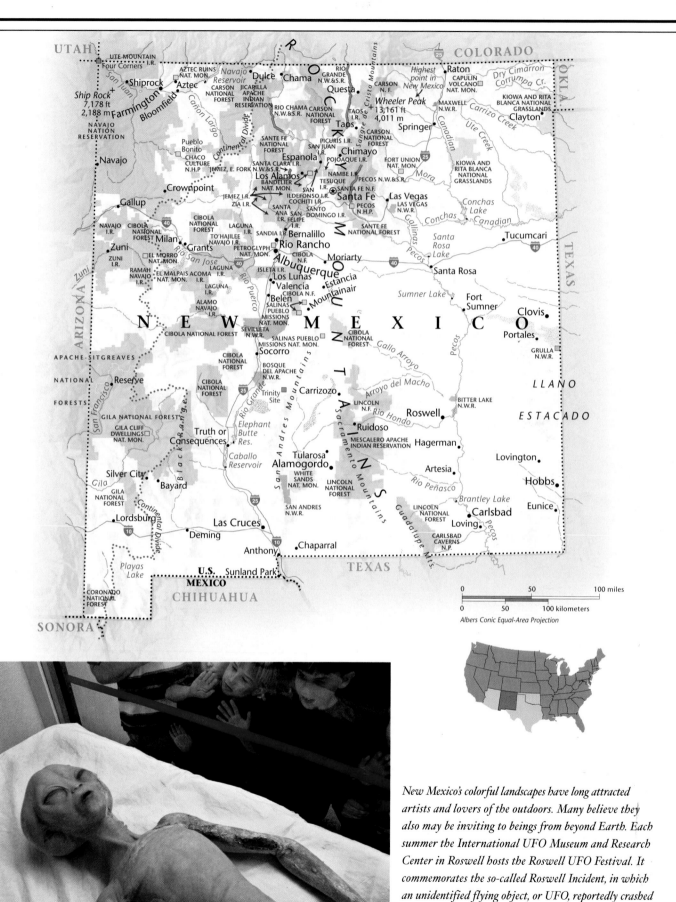

New Mexico's colorful landscapes have long attracted artists and lovers of the outdoors. Many believe they also may be inviting to beings from beyond Earth. Each summer the International UFO Museum and Research Center in Roswell hosts the Roswell UFO Festival. It commemorates the so-called Roswell Incident, in which an unidentified flying object, or UFO, reportedly crashed near the town in 1947. The alien shown here is a prop from a movie about the event.

more Americans, conflicts arose that sparked the Mexican-American War. New Mexico became a U.S. territory in 1850, soon after the war ended. More migrants arrived from the East, first by wagon train and then rail. They mined silver and gold, raised cattle and sheep, and irrigated crops in river valleys. Statehood came late, with New Mexico becoming the 47th state in 1912.

New kinds of immigrants arrived in the 20th century. Artists were lured by the state's colorful landscapes and dramatic skies. Historic Taos Pueblo and Sante Fe became world-famous art centers. Another group arrived—quietly—in 1943. Government scientists came to isolated Los Alamos to build a top-secret weapon. Their success was marked by the explosion of the first atomic bomb in the New Mexico desert in July 1945.

Today, New Mexico is still home to many specialists in military, nuclear, and space program research. Much high-tech work is concentrated around Albuquerque. Mines produce uranium, potash, and lead. Oil and natural gas wells dot the eastern plains, and mountain forests grow ponderosa pines for lumber. Cattle ranches can be upwards of a hundred square miles in area. A farming specialty is chili peppers, with New Mexico producing more than any other state. Tourists in increasing numbers visit historic sites, enjoy desert vistas, and hike wild landscapes.

New Mexico takes pride in its ethnic diversity. More than 42 percent of its population claims Hispanic heritage, the highest level in the nation, and there are more than a dozen American Indian groups. But poverty is a problem—especially among native peoples—and an overall population increase has created water-use issues that New Mexico's people must solve if their state is to remain the Land of Enchantment.

NEW MEXICO
Land of Enchantment

STATEHOOD	January 6, 1912; 47th state
CAPITAL	Santa Fe
LARGEST CITY	Albuquerque Population 463,874
TOTAL AREA	121,590 sq mi; 314,915 sq km
LAND AREA	121,356 sq mi; 314,309 sq km
POPULATION	1,874,614
POPULATION DENSITY	15.3 people per sq mi
MAJOR RACIAL/ ETHNIC GROUPS	66.8% white; 9.5% Native American; 1.9% African American; 1.1% Asian. Hispanic (any race) 42.1%.
INDUSTRY	electronic equipment, state and local government, real estate, business services, federal government, oil and gas extraction, health services
AGRICULTURE	cattle, dairy products, hay, chilies, onions

ROADRUNNER   YUCCA

Did you know?

1. In 1950 the town of Hot Springs volunteered to change its name to Truth or Consequences. It is the only city in the country named for a game show.
2. The roadrunner, New Mexico's state bird, can reach ground speeds of 15 miles an hour (24 kph).
3. The Big Room, the largest underground chamber in Carlsbad Caverns National Park, is big enough to hold six football fields.
4. The largest gypsum dune field in the world is in White Sands National Monument.
5. In terms of percent of its total population, New Mexico has more Native Americans and Hispanic people than any other state in the lower 48.

OKLAHOMA

★ *Sooner State* ★

THEY JUST COULDN'T WAIT to get there. Eager 1880s homesteaders who couldn't stand the wait for Oklahoma Territory to open were called "Sooners." Later, as many as 50,000 immigrants made wild "land runs," claiming lands to settle. The most famous land run, on April 22, 1889, saw a patch of prairie turn into a city of 10,000 newcomers in just a few hours. The place? Oklahoma City.

More than half a century earlier, a much different and sadder migration had begun to create the Oklahoma of today. Federal troops pushed Cherokee, Choctaw, Chickasaw, Creek, and Seminole people from their homes in the Southeast to lands west of the Mississippi River. Fifteen thousand Cherokee people endured the most tragic of these journeys during the winter of 1838–39. As many as 4,000 died along this Trail of Tears. The journey ended in what became known as Indian Territory, then much larger than present-day Oklahoma. These immigrants joined other groups already there, including the Osage, Pawnee, and Comanche. Not surprisingly, when a Choctaw chief was asked to name the re-divided territory in 1866, he chose "okla" ("people") and "homa" ("red"). The state kept the name when it entered the Union in 1907. Today, members of 67 tribes live here, making up almost 8 percent of the total population.

Perhaps the easiest state shape to recognize, Oklahoma resembles a cooking pan, complete with handle. Landforms range from mountains to flatlands, and habitats from deep woods to sparse grasslands. The Ozark Plateau, shared with Missouri and Arkansas, covers the state's northeast corner. This rugged region is eroded by fast-flowing streams, many of which have been dammed for hydropower, flood control, and recreation. Other highlands include the forested Ouachita Mountains in the southeast

1830-42

The forced march of the Cherokee from their homes in the Southeast to Indian Territory became known as the Trail of Tears.

1889

When the government opened former Indian land to settlement, thousands rushed in to stake their claims. Each settler got 160 acres.

1930s

Drought and poor conservation practices stripped farms of topsoil, forcing thousands of farmers to abandon their land.

1995

In an act of domestic terrorism, antigovernment militants destroyed the Murrah Federal Building in Oklahoma City.

Oklahoma is right in the middle of Tornado Alley, a region of the Great Plains where more twisters strike than any place else on Earth. Critical research is carried out here by scientists who attempt to predict tornadoes and their destructive paths.

OKLAHOMA
Sooner State

OKLAHOMA

STATEHOOD	November 16, 1907; 46th state
CAPITAL	Oklahoma City
LARGEST CITY	Oklahoma City Population 519,034
TOTAL AREA	69,898 sq mi; 181,036 sq km
LAND AREA	68,667 sq mi; 177,847 sq km
POPULATION	3,511,532
POPULATION DENSITY	50.9 people per sq mi
MAJOR RACIAL/ ETHNIC GROUPS	76.2% white; 7.9% Native American; 7.6% African American; 1.4% Asian. Hispanic (any race) 5.2%.
INDUSTRY	manufacturing, services, government, finance, insurance, real estate
AGRICULTURE	cattle, wheat, hogs, poultry, nursery stock

SCISSOR-TAILED FLYCATCHER

MISTLETOE

Did you know?

1. The country's first parking meters were installed in Oklahoma City in 1935.
2. In 1930 an oil gusher called Wild Mary Sudik sprayed so much oil and gas that people in Oklahoma City couldn't light matches for fear of causing explosions.
3. The famous ballerina Maria Tallchief was an Osage from Fairfax, Oklahoma. The ballerina mural in the rotunda of the state capitol honors this Native American's talent.
4. Oklahoma has had 14 official flags during its history.
5. The state capitol building in Oklahoma City has a working oil well on its grounds.
6. Tulsa is known as the Oil Capital of the World.
7. Oklahoma has more artificial lakes than any other state, with over one million surface acres of water.
8. Until statehood, Oklahoma was known as Indian Territory. Today 39 tribes have their headquarters in the state.

and the Wichita Mountains in the southwest. Much of the rest of the pan is filled with a mixture of hills and plains, rolling out to the Panhandle. There, the drier High Plains are topped by Black Mesa, Oklahoma's highest point, at 4,973 feet (1,516 m).

COLORADO
Black Mesa
4,973 ft Cima
1,516 m
Bo
Highest point Cit
in Oklahoma
KIOWA AND
RITA BLANCA
NATIONAL
GRASSLAND

Oklahoma's resources lie both below and above ground. Oil is found all across the varied landscape, with "black gold" pumped even on the state capitol grounds in Oklahoma City. Oil refining is a major industry, as is manufacturing of aviation components, auto parts, and electronics. Data processing is a growing service business. Top agricultural activities include cattle ranching and wheat growing. Peanuts, cotton, and vegetables are grown in the Red River Valley bordering Texas.

In the 1930s Oklahoma farmers fell victim to drought and to farming practices that had stripped the soil of its natural protection. Wind eroded their plowed fields, sending thousands of "Okies" on the road, some as far as California. Better care of the fragile soil has allowed much of the farmland to recover, but the wind still troubles Oklahoma. Cold fronts clash with warm and humid air each spring, sometimes producing destructive tornadoes. One twister struck near Oklahoma City in 1999, with winds of 318 miles per hour (513 kph)—the highest ever recorded!

Oklahoma today has great promise, but problems as well. Average income is among the lowest in the nation, with many Native Americans living in poverty. Farms and ranches are struggling to survive. The state is still recovering from the terrible tragedy of the Oklahoma City bombing that killed 168 people in 1995. But with its diversity and a wealth of natural resources, Oklahoma is bound to prosper "sooner" rather than later.

KANSAS

MO.

Beaver • Beaver

Buffalo •

Miami •

Alva • ● Blackwell

OSAGE NATION RESERVATION

Bartlesville •

Vinita

uymon •
OPTIMA N.W.R.
Optima Lake

HIGH

LAINS

TEXAS

Woodward •

SALT PLAINS N.W.R.
Salt Fork
Great Salt Plains Lake

Rock Cr.

Ponca City •

Oologah Lake

Grove •

Pawhuska •

Skiatook Lake

Pryor •

Owasso •

Lake O' The Cherokees
Lake Hudson

Wolf Creek

Fairview •

North Canadian

Enid •

Perry •

Sooner Lake

Will Rogers Tpk.

Claremore •

OZARK PLATEAU

Cimarron

Stillwater •

Keystone Lake

Tulsa ●

Sand Springs •

Broken Arrow •

Wagoner •

Illinois

Tahlequah •

Cushing •

Jenks •

Ft. Gibson L.

Stilwell •

Sapulpa •

Guthrie •

Bixby •

BLACK KETTLE NATIONAL GRASSLAND

WASHITA N.W.R.

Watonga •

Kingfisher •

Edmond •

Bristow •

Muskogee •

Tenkiller Lake

Sallisaw •

TURNER TURNPIKE

OKLAHOMA

Deep Fork

Oklahoma City ●

DEEP FORK N.W.R.

Okmulgee •

Checotah •

SEQUOYAH N.W.R.

WASHITA BATTLEFIELD N.H.S.

Weatherford •

Yukon •

Henryetta •

Clinton •

El Reno •

Bethany •

Canadian

Arkansas

Sayre •

Elk City •

Moore •

Shawnee •

Robert S. Kerr Lake

Poteau •

Hobart •

Anadarko •

Tecumseh •

Norman •

Seminole •

Holdenville •

Eufaula Lake

Wilburton •

Mangum •

Lake Altus

Wewoka •

INDIAN NATION TURNPIKE

McAlester •

Heavener •

Purcell •

Chickasha •

Canadian

Sardis Lake

OUACHITA NATIONAL FOREST

WICHITA MTS. WILDLIFE REFUGE

Wichita Mts.

H.E. BAILEY TURNPIKE

Marlow •

Pauls Valley •

Ada •

McGee Creek Lake

Kiamichi

Ouachita Mountains

Hollis •

Altus •

Lawton •

Duncan •

Sulphur •

CHICKASAW N.R.A.

Atoka •

Tishomingo •

Antlers •

Broken Bow Lake

Frederick •

Walters •

Waurika Lake

Arbuckle Mts.

Coleman •

Hugo Lake

LITTLE RIVER N.W.R.

Broken Bow

Lone Grove •

Ardmore •

Madill •

TISHOMINGO N.W.R.

Hugo •

OUACHITA NATIONAL FOREST

Idabel •

Durant •

Red

Lake Texoma

TEXAS

0   40   80 miles
0   40   80 kilometers
Albers Conic Equal-Area Projection

Oil wells, like the one shown here, can be found all across Oklahoma. While Bartlesville was the site of the first commercial oil well in 1897, nearby Tulsa soon became—and remains—the state's oil center. The Sooner State ranks sixth among U.S. states in oil production and fourth in output of natural gas, which has recently become a more valuable resource for the state.

TEXAS

★ *Lone Star State* ★

TEXAS IS BIGGER than most countries—and it once was one! In 1836, Texans fought Mexico for independence. The best-known battle took place in San Antonio at a mission called the Alamo. There, a band of volunteers fought for days against General Antonio Lopez de Santa Anna's Mexican Army—and died. But six weeks later, on April 21, other Texans defeated Santa Anna near San Jacinto. Their famous battle cry? "Remember the Alamo!"

When it entered the Union in 1845 as the 28th state, Texas was considered so large that Congress gave it the chance to split into five separate states. It never did divide itself, so it's not surprising that sprawling Texas has an amazing mix of environments. Sun-baked deserts and cold peaks in the west contrast with warm, swampy bayous along the Louisiana border. Ranchers in the Texas Panhandle may endure bitter winter winds on the same day that grapefruit is picked in the Rio Grande Valley 800 miles (1,280 km) to the south.

The Spanish first arrived on Texas's Gulf shores in 1519, and the area became part of New Spain. For nearly two centuries France struggled with Spain for control of the region. Then New Spain won its independence in 1821 and became Mexico. Texas became an independent republic in 1836, and nine years later, it joined the United States.

By that time, cattle was king in Texas. Cowboys on horseback let their longhorns graze freely across the range. Huge herds were driven to market along the Chisholm Trail all the way to Kansas. Such cattle drives ended as the open range was fenced. Angus, Hereford, and other cattle breeds now join longhorns on Texas ranches large and small. Cattle ranching is still big business, and the rugged individualism of "cowboy culture" lives on in Texas.

1718

San Antonio de Valero, later known as the Alamo, was one of several missions built throughout Texas by the Spanish.

1836

Sam Houston defeated Santa Anna in the Battle of San Jacinto, winning Texas independence from Mexico.

1901

The discovery of oil at Spindletop near Beaumont led to the building of refineries that support the state's oil and gas industries.

Present day

The Lyndon B. Johnson Space Center, site of this mission simulator, is the foundation of the space technology industry in Houston.

While most Texans today live in urban and suburban areas, real-life cowboys—some on horseback—still herd cattle on ranches in the Lone Star State.

TEXAS
Lone Star State

STATEHOOD	December 29, 1845; 28th state
CAPITAL	Austin
LARGEST CITY	Houston Population 2,009,834
TOTAL AREA	268,581 sq mi; 695,621 sq km
LAND AREA	261,797 sq mi; 678,051 sq km
POPULATION	22,118,509
POPULATION DENSITY	83.2 people per sq mi
MAJOR RACIAL/ ETHNIC GROUPS	71.0% white; 11.5% African American; 2.7% Asian; .6% Native American. Hispanic (any race) 32%.
INDUSTRY	chemicals, machinery, electronics and computers, food products, petroleum and natural gas, transportation equipment
AGRICULTURE	cattle, sheep, poultry, cotton, sorghum, wheat, rice, hay, peanuts, pecans

MOCKINGBIRD

BLUEBONNET

Did you know?

1. Texas is bigger than the combined area of all seven countries in Central America. It is also bigger than every country in Europe except Russia.
2. In 1900 a storm surge caused by a hurricane killed 6,000 people in Galveston.
3. Six national flags have flown over Texas during the course of its history: Spanish, French, Mexican, Texan, Confederate, and American.
4. Texas is noted for having towns with strange names, such as Goodnight, Cut and Shoot, Wink, Muleshoe, North Zulch, Birthright, Turkey, and Noodle. A city named Iraan is made up of the first names of Ira and Ann Yates who struck oil on their farm in 1926.
5. Both the silicon computer chip and the electronic calculator were invented by engineers at a company named Texas Instruments.

The Panhandle has some of the state's best farmlands, where wheat, sorghum, and soybeans are grown. Year-round warmth allows winter vegetables and citrus fruits to be produced in the far south. Irrigated cotton and sugar beets are grown on the dry plains. Scenic rivers run from the higher lands of west and central Texas southeast across the coastal plain to the Gulf of Mexico. Shrimp, crabs, and oysters are caught in Gulf waters.

The discovery of East Texas oil in 1901 brought wealth and propelled the state into the modern era. World War II fueled state manufacturing. San Antonio became a major military hub and biotechnology research center. In recent decades, Texas cities have become leaders in banking, electronics, and many high-tech industries.

Today Texas is second only to Alaska in area and second only to California in population (about 22 million). In 2001, another "second" was achieved when George W. Bush became the second Texas Bush to live in the White House. The state ranks first among states in number of counties (254), number of farms and amount of farmland, cattle and beef production, and oil and gas output. Texas surely ranks high in the influence of Hispanic, mostly Mexican, culture. One-third of its people are Hispanic. By 2010, Hispanic Texans are expected to be in the majority.

Texans face problems, too. A long border and massive immigration sometimes brings trouble. The U.S. Border Patrol works to keep out illegal migrants and drugs. The Texas economy rides unsteady oil prices. Pollution comes from oil industries and millions of Texas cars and trucks. State population has increased by five million since 1990. But the promise of the Lone Star State shines for newcomers and old hands alike. The future for big, friendly Texas sure seems bright.

COLORADO KANSAS

KIOWA AND
RITA BLANCA
NATIONAL
GRASSLAND

HIGH

PLAINS

Canadian

Perryton

Dumas

LAKE MEREDITH N.R.A.
ALIBATES FLINT QUARRIES NAT. MON.

Borger BLACK
KETTLE
N.G.
Pampa N. Fork

McCLELLAN CREEK N.G.

NEW
MEXICO

Amarillo

BUFFALO LAKE
N.W.R.

Canyon

Hereford

PALO DURO
CANYON
S.P.

Prairie Dog

OKLAHOMA

Plainview

MULESHOE
N.W.R.

Town Fk.

Childress

Red

Lake
Texoma

ARK.

LLANO

Levelland

Lubbock

Vernon
Burkburnett
Nocona

Pease

Wichita

Wichita
Falls

HAGERMAN
N.W.R.

Denison
Sherman

Paris

CADDO
N.G.

Texarkana

ESTACADO

Brownfield

Snyder

Brazos

LYNDON B.
JOHNSON N.G.

Denton
Plano

Mt. Pleasant

Fort Worth

Irving

Sulphur
Springs

Marshall

Lamesa

Sweetwater

Breckenridge

Abilene

Mineral
Wells

Garland
Dallas
Arlington

Tyler

Longview

Andrews

Stephenville

Corsicana

Palestine

Henderson

SABINE
NATIONAL
FOREST

Toledo
Bend
Reservoir

Guadalupe Peak
8,749 ft
2,667 m

GUADALUPE MTS.
NATIONAL PARK

Big Spring

Midland

Leon

Waco

Lufkin

Nacogdoches

U.S.
MEXICO

El Paso

Fabens Highest
point in
Texas

YSLETA
DEL SUR
I.R.

Odessa

San
Angelo

Coleman

Brownwood
Gatesville

Copperas
Cove

Temple

DAVY
CROCKETT
N.F.

ANGELINA
N.F.

ALABAMA &
COUSHATTA
I.R.

Sam Rayburn Res.

LA.

Pecos

Monahans

Brady

EDWARDS

Belton

Killeen

Bryan

SAM
HOUSTON
N.F.

BIG THICKET
N.P.

Ozona

Georgetown

Round Rock

College
Station Conroe

Sabine

T E X A S

Sonora

Brenham

Beaumont

Fort
Stockton

Davis Mts. FORT
DAVIS
N.H.S.

PLATEAU

Llano

LYNDON B.
JOHNSON N.H.P.

San Marcos

Houston

Baytown

Port Arthur

TEXAS POINT N.W.R.

Marfa

Alpine

Big Canyon

Kerrville

New
Braunfels

ATTWATER PRAIRIE
CHICKEN N.W.R.

Sugar
Land

McFADDIN N.W.R.
ANAHUAC N.W.R.

Presidio

AMISTAD
N.R.A.

HILL COUNTRY

Yoakum

El Campo

Galveston

BRAZORIA N.W.R.

BIG BEND
NATIONAL
PARK

Amistad
Res.

RIO GRANDE
WILD AND
SCENIC RIVER

San Antonio

Del Rio

Uvalde

Victoria

Bay City

Freeport

SAN BERNARD N.W.R.
BIG BOGGY N.W.R.

CHIHUAHUA

COAHUILA

Eagle Pass

Pearsall

Beeville

Port Lavaca

GULF

Carrizo
Springs

Nueces

Rockport

Portland

OF

Alice

Corpus Christi

MEXICO

Laredo

Robstown

Kingsville

Zapata

Falfurrias

PADRE
ISLAND
NATIONAL
SEASHORE

Falcon
Res.

Rio
Grande
City Mission

LAGUNA ATASCOSA N.W.R.

Harlingen

NUEVO
LEÓN

PALO ALTO BATTLEFIELD N.H.S.

McAllen

SANTA ANA N.W.R.

Brownsville

TAMAULIPAS

Rio Grande

Guadalupe

San Antonio

Frio

Nueces

0   100   200 miles
0   100   200 kilometers

Albers Conic Equal-Area Projection

PUENTE INTERNACIONAL PASO DEL NORTE

*Many Mexicans along the 1,250-mile-
(2,000-km-) long Texas-Mexico border
have developed a cross-border life.
Thousands, like this taxi driver, live
in their home country and commute
each day across the international
boundary to work in El Paso and
other Texas border cities. Others risk
their lives to enter the U.S. illegally
by crossing the Rio Grande.*

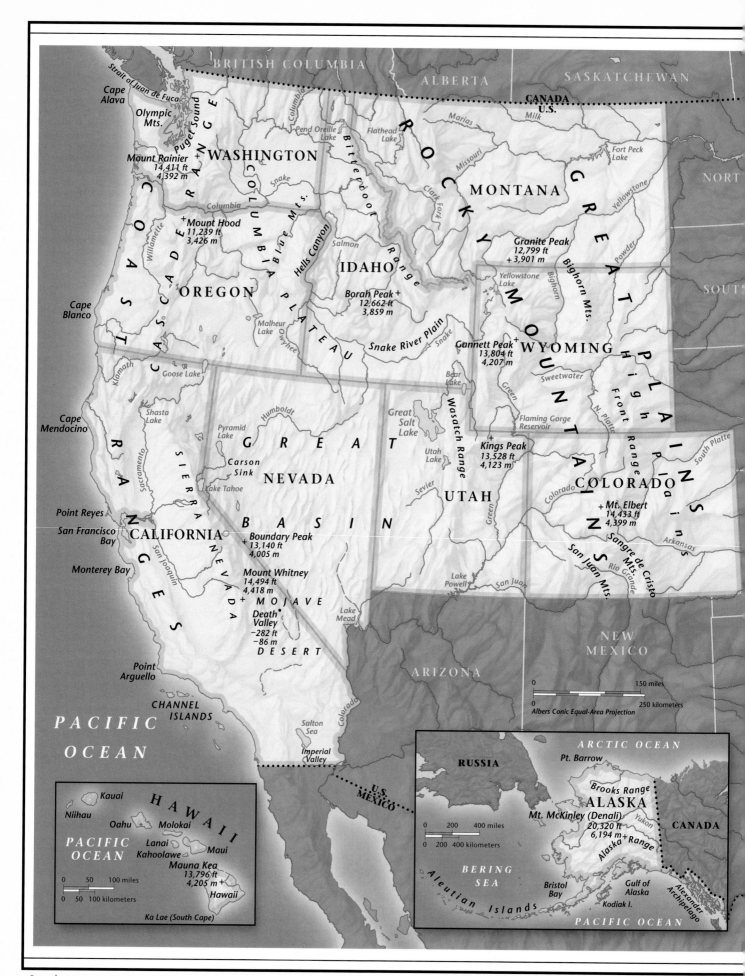

BRITISH COLUMBIA
ALBERTA
SASKATCHEWAN

Strait of Juan de Fuca
Cape Alava
Olympic Mts.
Puget Sound
Mount Rainier
14,411 ft
4,392 m

WASHINGTON

CANADA
U.S.

Columbia
Pend Oreille Lake
Flathead Lake

ROCKY

Marias
Milk

NORT

MONTANA

Fort Peck Lake

Snake
Columbia

Blue Mts.
Hells Canyon
Bitterroot Range

Missouri
Clark Fork

Yellowstone

+ Mount Hood
11,239 ft
3,426 m

Salmon

IDAHO

Granite Peak
12,799 ft
+ 3,901 m

Powder

SOUT

OREGON

Cascade Range
Columbia Plateau

Borah Peak +
12,662 ft
3,859 m

Yellowstone Lake
Bighorn
Bighorn Mts.

GREAT

Cape Blanco

Malheur Lake
Owyhee

Snake River Plain
Snake

WYOMING

Cape Mendocino

Klamath

Goose Lake

Humboldt

Gannett Peak +
13,804 ft
4,207 m

Bear Lake

Green

Sweetwater

High

PLAINS

Front Range

Shasta Lake
Pyramid Lake

GREAT

Great Salt Lake

Wasatch Range
Utah Lake

Flaming Gorge Reservoir

MOUNTAIN

South Platte

Sacramento

COAST RANGES
SIERRA

Carson Sink
Lake Tahoe

NEVADA

BASIN

Sevier

UTAH

Kings Peak +
13,528 ft
4,123 m

Colorado

COLORADO

Plains

Point Reyes
San Francisco Bay

Boundary Peak
+ 13,140 ft
4,005 m

+ Mt. Elbert
14,433 ft
4,399 m

Arkansas

Monterey Bay

San Joaquin

CALIFORNIA

NEVADA

Mount Whitney
14,494 ft
4,418 m
+

Lake Powell

Green

San Juan

Rio Grande

San Juan Mts.
Sangre de Cristo Mts.

MOJAVE
Death Valley
-282 ft
-86 m

DESERT

Lake Mead

NEW
MEXICO

Point Arguello

CHANNEL ISLANDS

Salton Sea

ARIZONA

0   150 miles
0   250 kilometers
Albers Conic Equal-Area Projection

PACIFIC
OCEAN

Imperial Valley

Colorado

U.S.
MEXICO

ARCTIC OCEAN

RUSSIA

Pt. Barrow

Brooks Range

ALASKA

CANADA

Kauai
Niihau

HAWAII

Oahu
Molokai

Mt. McKinley (Denali)
20,320 ft
6,194 m + Range

PACIFIC
OCEAN

Lanai
Kahoolawe

Maui

Yukon

Mauna Kea
13,796 ft
4,205 m +

Hawaii

Alaska Range

Alexander Archipelago

0   50   100 miles
0   50   100 kilometers

0   200   400 miles
0   200   400 kilometers

BERING
SEA

Gulf of Alaska

Ka Lae (South Cape)

Aleutian Islands

Bristol Bay

Kodiak I.

PACIFIC OCEAN

The West

THE WEST BEGINS where the Great Plains meet the Rocky Mountains. Between the Rockies and the Sierra Nevada is a vast, crumpled land called the Great Basin where rivers vanish beneath desert sand or drain into seasonal lakes. North of the Great Basin, rich volcanic soils from ancient lava flows cover the Columbia Plateau.

Along the western rim, coastal mountains wring moisture from Pacific storms. The rain and snow nourish forests of spruce, cedar, hemlock, and redwood. The great Central Valley in California and the Willamette Valley in Oregon are the largest of many fertile lowlands. The vast Alaskan peninsula stretches from its forested panhandle in the southeast, over towering peaks and treeless plains to the Arctic Ocean, then west almost to Asia. Tropical Hawaii, a chain of volcanic islands, is located in the Pacific Ocean more than 2,400 miles (4,000 km) from the U.S. mainland.

A Restless and Enduring Frontier

GEOGRAPHIC EXTREMES rule in the West. The nation's highest, lowest, wettest, and driest places are here, along with volcanoes, earthquakes, flash floods, mudslides, and wildfires. For thousands of years the Nez Perce thrived in the northwest by spearing salmon and collecting berries. Paiute irrigated fields of corn and squash in the Great Basin, and Blackfeet hunted game in the Rockies.

Europeans did not reach this region of the New World until 1542 when Juan Cabríllo sailed up the coast to Oregon. Vitus Bering navigated the Alaska Panhandle during 1741, and in 1778 Captain James Cook reached Hawaii. The Spanish built a string of missions along the California coast beginning in 1769. But the rest of the region remained largely unsettled until the 1840s, when thousands of people followed the Oregon and California Trails into the Pacific states. Other groups, such as Brigham Young's Mormon pioneers, settled Utah's Salt Lake Valley. With the discovery of gold in California in 1848, the world literally rushed in.

By 1869 the Transcontinental Railroad, built with the help of Chinese and Irish labor, linked the eastern and western halves of the country. New arrivals from every corner of the globe fanned out across the West to take advantage of the untapped riches of America's newest frontier. In Oregon and Washington logging employed thousands of workers. The introduction of cattle and other domestic stock and crops, followed by the invention of barbed wire, altered natural grasslands forever. Mineral strikes created boom towns as far away as Alaska. In Hawaii lush tropical forests gave way to sugarcane and fruit fields. By the early 1900s—50 years after the California gold rush—Americans had largely displaced Mexicans in California, Native Hawaiians, and Indians throughout the West. At the same time the American conservation movement emerged when Congress created the world's first national park: Yellowstone (1872).

Today, mining, logging, ranching, and fishing remain important in rural areas. Every Western state depends upon farming, especially California where huge corporate operations employ migrant field workers from Mexico and other Latin American countries. However, providing water both to farms and growing cities in this mostly arid land is an enormous challenge that will require creative leadership to solve.

Since the 1920s, a variety of new industries has emerged to energize the economies and cultures of this vast region. Southern California and Las Vegas are famous for entertainment. Seattle is home to software giant Microsoft, and electricity harnessed from the Columbia River powers aerospace and aluminum industries. California's Silicon Valley, southeast of San Francisco, is a global hub of high-tech industries. Hawaii tops the nation in macadamia nuts and some tropical fruits. Alaska's North Slope is a leading source of crude oil, but proposals to lessen the country's dependency on foreign oil by drilling in the Arctic National Wildlife Refuge stir controversy among oil companies, conservationists, government leaders, and ordinary citizens. For mountain states, ski resorts and vacation/retirement homes now make up an increasingly important part of their economies.

> "Out where the hand clasp's a little stronger, Out where the smile dwells a little longer, That's where the West begins."
>
> ARTHUR CHAPMAN,
> "OUT WHERE THE WEST BEGINS"

Although the West clings to its frontier image, most people live in rapidly growing and ethnically diverse cities such as Seattle, Los Angeles, and Denver. The continuing challenge will be to provide a decent standard of living for the millions of people who live here while preserving the scenic beauty and natural resources that attracted them to the region.

This brown bear gets ready to enjoy a meal of fresh salmon from a river in southeastern Alaska. Known as grizzlies in some areas, brown bears are smart and adapt readily to their environment, eating roots, insects, small mammals, and berries as well as fish.

ALASKA
★ *Last Frontier* ★

"SEWARD'S ICEBOX." That's what critics called the continent's vast, mostly unexplored northwestern peninsula when William Seward arranged for its purchase from Russia in 1867. But few complained when Joe Juneau discovered gold in 1880. By the end of the century, people were pouring through the Chilkoot Pass to the nearby Klondike goldfields—a scene now shown on some Alaska license plates.

The newcomers found more than gold. There were huge catches of salmon and impressive timber harvests. Today the state is still a leading source for salmon, crab, halibut, and herring. Although Alaska ranks first among the states in amount of forestland, only 10 percent of it is used for timber.

Alaska's strategic importance to the United States became critical when the Japanese invaded the Aleutian Islands during World War II. The 1,522-mile (2,450-km) Alaska-Canada (Alcan) Highway was completed in just eight months. Originally built as a military supply road, it is still the only land route to Alaska. Population in the territory grew steadily after the war, and the Last Frontier became the 49th state in 1959.

More than twice as large as Texas, the state totals one-sixth of the country's entire area. Mountains abound, topped by massive Mount McKinley (Denali), North America's highest peak. Snow-fed rivers rush to the sea while tens of thousands of blue-ice glaciers inch their way across the land. Cold northern treeless plains called tundra contrast with the dense evergreen trees of the Tongass National Forest a thousand miles to the milder southeast. Alaska's position on the Arctic Circle brings long and sometimes warm "midnight sun" summer days, while winters can be brutally cold with long hours of darkness.

Powerful forces are at work far beneath the land. The 1912 eruption of Mount Katmai was

1867

The agreement to purchase Alaska from Russia was a bold and controversial move to expand U.S. territory.

1896–1902

Gold rushes, first in Canada's Klondike region and then in Alaska, focused U.S. attention on the territory's vast resources.

1942

The Japanese invasion of the Aleutians in World War II led to the building of a military supply route called the Alcan Highway.

1968–Present

Each day the Trans Alaska Pipeline carries almost a million gallons of oil from Prudhoe Bay to Valdez, on the Gulf of Alaska.

Massive Hubbard Glacier loses a chunk of its ice to Russell Fiord (opposite) through a process called calving. One of more than 600 named glaciers in the state, the Hubbard flows from the St. Elias Mountains to the sea near the north end of Alaska's southeast panhandle.

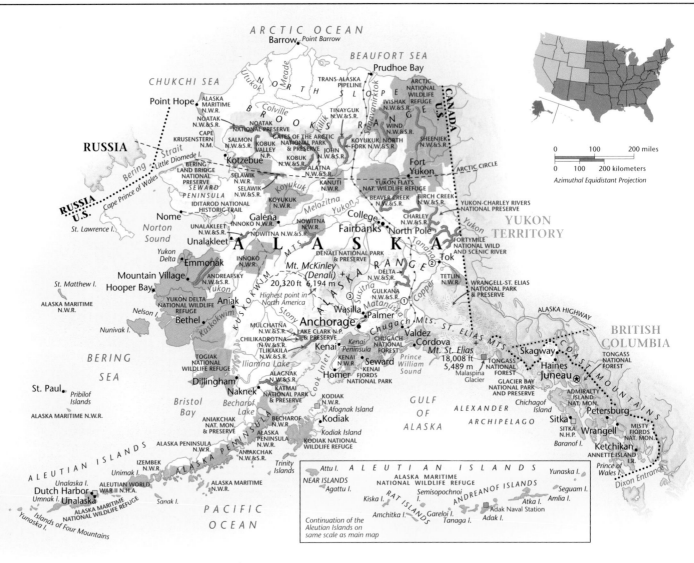

ARCTIC OCEAN
Barrow • Point Barrow

BEAUFORT SEA
Prudhoe Bay

CHUKCHI SEA

NORTH SLOPE

TRANS-ALASKA PIPELINE

ARCTIC NATIONAL WILDLIFE REFUGE

CANADA U.S.

Point Hope
ALASKA MARITIME N.W.R.
NOATAK N.W.&S.R.
CAPE KRUSENSTERN N.M.
Colville
NOATAK NATIONAL PRESERVE

BROOKS RANGE

IVISHAK N.W.&S.R.
WIND N.W.&S.R.

RUSSIA
Bering Strait
Little Diomede I.
Cape Prince of Wales

SALMON N.W.&S.R.
KOBUK VALLEY N.P.
GATES OF THE ARCTIC NATIONAL PARK & PRESERVE
JOHN N.W.&S.R.
KOYUKUK, NORTH FORK N.W.&S.R.
SHEENJEK N.W.&S.R.

Kotzebue
KOBUK N.W.&S.R.
ALATNA N.W.&S.R.
KANUTI N.W.R.
Fort Yukon
ARCTIC CIRCLE

RUSSIA U.S.
BERING LAND BRIDGE NATIONAL PRESERVE
SEWARD PENINSULA
SELAWIK N.W.R.
SELAWIK N.W.&S.R.
KOYUKUK N.W.R.
YUKON FLATS NAT. WILDLIFE REFUGE
BEAVER CREEK N.W.&S.R.
BIRCH CREEK N.W.&S.R.
YUKON-CHARLEY RIVERS NATIONAL PRESERVE

YUKON TERRITORY

Nome
IDITAROD NATIONAL HISTORIC TRAIL
Galena
College
CHARLEY N.W.&S.R.

St. Lawrence I.
Norton Sound
Unalakleet
INNOKO N.W.R.
NOWITNA N.W.R.
Fairbanks
North Pole
FORTYMILE NATIONAL WILD AND SCENIC RIVER

Yukon Delta
Emmonak
NOWITNA N.W.&S.R.
A L A S K A   M T S .
DENALI NATIONAL PARK & PRESERVE
Tok

St. Matthew I.
Mountain Village
ANDREAFSKY N.W.&S.R.
INNOKO N.W.R.
Mt. McKinley (Denali) 20,320 ft 6,194 m
DELTA N.W.&S.R.
TETLIN N.W.R.
WRANGELL-ST. ELIAS NATIONAL PARK & PRESERVE

Hooper Bay
Yukon
Highest point in North America
A L A S K A   R A N G E
GULKANA N.W.&S.R.
Copper
ALASKA HIGHWAY

ALASKA MARITIME N.W.R.
Nelson I.
YUKON DELTA NATIONAL WILDLIFE REFUGE
Bethel
Aniak
Wasilla
Palmer
St. Elias Mts.

Nunivak I.
MULCHATNA N.W.&S.R.
Anchorage
Chugach Mts.
ST. ELIAS MTS.
BRITISH COLUMBIA

BERING SEA
CHILIKADROTNA N.W.&S.R.
TLIKAKILA N.W.&S.R.
LAKE CLARK N.P. & PRESERVE
Kenai
CHUGACH NATIONAL FOREST
Valdez
Cordova
Mt. St. Elias 18,008 ft 5,489 m
Skagway
COAST MOUNTAINS
TONGASS NATIONAL FOREST

Dillingham
TOGIAK NATIONAL WILDLIFE REFUGE
Iliamna Lake
KENAI N.W.R.
Kenai Peninsula
Seward
KENAI FJORDS NATIONAL PARK
Prince William Sound
Malaspina Glacier
TONGASS NATIONAL FOREST
Haines
Juneau

St. Paul
Pribilof Islands
ALAGNAK N.W.&S.R.
KATMAI NATIONAL PARK & PRESERVE
Homer
GLACIER BAY NATIONAL PARK AND PRESERVE
ADMIRALTY ISLAND NAT. MON.
Chichagof Island

Bristol Bay
Becharof Lake
KODIAK N.W.R.
Afognak Island
GULF OF ALASKA
ALEXANDER ARCHIPELAGO
Sitka
Petersburg

ALASKA MARITIME N.W.R.
Naknek
BECHAROF N.W.R.
Kodiak
Kodiak Island
KODIAK NATIONAL WILDLIFE REFUGE
Baranof I.
SITKA N.H.P.
Wrangell

ALASKA PENINSULA N.W.R.
ANIAKCHAK NAT. MON. & PRESERVE
ALASKA PENINSULA N.W.R.
Trinity Islands
Ketchikan
ANNETTE ISLAND I.R.
MISTY FIORDS NAT. MON.

ALEUTIAN ISLANDS
ANIAKCHAK N.W.&S.R.
Prince of Wales I.
Dixon Entrance

IZEMBEK N.W.R.
ALASKA WORLD WAR II N.H.A.
ALASKA PENINSULA N.W.R.

A L E U T I A N   I S L A N D S
ALASKA MARITIME NATIONAL WILDLIFE REFUGE
Yunaska I.

Unimak I.
NEAR ISLANDS
Attu I.
Agattu I.
Kiska I.
Semisopochnoi
ANDREANOF ISLANDS
Seguam I.
Amlia I.

Dutch Harbor
Umnak I.
Unalaska
ALASKA MARITIME NATIONAL WILDLIFE REFUGE
Sanak I.
PACIFIC OCEAN
RAT ISLANDS
Amchitka I.
Gareloi I.
Tanaga I.
Atka I.
Adak I.
Adak Naval Station

Yunaska I.
Islands of Four Mountains
Continuation of the Aleutian Islands on same scale as main map

RUSSIA

0   100   200 miles
0   100   200 kilometers
Azimuthal Equidistant Projection

A bull moose pays a surprise visit to a home in downtown Anchorage. Standing as tall as seven feet (2 m) and weighing as much as 1,200 pounds (554 kg), they are the world's largest deer. In Alaska, moose have traditionally been sources of food, hides, and bone for tools. Today, hunters kill 6,000 to 8,000 moose a year in Alaska, yielding some 3.5 million pounds (1.6 million kg) of meat. The animals are also a favorite with tourists, who love to photograph them.

the largest in North America in the last century, and the 1964 earthquake that rocked Anchorage was among the most powerful ever recorded.

The discovery of huge oil reserves on the North Slope in 1968 spurred the state's most recent growth. Workers by the thousands moved from other states to help build an 800-mile- (1,280-km-) long pipeline from Prudhoe Bay to the ice-free port of Valdez. As many as 88 barrels of crude oil an hour move through the pipeline, making Alaska a leading oil-producing state.

Thanks to wise legislation, every Alaskan shares in these oil earnings. But costs to the environment can be high. The biggest oil spill in the country's history blackened hundreds of miles of shoreline in 1989. Coastal ecosystems and fishing towns still feel the effects. A debate over plans to drill for oil in the Arctic National Wildlife Refuge pits those who want to preserve the wilderness against those who want to exploit its energy reserves. The issue is far from being resolved.

Alaskans today are still pioneers in many ways. Their state is a mix of wild and tamed that is unlike any other. Huge moose and brown bears sometimes stroll right into Alaskan cities. Legislators must travel to the state capital by water or air because no road connects Juneau to the rest of the world. Where schools are few and far between, children attend school over the Internet, and doctors often travel by bush plane to see patients. Alaska's Native peoples make up a higher percentage of the population than in any other state, and many follow their traditional lifestyles. Alaskans face amazing opportunities and tough challenges—especially concerning the state's rich natural resources and fragile environments. But it's easy for them to see that Seward got a great bargain in buying this great land.

ALASKA
Last Frontier

STATEHOOD	January 3, 1959; 49th state
CAPITAL	Juneau
LARGEST CITY	Anchorage Population 268,983
TOTAL AREA	663,267 sq mi; 1,717,854 sq km
LAND AREA	571,951 sq mi; 1,481,347 sq km
POPULATION	648,818
POPULATION DENSITY	1.1 people per sq mi
MAJOR RACIAL/ ETHNIC GROUPS	69.3% white; 15.6 % Native American; 4.0% Asian; 3.5% African American. Hispanic (any race) 4.1%.
INDUSTRY	petroleum products, state, local, and federal government, services, trade
AGRICULTURE	shellfish, seafood, nursery stock, vegetables, dairy products, feed crops

WILLOW PTARMIGAN

FORGET-ME-NOT

Did you know?

1. Alaska has the northernmost, westernmost, and easternmost points in the United States.
2. The distance from southeast Alaska to the tip of the Aleutian chain roughly equals the distance from Miami to Los Angeles.
3. The most powerful earthquake ever recorded in North America struck Anchorage in 1964. It was 80 times more powerful than the 1906 San Francisco quake and measured 9.2 on the Richter scale.
4. Little Diomede Island is only 2.5 miles (4 km) from Russian territory.
5. Barrow, the northernmost U.S. city, has 69 days of continuous darkness in winter and 84 days of continuous daylight in summer.
6. Alaska was first populated 7,000 years ago by people from Asia who migrated across an Ice-Age land bridge.

CALIFORNIA
★ *Golden State* ★

"JUST ADD WATER." Californians have followed this simple recipe for more than a century to grow their state. Snowmelt from Sierra Nevada slopes and Colorado River water make distant deserts produce and temperate croplands produce more. Water sharing also helped propel the state into the modern era by allowing industries to sprout and cities to bloom.

California's fields and factories make it the nation's leading producer of food and manufactured goods. So colossal is the state's economy that if California were an independent country it would be among the ten richest in the world. In terms of money earned, milk and grapes are the state's leading farm products. It also grows more than 99 percent of the nation's total of more than a dozen specialty crops, including artichokes, raisins, walnuts, and kiwifruit. California is an industrial powerhouse, too. The state's assembly lines turn out a multitude of products—everything from jets and missiles to high-tech hardware and software.

The Golden State has a stunning array of natural resources and environments. There is an abundance of minerals, vast forests of gigantic pines and redwoods, and unrivaled fisheries along its nearly thousand-mile coast. In the north stand the majestic peaks of the Cascade Range. Deep within Death Valley, the driest and hottest place on the continent, lies Badwater. At 282 feet (86 m) below sea level, it is North America's lowest point. Seventy miles west—and nearly three miles higher—stands 14,494-foot (4,418-m) Mount Whitney in the Sierra Nevada. The Coast Ranges rise along the Pacific Ocean. In between lies the fertile Central Valley, source of most of California's agricultural wealth.

1769

Mission San Diego de Alcalá was the first of 21 missions built by the Spanish in an effort to convert native people to Christianity.

1848

The discovery of gold brought fortune seekers from around the world and sparked the westward movement across the country.

1906

The San Francisco earthquake led to the first government-sponsored study of the cause of earthquakes in the U.S.

2003

In a special recall election, California voted to remove its governor from office, the first state ever to take such action.

The Golden Gate Bridge (opposite) rises above the fog over San Francisco Bay. Each day thousands travel back and forth across the bridge from homes in northern suburbs to high-tech jobs in the Silicon Valley between Palo Alto and San Jose.

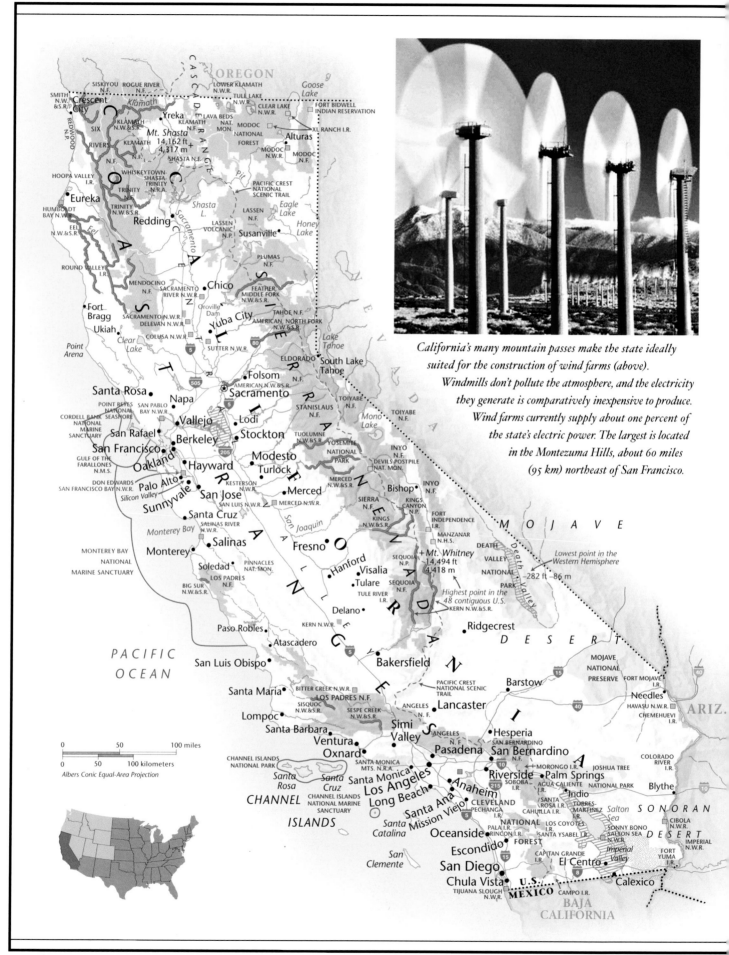

California's many mountain passes make the state ideally
suited for the construction of wind farms (above).
Windmills don't pollute the atmosphere, and the electricity
they generate is comparatively inexpensive to produce.
Wind farms currently supply about one percent of
the state's electric power. The largest is located
in the Montezuma Hills, about 60 miles
(95 km) northeast of San Francisco.

OREGON

SISKIYOU N.F.
ROGUE RIVER N.F.
LOWER KLAMATH N.W.R.
TULE LAKE N.W.R.
CLEAR LAKE N.W.R.
FORT BIDWELL INDIAN RESERVATION
Goose Lake

SMITH N.W. &S.R.
Crescent City
Klamath
Yreka
KLAMATH N.W. &S.R.
LAVA BEDS NAT. MON.
MODOC NATIONAL FOREST
Alturas
XL RANCH I.R.

SIX RIVERS N.F.
KLAMATH N.F.
Mt. Shasta 14,162 ft. 4,317 m
SHASTA N.F.
MODOC N.W.R.
MODOC N.F.

HOOPA VALLEY I.R.
WHISKEYTOWN-SHASTA-TRINITY N.R.A.
TRINITY N.F.
Pit

Eureka
HUMBOLDT BAY N.W.R.
TRINITY N.W. &S.R.
Eel
Shasta L.
LASSEN VOLCANIC N.P.
LASSEN N.F.
Eagle Lake
Honey Lake

ROUND VALLEY I.R.
Redding
Sacramento River

EEL N.W. &S.R.

Fort Bragg
MENDOCINO N.F.
SACRAMENTO RIVER
Chico
FEATHER MIDDLE FORK N.W. &S.R.
PLUMAS N.F.

Ukiah
SACRAMENTO N.W.R.
DELEVAN N.W.R.
COLUSA N.W.R.
Oroville Dam
Yuba City
AMERICAN, NORTH FORK N.W. &S.R.
TAHOE N.F.

Point Arena
Clear Lake
SUTTER N.W.R.
Lake Tahoe

Santa Rosa
Napa
Folsom
ELDORADO N.F.
South Lake Tahoe

POINT REYES NATIONAL SEASHORE
SAN PABLO BAY N.W.R.
AMERICAN N.W. &S.R.
Sacramento
TOIYABE N.F.

CORDELL BANK NATIONAL MARINE SANCTUARY
San Rafael
Vallejo
Lodi
STANISLAUS N.F.
Mono Lake
TOIYABE N.F.

San Francisco
Berkeley
Stockton
TUOLUMNE N.W. &S.R.
INYO N.F.

GULF OF THE FARALLONES N.M.S.
Oakland
Modesto
YOSEMITE NATIONAL PARK
DEVILS POSTPILE NAT. MON.

DON EDWARDS SAN FRANCISCO BAY N.W.R.
Hayward
Turlock
MERCED N.W. &S.R.

Palo Alto
Silicon Valley
KESTERSON N.W.R.
Merced
MERCED N.W.R.
Bishop
INYO N.F.

Sunnyvale
San Jose
SAN LUIS N.W.R.
SIERRA N.F.
KINGS CANYON N.P.

Santa Cruz
SALINAS RIVER N.W.R.
San Joaquin
KINGS N.W. &S.R.
FORT INDEPENDENCE I.R.

Monterey Bay
Fresno
MANZANAR N.H.S.

MONTEREY BAY NATIONAL MARINE SANCTUARY
Salinas
Hanford
Visalia
SEQUOIA N.P.
Mt. Whitney 14,494 ft 4,418 m
DEATH VALLEY NATIONAL PARK
Lowest point in the Western Hemisphere -282 ft -86 m

Monterey
Soledad
PINNACLES NAT. MON.
Tulare
SEQUOIA N.F.
Highest point in the 48 contiguous U.S.
KERN N.W. &S.R.

LOS PADRES N.F.
BIG SUR N.W. &S.R.
Delano
TULE RIVER I.R.

MOJAVE DESERT

Paso Robles
KERN N.W.R.
Ridgecrest

Atascadero

PACIFIC OCEAN

San Luis Obispo
Bakersfield
Barstow
MOJAVE NATIONAL PRESERVE
FORT MOJAVE I.R.

Santa Maria
BITTER CREEK N.W.R.
Lancaster
I-15
Needles
HAVASU N.W.R.
CHEMEHUEVI I.R.

Lompoc
SISQUOC N.W. &S.R.
LOS PADRES N.F.
SESPE CREEK N.W. &S.R.
ANGELES N.F.
Simi Valley
ANGELES N.F.
Hesperia
ARIZ.

Santa Barbara
Ventura
Oxnard
Pasadena
San Bernardino
SAN BERNARDINO N.F.
COLORADO RIVER I.R.

CHANNEL ISLANDS NATIONAL PARK
SANTA MONICA MTS. N.R.A.
Santa Monica
Los Angeles
Riverside
Palm Springs
MORONGO I.R.
JOSHUA TREE NATIONAL PARK
Blythe

Santa Rosa
Santa Cruz
CHANNEL ISLANDS NATIONAL MARINE SANCTUARY
Long Beach
Anaheim
SOBOBA I.R.
AGUA CALIENTE I.R.
Indio

CHANNEL ISLANDS
Santa Catalina
Santa Ana
Mission Viejo
SANTA ROSA I.R.
SANTA YSABEL I.R.
TORRES-MARTINEZ I.R.
Salton Sea
SONORAN DESERT

Oceanside
PALA I.R.
RINCON I.R.
CLEVELAND NATIONAL FOREST
PECHANGA I.R.
LOS COYOTES I.R.
SONNY BONO SALTON SEA N.W.R.
CIBOLA N.W.R.
IMPERIAL N.W.R.

San Clemente
Escondido
CAPITAN GRANDE I.R.
Imperial Valley
FORT YUMA I.R.

San Diego
Chula Vista
U.S.
El Centro
Calexico

TIJUANA SLOUGH N.W.R.
MEXICO
CAMPO I.R.
BAJA CALIFORNIA

0 50 100 miles
0 50 100 kilometers
Albers Conic Equal-Area Projection

The seafaring explorer Juan Rodríguez Cabríllo claimed California for Spain in 1542. But it was not until 1769 that colonization began. Father Junípero Serra established the first of a string of missions. There, priests worked to convert the native people to Christianity. With the missions came presidios (forts) and pueblos (towns). Some of these, such as San Francisco, San Jose, and San Diego, now rank among the nation's largest urban areas. In 1821 control passed to Mexico and then in 1848 to the United States after the Mexican-American War. That same year gold was discovered on the American River. In 1849 thousands of "forty-niners" headed for California to strike it rich. By the time statehood was achieved in 1850, the population had grown to almost 100,000.

Today, nearly one out of eight Americans lives in California, making it by far the most populous state. More than 90 percent of the people live in urban areas. One in three Californians is Hispanic, and one in ten is of Asian descent.

Such a diverse land is not without problems. There are frequent earthquakes, forest fires, and other natural disasters. A downturn in the high-tech industry boosted unemployment figures, and recurring problems with water supply, freeway congestion, and air quality have been joined by massive power outages and budget shortages. In 2003 Californians expressed their frustration by recalling their governor. In a special election, actor-turned-politician Arnold Schwarzenegger replaced Gray Davis as chief executive. Whether he can solve California's problems remains to be seen, but one thing is certain. There are plenty of opportunities. People will continue to seek their fortunes in the Golden State.

CALIFORNIA
Golden State

STATEHOOD	September 9, 1850; 31st state
CAPITAL	Sacramento
LARGEST CITY	Los Angeles Population 3,798,981
TOTAL AREA	163,696 sq mi; 423,970 sq km
LAND AREA	155,959 sq mi; 403,933 sq km
POPULATION	35,484,453
POPULATION DENSITY	225.2 people per sq mi
MAJOR RACIAL/ ETHNIC GROUPS	59.5% white; 10.9% Asian; 6.7% African American; 1 % Native American. Hispanic (any race) 32.4%.
INDUSTRY	electronic components and equipment, computers and computer software, tourism, food processing, entertainment, clothing
AGRICULTURE	fruits and vegetables, dairy products, cattle, forest products, commercial fishing

CALIFORNIA QUAIL

GOLDEN POPPY

Did you know?

1. Lake Tahoe has enough water to flood California to a depth of 14 inches (35 cm).
2. California has the highest and lowest points in the lower 48 states: Mount Whitney at 14,494 feet (4,418 m) and Death Valley at 282 feet (86 m) below sea level.
3. California contains the tallest, biggest, and oldest trees in the world: a 368-foot- (112-m-) tall coast redwood, a giant sequoia measuring 275 feet (84 m) high by 103 feet (31 m) around, and a 4,700-year-old bristlecone pine.
4. The world's largest solar power plant is located near San Luis Obispo.
5. California grows more than half the nation's fruits, nuts, and vegetables, and produces more milk than the state of Wisconsin.
6. More Native Americans live in California than in any other U.S. state.

COLORADO

★ *Centennial State* ★

REACH FOR THE SKY! Colorado is known around the world for its lofty mountains and its Mile-High City of Denver. The state has more than 50 peaks higher than 14,000 feet (4,270 m), and averages an elevation of 6,800 feet (2,100 m). No other state measures up to that.

Yet Colorado is more than snow-capped peaks. The flatter, drier High Plains cover its eastern third. Here cattle are ranched where buffalo once roamed. In a broad southern valley that was once the bed of an ancient sea lies Great Sand Dunes National Monument, with dunes topping 700 feet (220 m). The state's western third is rugged plateau, cut by rivers into deep valleys and flat-topped mesas.

Colorado's snow-capped peaks provide water for wildlife, farms, and cities far from the state. Like spokes of a wheel, life-giving rivers flow from high peaks to drier lands around. The state takes its name from its most famous river.

Spanish explorers, who saw the rusty-colored waters cutting through red stone canyons far downstream from its source in what is now Rocky Mountain National Park, named it Colorado, meaning "colored red." The Rio Grande runs south and east all the way to the Gulf of Mexico. To the northeast flows the South Platte; to the southeast the Arkansas.

Along a creek flowing from the Front Range, prospectors found another Colorado treasure in 1858 — gold. Thousands of fortune-seekers moved in, and the city of Denver was founded. The Cheyenne and Arapaho fought to hold onto their lands, but the settlers won out. By 1870, railroads linked the territory with the rest of the country, bringing more people. Some settlers ranched cattle on the High Plains, while others farmed crops in irrigated fields. Towns sprang up in mountain valleys across the territory with the discovery of silver, other minerals,

1833

Bent's Fort, a prominent landmark and trading center on the Santa Fe Trail, was Colorado's first permanent settlement.

1858

With the discovery of gold in the Front Range north of Pikes Peak, thousands of fortune seekers headed to Colorado in covered wagons.

1954

President Eisenhower toured reclamation projects that carry water from western Colorado to irrigate dry plains in the east.

Present day

The North American Aerospace Defense Command (NORAD) keeps watch for air attacks directed at the U.S. or Canada.

Ancestral Puebloans built spectacular villages into the sandstone walls of canyons. Cliff Palace (opposite), preserved in Mesa Verde National Park, once housed up to 250 people in its 200 rooms. It was mysteriously abandoned more than 700 years ago.

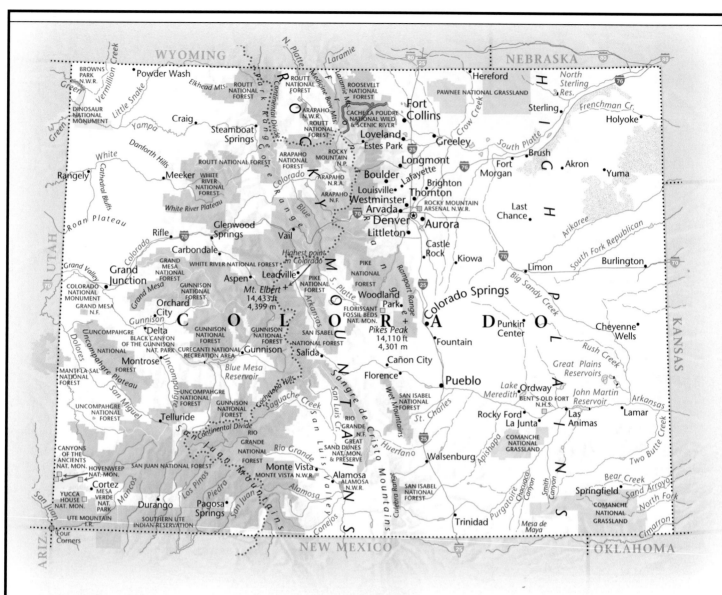

NEBRASKA

BROWNS
PARK
N.W.R.
Powder Wash
DINOSAUR
NATIONAL
MONUMENT
Little Snake
Elkhead Mts.
ROUTT
NATIONAL
FOREST
Medicine Bow Mts.
ROUTT
NATIONAL
FOREST
ROOSEVELT
NATIONAL
FOREST
PAWNEE NATIONAL GRASSLAND
Hereford
North
Sterling
Res.
Sterling
Holyoke
Craig
Steamboat
Springs
Yampa
ARAPAHO
N.W.R.
ARAPAHO
NATIONAL
FOREST
ROCKY
MOUNTAIN
N.P.
CACHE LA POUDRE
NATIONAL WILD
& SCENIC RIVER
Fort
Collins
Frenchman Cr.
Rangely
Danforth Hills
Meeker
WHITE
RIVER
NATIONAL
FOREST
Colorado
Loveland
Estes Park
ROCKY
MOUNTAIN
N.P.
Greeley
Longmont
Fort
Morgan
Brush
Akron
Yuma
White River Plateau
ARAPAHO
NATIONAL
FOREST
Boulder
Lafayette
Louisville
Brighton
Thornton
Westminster
Arvada
Roan Plateau
Glenwood
Springs
Vail
Blue
ARAPAHO
N.R.A.
ARAPAHO
N.F.
Denver
Aurora
Littleton
ROCKY MOUNTAIN
ARSENAL N.W.R.
Last
Chance
Rifle
Carbondale
GRAND
MESA
NATIONAL
FOREST
WHITE RIVER NATIONAL FOREST
Highest point
in Colorado
Castle
Rock
Kiowa
Grand Valley
Grand
Junction
COLORADO
NATIONAL
MONUMENT
Grand Mesa
Aspen
Leadville
PIKE
NATIONAL
FOREST
PIKE
NATIONAL
FOREST
Woodland
Park
Colorado
Springs
Limon
Burlington
GRAND MESA
N.F.
GUNNISON
NATIONAL
FOREST
Mt. Elbert +
14,433 ft
4,399 m
FLORISSANT
FOSSIL BEDS
NAT. MON.
Orchard
City
UNCOMPAHGRE
NATIONAL
FOREST
Delta
BLACK CANYON
OF THE GUNNISON
NAT. PARK
GUNNISON
NATIONAL
FOREST
GUNNISON
NATIONAL
FOREST
SAN ISABEL
NATIONAL FOREST
Pikes Peak
14,110 ft
4,301 m
Cañon City
Punkin
Center
Cheyenne
Wells
Montrose
CURECANTI NATIONAL
RECREATION AREA
Gunnison
Salida
Florence
Great Plains
Reservoirs
MANTI-LA-SAL
NATIONAL
FOREST
Blue Mesa
Reservoir
UNCOMPAHGRE
NATIONAL
FOREST
Pueblo
Lake
Meredith
Ordway
BENT'S OLD FORT
N.H.S.
John Martin
Reservoir
Telluride
GUNNISON
NATIONAL
FOREST
SAN ISABEL
NATIONAL
FOREST
Rocky Ford
La Junta
Las
Animas
Lamar
UNCOMPAHGRE
NATIONAL
FOREST
Continental Divide
RIO
GRANDE
N.F.
RIO
GRANDE
NATIONAL
FOREST
GREAT
SAND DUNES
NAT. MON.
& PRESERVE
COMANCHE
NATIONAL
GRASSLAND
CANYONS
OF THE
ANCIENTS
NAT. MON.
HOVENWEEP
NAT. MON.
SAN JUAN NATIONAL FOREST
Monte Vista
MONTE VISTA N.W.R.
Alamosa
ALAMOSA
N.W.R.
Walsenburg
SAN ISABEL
NATIONAL
FOREST
Springfield
COMANCHE
NATIONAL
GRASSLAND
Cortez
YUCCA
HOUSE
NAT. MON.
MESA
VERDE
NAT.
PARK
Durango
Pagosa
Springs
Trinidad
Mesa de
Maya
UTE MOUNTAIN
T.R.
SOUTHERN UTE
INDIAN RESERVATION
Four
Corners
OKLAHOMA

UTAH
ARIZ.
KANSAS

ROCKY MOUNTAIN

COLORADO

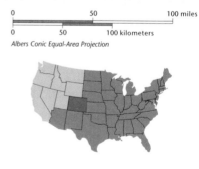

0   50   100 miles
0   50   100 kilometers
Albers Conic Equal-Area Projection

A skier goes spread eagle off a slope in the Colorado Rockies. Millions of snow enthusiasts bring their skis and boards— plus billions of dollars—to the state each year. In 2002, Colorado hosted more than 1.6 million ski trips and was the nation's number one destination for overnight ski vacations.

and more gold. In 1876, on the nation's 100th birthday, the Centennial State entered the Union.

Colorado grew rapidly through the 20th century. Oil and natural gas deposits were tapped in both the eastern plains and western plateaus. Coal and iron helped Pueblo become a steel center. Denver, located where the Plains meet the mountains, grew into the trade, transportation, and financial center for the entire Rocky Mountain region. Its many federal government offices and nearby military facilities have earned it the nickname Washington of the West. As the population grew so did the demand for water. Most of the runoff from rain and snow flows into rivers on the western side of the Rockies, but most of the people live and work on the eastern side. To solve this problem rivers have been dammed and tunnels built to carry water through the mountains for homes, industry, and irrigation.

Colorado's fresh, powdery snow attracts millions of skiers and snowboarders to its slopes each year. Reborn mining towns, such as Aspen and Telluride, boom each winter, and Vail is one of the country's largest ski resorts. Some people even move to Colorado just for the snow!

Colorado's treasures can be the source of problems, too. Sand laced with deicing chemicals is damaging mountain streams. Toxic minerals from abandoned mines pollute water supplies. Since 1990 the population has increased from 3.3 million to more than 4.5 million. The heavy volume of traffic and industry creates smog that hangs like a huge brown cloud over the Denver region. Although progress has been made in cleaning up the air, there is pressure to weaken some of the controls. These are a few of the issues the people of Colorado must try to solve to preserve the quality of life they prize so highly.

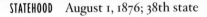

COLORADO
Centennial State

STATEHOOD	August 1, 1876; 38th state
CAPITAL	Denver
LARGEST CITY	Denver Population 560,415
TOTAL AREA	104,094 sq mi; 269,601 sq km
LAND AREA	103,718 sq mi; 268,627 sq km
POPULATION	4,550,688
POPULATION DENSITY	43.4 people per sq mi
MAJOR RACIAL/ ETHNIC GROUPS	82.8% white; 3.8% African American; 2.2% Asian; 1% Native American. Hispanic (any race) 17.1%.
INDUSTRY	real estate, state, local, and federal government, durable goods, communications, health and other services, non-durable goods, transportation
AGRICULTURE	cattle, corn, wheat, dairy products, hay

LARK BUNTING

COLUMBINE

Did you know?

1. As protection against earthquakes or nuclear explosions, the Cheyenne Mountain Operations Center of NORAD is mounted on 1,319 giant springs that allow it to sway up to 12 inches (30 cm) in any direction.
2. The 700-foot- (213-m-) high, wind-shaped sand dunes in Great Sand Dunes National Monument occupy an area that was covered by an ancient sea more than one million years ago.
3. The benefits of fluorides for healthy teeth were discovered when a study determined that fluoride in the drinking water of Colorado Springs caused residents to have fewer cavities.
4. The Unsinkable Molly (Margaret Tobin) Brown was a citizen of Leadville where her husband struck it rich when he found gold in 1893. She earned her nickname by helping women and children leave the *Titanic* before the luxury liner sank in 1912.

HAWAII

★ *Aloha State* ★

MARK TWAIN CALLED THEM "the loveliest fleet of islands that lies anchored in any ocean." Though they look like green jewels in an ocean-blue setting, these islands were formed by a red-glowing force of nature. As the Pacific plate grinds slowly to the northwest, molten rock pushes up through a "hot spot" to form the islands one by one. The oldest, worn down by millions of years of weather and waves, lie near Russia's Kamchatka Peninsula, far to the northwest of today's main islands. The newest is the "Big Island" of Hawaii where eruptions from Kilauea and gigantic Mauna Loa continue to build new land. Thousands of years from now there will be a new island. Molten material is slowing pushing a seamount called Loihi toward the surface.

The first settlers were Polynesians who paddled double-hulled canoes from islands farther west, perhaps 1,500 years ago. They established thriving communities on each of the eight major islands. Captain James Cook claimed the islands for the British Empire in 1788, naming them the Sandwich Islands for the Earl of Sandwich. But the name didn't last long. By 1810 a native chieftan, King Kamehameha I, had succeeded in unifying the islands, and the entire island group became known as Hawaii.

Change came rapidly. Hawaii became a center of the Pacific whaling industry. Imported Christianity took root among many native Hawaiians, while imported diseases took the lives of many more. A special trade agreement allowed American businesses to export sugar tax-free. This led to a boom in sugarcane production. Workers were brought in mostly from Asia to work the plantations. Eventually, this resulted in greater ethnic diversity and fewer pure Hawaiians. In 1893, the powerful sugar barons helped overthrow Queen Liliuokalani,

1782-1810

King Kamehameha gained control of the islands from local chiefs and became the first king of a unified Hawaii.

1898

Profits from sugarcane, shown being harvested, led U.S. businessmen to pressure the government to make Hawaii part of the U.S.

1941

Japan's attack on the naval base at Pearl Harbor on December 7 caused the United States to officially enter World War II.

Present day

Resort areas like Waikiki (above), in the shadow of Diamond Head, have made tourism Hawaii's most important industry.

Kilauea (opposite), the world's most active volcano, has been spilling lava down its slopes in one eruption after another since 1983. Where it flows into the sea, lava extends the coast. More than 380 acres (154 ha) have been added to the Big Island's edge.

HAWAII
Aloha State

STATEHOOD	August 21, 1959; 50th state
CAPITAL	Honolulu
LARGEST CITY	Honolulu Population 378,155
TOTAL AREA	10,931 sq mi; 28,311 sq km
LAND AREA	6,423 sq mi; 16,635 sq km
POPULATION	1,257,608
POPULATION DENSITY	193.8 per sq mi
MAJOR RACIAL/ ETHNIC GROUPS	41.6% Asian; 24.3% white; 9.4% Hawaiian/Pacific Islander; 1.8% African American. Hispanic (any race) 7.2%.
INDUSTRY	tourism, trade, finance, food processing, petroleum refining, stone, clay, and glass products
AGRICULTURE	sugarcane, pineapples, nursery stock, tropical fruit, livestock, macadamia nuts

HAWAIIAN GOOSE (NENE)   HIBISCUS

Did you know?

1. There are no racial or ethnic minorities in Hawaii. Everyone is a minority.
2. More animals and plants native to Hawaii are on the endangered species list than in any other state. Even its state bird is endangered.
3. You can ski two different ways on the same day in Hawaii: on water at the beach and on snow on the slopes of Mauna Kea, a 13,796-foot- (4,205-m-) high volcano on the Big Island.
4. Mount Waialeale, on the island of Kauai, is the wettest place in the United States, with 460 in (1,170 cm) of rainfall per year.
5. Hawaii's state fish is the humuhumunukunukuakua'a, or trigger fish.
6. There are only 12 letters in the Hawaiian alphabet: *A, E, I, O, U, H, K, L, M, N, P,* and *W.*

Hawaiian surfer Megan Abubo performs at a competition on Maui in 2003. Surfers from around the world visit the Aloha State to experience what many think is the world's best surfing. The biggest waves, as high as 12 feet (4 m) or more, usually crash against Oahu's North Shore beaches during winter, generated by North Pacific storms. Smaller waves for beginning surfers are found on other beaches.

the last monarch. Hawaii became a U.S. territory in 1900. By the following year the naval station at Pearl Harbor was under construction.

The Japanese attack on Pearl Harbor brought the United States into World War II and brought Hawaii into the modern era. Thousands of people from the U.S. mainland moved in to work for the war effort, and many stayed on after peace was restored. More people immigrated in the post-war years. In 1959 Hawaii entered the Union as the 50th state.

The introduction of jet airline passenger service to Hawaii opened the doors to tourism. By 1970 this industry had replaced agriculture as the state's chief economic activity. These days the

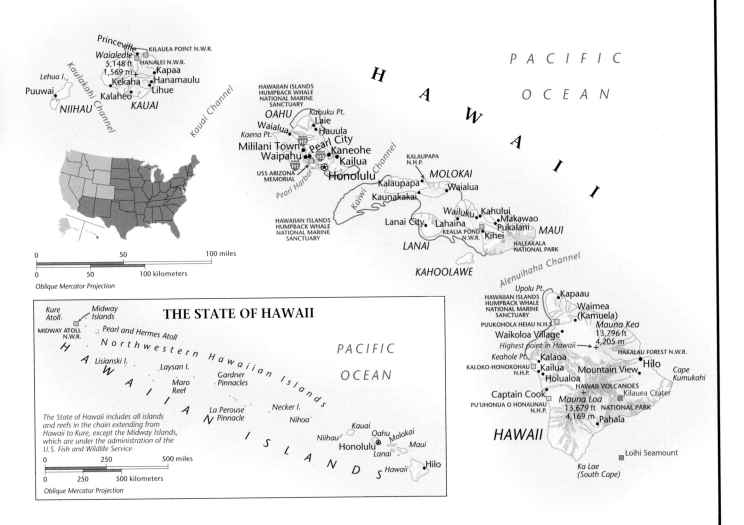

THE STATE OF HAWAII

Map labels (Northwestern Hawaiian Islands inset):

Kure Atoll
MIDWAY ATOLL N.W.R.
Midway Islands
Pearl and Hermes Atoll
Lisianski I.
Northwestern Hawaiian Islands
PACIFIC OCEAN
Laysan I.
Maro Reef
Gardner Pinnacles
La Perouse Pinnacle
Necker I.
Nihoa
Kauai
Niihau
Oahu
Molokai
Honolulu
Lanai
Maui
Hawaii
Hilo

HAWAIIAN ISLANDS

The State of Hawaii includes all islands and reefs in the chain extending from Hawaii to Kure, except the Midway Islands, which are under the administration of the U.S. Fish and Wildlife Service

0   250   500 miles
0   250   500 kilometers
Oblique Mercator Projection

Main map labels:

Princeville, KILAUEA POINT N.W.R.
Waialeale 5,148 ft 1,569 m, HANALEI N.W.R.
Lehua I.
Kapaa
Kekaha, Hanamaulu
Puuwai
Kalaheo, Lihue
NIIHAU, KAUAI
Kaulakahi Channel
Kauai Channel

PACIFIC OCEAN

HAWAII

HAWAIIAN ISLANDS HUMPBACK WHALE NATIONAL MARINE SANCTUARY
OAHU
Kahuku Pt.
Waialua, Laie, Hauula
Kaena Pt.
Mililani Town, Pearl City, Kaneohe
Waipahu, Kailua
USS ARIZONA MEMORIAL
Honolulu
Pearl Harbor
Kaiwi Channel

KALAUPAPA N.H.P.
MOLOKAI
Kalaupapa, Waialua
Kaunakakai

HAWAIIAN ISLANDS HUMPBACK WHALE NATIONAL MARINE SANCTUARY
Lanai City
Wailuku, Kahului
Lahaina, Makawao, Pukalani
KEALIA POND N.W.R., Kihei, MAUI
LANAI
HALEAKALA NATIONAL PARK
KAHOOLAWE
Alenuihaha Channel

Upolu Pt.
HAWAIIAN ISLANDS HUMPBACK WHALE NATIONAL MARINE SANCTUARY
Kapaau
Waimea (Kamuela)
PUUKOHOLA HEIAU N.H.P.
Mauna Kea 13,796 ft 4,205 m
Waikoloa Village
Highest point in Hawaii
Keahole Pt.
HAKALAU FOREST N.W.R.
KALOKO-HONOKOHAU N.H.P.
Kailua, Mountain View, Hilo
Kalaoa
Holualoa
Cape Kumukahi
Captain Cook
PU'UHONUA O HONAUNAU N.H.P.
HAWAII VOLCANOES
Mauna Loa 13,679 ft 4,169 m
Kilauea Crater
NATIONAL PARK
Pahala
HAWAII
Loihi Seamount
Ka Lae (South Cape)

0   50   100 miles
0   50   100 kilometers
Oblique Mercator Projection

---

islands are a peaceful getaway for vacationers especially from Japan and the U.S. mainland. Millions each year enjoy the state's scenic delights and tropical climate. Tourists hike in lush Kauai rain forests, view volcanoes on the Big Island and whales off Maui, or shop in the famous Waikiki district of Oahu. Many enjoy surfing or sunning on beautiful beaches—some of volcanic black sand—all over the islands.

Hawaii has the greatest ethnic diversity of any U.S. state. Fewer than one in four residents are white, and roughly four in ten are of primarily Asian descent. Though few "pure" Hawaiians remain, it is estimated that a majority of people here are part Hawaiian. There is a movement among Native Hawaiians for some form of self-government that ranges from leaving the Union to reclaiming land taken from them when the monarchy was overthrown. Other issues affect daily lives. A heavy dependence on tourism means that a drop in the number of visitors can cause difficulty for residents who live in a state where the high cost of importing goods makes everyday items expensive. The loss of habitat, which places more and more native plants and animals on the endangered species list, is also linked to this industry. The state has its problems. But it also has what Hawaiians call a "spirit of aloha" that places value on working together for the betterment of their island home.

IDAHO

★ *Gem State* ★

GEM OF THE MOUNTAINS, another nickname for Idaho, fits the state in several ways. Among the rich variety of minerals found here, the deep purple Idaho star garnet is treasured by gem collectors. The state's snow-topped peaks sparkle jewel-like in the sun. And cold, clear streams, like the Clearwater and Salmon Rivers, are strung like sparkling necklaces through the state's mountain valleys. The state's official name comes from the *Idaho,* a Columbia River steamship. With the discovery of gold in 1860 along the Clearwater River, the diggings came to be called the Idaho mines. When a state name was needed, Idaho won the prize.

Prospectors traveled up the Columbia and Snake Rivers, staking claims to gold, silver, and other minerals in the mountain valleys north of present-day Boise. Ranchers and others followed the miners, and by 1890 the population reached 90,000. That year, with "leftover" lands from neighboring Wyoming and Montana, Idaho was admitted as the 43rd state with Boise as its capital.

Today, most residents live south and east of Boise on the Snake River Plain. This broad valley, though poor in rainfall, is rich with both hydro-electricity and water for fields thanks to a series of dams built across the river. Fertile volcanic soils combine with mild temperatures to support the state's famous potato crop.

Forested mountains cover most of sparsely populated central Idaho and the northern panhandle. Lewis and Clark crossed the Bitterroot Range in 1805, opening the region to trappers who supplied beaver pelts for markets in the East. Until the 1830s, these mountain men would gather to trade furs, supplies, and tall tales. One popular spot for these rendezvous was near Bear Lake on the Idaho-Utah border.

The natural resources that first brought

1805

With the help of Indian guides, Lewis and Clark crossed the Bitterroot Range on their quest to find the Pacific Ocean.

1877

The Army's arrest of a Nez Perce chief (above) led to a war that ended with the Indians being forced to move to reservations.

1976

The Teton Dam collapse increased inspections of existing dams, cancelled some projects, and promoted the use of concrete in future dams.

Present day

Idaho's mountains, lakes, rivers, and wildlife have made tourism, including snow sports, an important year-round industry.

Posing serious hazards for trappers and other early travelers, Idaho's whitewater rivers provide thrills and chills for today's tourists. This group of rafters (opposite) flashes through rapids on the Selway River in central Idaho.

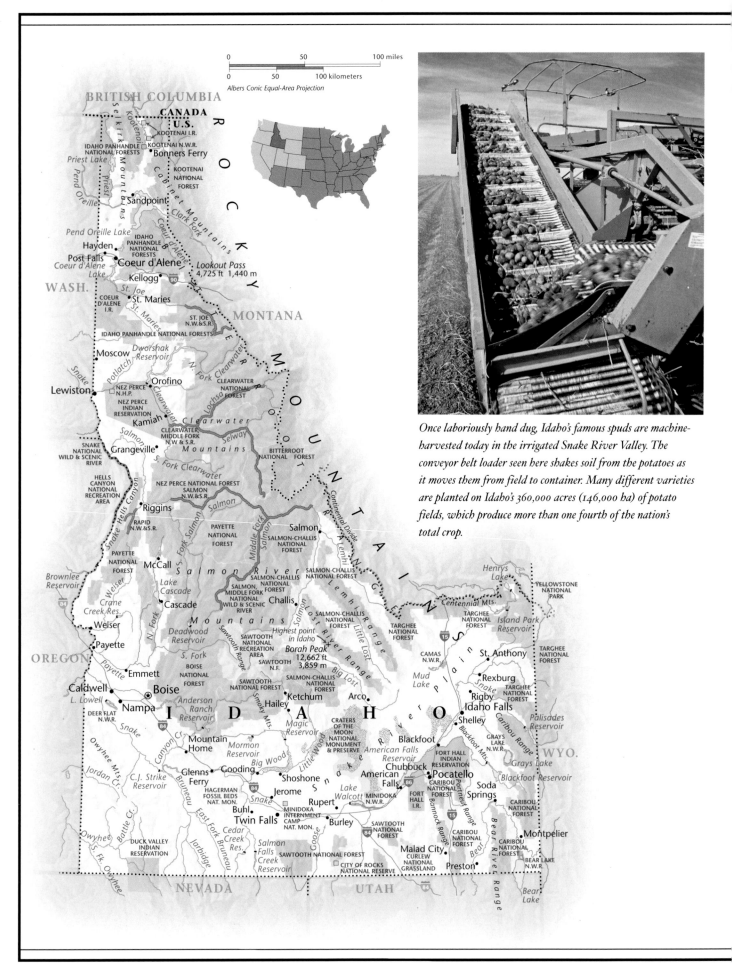

Once laboriously hand dug, Idaho's famous spuds are machine-harvested today in the irrigated Snake River Valley. The conveyor belt loader seen here shakes soil from the potatoes as it moves them from field to container. Many different varieties are planted on Idaho's 360,000 acres (146,000 ha) of potato fields, which produce more than one fourth of the nation's total crop.

people to the state still provide Idahoans with work. Precious metals are declining in importance, but mining remains a key industry. Idaho supplies the nation with a broad array of industrial minerals, including lead, zinc, and copper. Phosphate, used as fertilizer and even in soft drinks, is mined in the arid far southeast. Processing of the huge potato crop into various frozen styles also provides work for residents. Many are employed in the harvesting and processing of spruce, fir, and pine trees from the state's vast forests. Indeed, national forests cover more than a third of the state, an area exceeded only by Alaska.

Among the most rugged and remote in the United States, Idaho's wild lands attract tourists who want to "get away from it all." Thrill-seekers come to raft roaring rivers, hike rocky trails, and fish icy streams in the Salmon, Sawtooth, and Bitterroot ranges. Winter sports are popular, too, such as skiing at one of the country's biggest resorts—Sun Valley.

Wild and scenic Idaho faces challenges, too. Its population of nearly 1.4 million places it just 40th among states—but it is the fifth fastest-growing state. Forests are being cut down as demands for housing increase. As mining and logging operations downsize, computer and other high-technology businesses provide increasing numbers of jobs. The rise of dairy farms has led to complaints about waste management. Adventure tourism provides an ever-growing economic boost to the state, but increasing visitor numbers may threaten the wilderness experience they seek. It is crystal clear that Idaho's people must seek a balance between the use and the protection of plentiful natural resources for their state to continue as a gem of the mountains.

IDAHO
Gem State

STATEHOOD	July 3, 1890; 43rd state
CAPITAL	Boise
LARGEST CITY	Boise Population 189,847
TOTAL AREA	83,570 sq mi; 216,446 sq km
LAND AREA	82,747 sq mi; 214,314 sq km
POPULATION	1,366,332
POPULATION DENSITY	16.2 people per sq mi
MAJOR RACIAL/ ETHNIC GROUPS	91.0% white; 1.4% Native American; .9% Asian; .4% African American. Hispanic (any race) 7.9%.
INDUSTRY	electronics and computer equipment, tourism, food processing, forest products, mining, chemicals
AGRICULTURE	potatoes, dairy products, cattle, wheat, alfalfa hay, sugar beets, barley, trout

MOUNTAIN BLUEBIRD   SYRINGA (MOCK ORANGE)

Did you know?

1. To prepare for missions to the Moon, NASA's Apollo astronauts spent time learning about volcanic rocks at Craters of the Moon National Monument.
2. The Big Wood River, sometimes known as the Upside Down River, has the curious feature of changing from 100 feet (30 m) wide by 4 feet (1 m) deep to 4 feet (1 m) wide by 100 feet (30 m) deep a short distance away.
3. Idaho's first sizable potato crop was planted by Mormon colonists from Salt Lake City. They found a ready market with the gold miners of 1860.
4. Crystal Ice Cave is a remarkable underground chamber containing a frozen river, waterfall, and other formations all preserved at a consistent 32°F (0°C) even when the outside temperature is 95–97°F (35–36°C)
5. Arco was the first city in the world to be lighted with electricity generated by nuclear power.

MONTANA

★ *Treasure State* ★

RECIPE FOR MONTANA: Take three parts shortgrass prairie and two parts mountain. Lace with small streams and large rivers. Sprinkle with gold, silver, copper, lots of animals, and a few people. Freeze in winter and warm in summer under a Big Sky.

Fourth largest state, sprawling Montana—a Spanish word meaning "mountainous"—has dozens of ranges in its west and flat to gently rolling prairies in its east. The Continental Divide winds along Rocky Mountain ridges that form its border with Idaho, splitting waterways along the way. To the west rivers flow to the Pacific; to the east the mighty Missouri River runs through grassy plains to the Mississippi then south to the Gulf of Mexico. Montana's climate divides there as well. The west is comparatively wet and mild year-round. Extremes are typical in the east, with very cold winters and hot, dry summers.

In a pattern typical of western settlement, mineral riches brought fortune seekers to Montana. Many cities trace their beginnings to mining in the 1860s. Prospectors found gold and silver along what is now state-capital Helena's main street. A massive copper deposit called "the richest hill on earth" put Butte on the map. Virginia City, once rich with gold, is now a ghost town. Mineral wealth propelled Montana to territorial status in 1864 and statehood in 1889.

Livestock grazing on open range in eastern Montana was followed by fenced cattle and sheep ranches and wheat farms. Miners were joined by loggers and sawmill workers, who turned spruce, fir, pine, and cedar trees into lumber and other wood products for the rest of the country. Gold, silver, and even sapphires are still mined in Montana's mountain west. But these days minerals even more vital for the

1860s

The arrival of steamboats at Fort Benton, a key trading post on the Missouri River, made it the world's most remote inland port.

1876

The Plains Indian victory at the Battle of the Little Bighorn was short-lived. Within a year they were forced onto reservations.

1886–1887

The bitter winter of 1886–87, coupled with too many cattle grazing on too little land, almost destroyed the cattle industry.

Present day

Efforts to treat unsafe water seeping into Berkeley Pit copper mine, closed since 1982, have turned it into an environmental laboratory.

Unlike its human-built namesake, this "Chinese Wall" (opposite) is a natural feature running along the Continental Divide in western Montana. It was created by mountain-building forces that lifted the limestone reef of an ancient seabed a thousand feet.

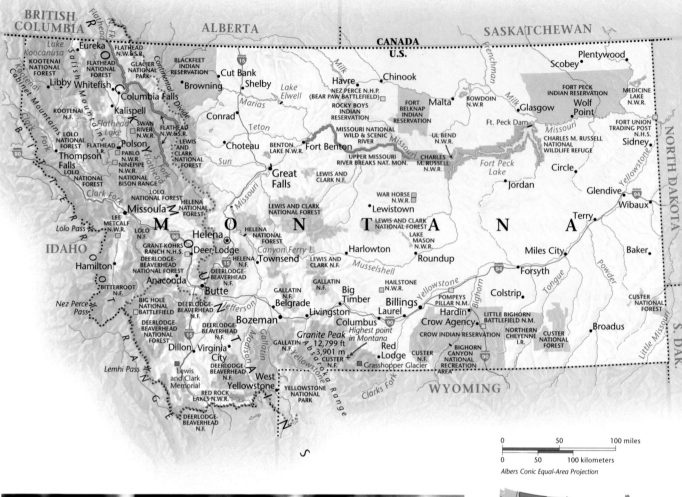

BRITISH COLUMBIA · **ALBERTA** · **SASKATCHEWAN**

CANADA
U.S.

Flathead R.

Lake Koocanusa

Eureka
FLATHEAD N.W.&S.R.
KOOTENAI NATIONAL FOREST
FLATHEAD NATIONAL FOREST
GLACIER NATIONAL PARK
BLACKFEET INDIAN RESERVATION
Cut Bank
Shelby
Havre
Chinook
Plentywood
Scobey

Libby
Whitefish
Columbia Falls
Browning
Lake Elwell
NEZ PERCE N.H.P. (BEAR PAW BATTLEFIELD)
Malta
BOWDOIN N.W.R
FORT PECK INDIAN RESERVATION
MEDICINE LAKE N.W.R.

KOOTENAI N.F.
Cabinet Mountains
Kalispell
Marias
ROCKY BOYS INDIAN RESERVATION
FORT BELKNAP INDIAN RESERVATION
Glasgow
Wolf Point
FORT UNION TRADING POST N.H.S.

LOLO NATIONAL FOREST
Satish Mountains
Flathead Lake
SWAN RIVER N.W.R.
FLATHEAD N.W.&S.R.
Conrad
Teton
MISSOURI NATIONAL WILD & SCENIC RIVER
Ft. Peck Dam
Sidney

Thompson Falls
Polson
PABLO N.W.R.
FLATHEAD I.R.
LEWIS AND CLARK NATIONAL FOREST
Choteau
Missouri
UL BEND N.W.R.
CHARLES M. RUSSELL N.W.R.
Fort Peck Lake
Circle

LOLO NATIONAL FOREST
NINEPIPE N.W.R.
NATIONAL BISON RANGE
Sun
BENTON LAKE N.W.R.
Fort Benton
UPPER MISSOURI RIVER BREAKS NAT. MON.
CHARLES M. RUSSELL NATIONAL WILDLIFE REFUGE

Missoula
Clark Fork
LOLO NATIONAL FOREST
HELENA NATIONAL FOREST
Great Falls
LEWIS AND CLARK N.F.
Glendive

M   O   N   T   A   N   A

Lolo Pass
LEE METCALF N.W.R.
LOLO N.F.
GRANT-KOHRS RANCH N.H.S.
HELENA NATIONAL FOREST
Lewistown
WAR HORSE N.W.R.
Wibaux

IDAHO
Hamilton
BITTERROOT N.F.
DEERLODGE-BEAVERHEAD NATIONAL FOREST
Helena
Deer Lodge
Canyon Ferry L.
Townsend
LEWIS AND CLARK N.F.
Harlowton
LEWIS AND CLARK NATIONAL FOREST
LAKE MASON N.W.R.
Roundup
Miles City
Terry
Baker

Nez Perce Pass
BIG HOLE NATIONAL BATTLEFIELD
Anaconda
Butte
DEERLODGE-BEAVERHEAD N.F.
Jefferson
Belgrade
GALLATIN N.F.
Musselshell
Big Timber
GALLATIN N.F.
HAILSTONE N.W.R.
Forsyth
Yellowstone
POMPEYS PILLAR N.M.
Bighorn
Colstrip
Tongue
CUSTER NATIONAL FOREST

DEERLODGE-BEAVERHEAD NATIONAL FOREST
Bozeman
Columbus
Billings
Hardin
LITTLE BIGHORN BATTLEFIELD N.M.

B   I   T   T   E   R   R   O   O   T   R   A   N   G   E
Dillon
DEERLODGE-BEAVERHEAD N.F.
Virginia City
Madison
Gallatin
Livingston
Laurel
Crow Agency
CROW INDIAN RESERVATION
NORTHERN CHEYENNE I.R.
Broadus

Lemhi Pass
Lewis and Clark Memorial
Granite Peak 12,799 ft 3,901 m Highest point in Montana
GALLATIN N.F.
Red Lodge
CUSTER N.F.
BIGHORN CANYON NATIONAL RECREATION AREA
CUSTER NATIONAL FOREST

RED ROCK LAKES N.W.R.
DEERLODGE-BEAVERHEAD N.F.
West Yellowstone
ABSAROKA RANGE
CUSTER N.F.
Grasshopper Glacier
Clarks Fork
WYOMING

YELLOWSTONE NATIONAL PARK

NORTH DAKOTA · **S. DAK.**

0   50   100 miles
0   50   100 kilometers
Albers Conic Equal-Area Projection

A boy connects the Old West to the New at a guest ranch in the Blackfoot River Valley in western Montana. These days visitors can help work cattle on real ranches, or relax at modern resorts. Horseback riding, river float trips, fly fishing, and hiking are all offered in summer, while winters bring out snowmobiles, skis, and snowshoes. For those who prefer a true Big Sky Country getaway, Montana maintains 14 wilderness areas.

nation—oil and coal—come from the state's Great Plains. More recently, there has been an increase in jobs in the tourist industry. People come to fish and canoe the state's plentiful rivers, and to hike and hunt the state's vast wild lands. Glacier National Park features snow-capped peaks, deep glacier-carved valleys, and spectacular lakes. The scenic Beartooth Highway passes through three of Montana's many national forests on its way to Yellowstone National Park.

There's lots of history to see in Montana, too. Lewis and Clark traveled more miles in Montana than in any other present-day state. They met mostly friendly and helpful native people as they followed the Missouri. On June 25, 1876, near another Montana river—the Little Big Horn—a meeting between whites and Indians was anything but friendly. Crazy Horse led 2,000 Lakota and Cheyenne warriors against George Armstrong Custer and about 215 U.S. Army troops. It was the last major victory by Native Americans in the Indian Wars. Blackfeet, Crow, Flathead, Cheyenne, Lakota, and other native peoples still live in Montana, making up more than 6 percent of the state's population. Most live on one of seven reservations across the state.

In recent years, a number of celebrities have bought homes and ranches in Montana. Some residents do not welcome the increased land prices and other changes this trend has brought. There is also a struggle over logging and mining decisions that impact the natural environment. Although Montana's population has increased by more than 100,000 since 1990, great expanses of the state remain largely untouched by people. While some of Montana's ingredients may change a little in the future, the state's basic recipe will continue to be treasured under its Big Sky.

MONTANA
Treasure State

STATEHOOD	November 8, 1889; 41st state
CAPITAL	Helena
LARGEST CITY	Billings Population 92,008
TOTAL AREA	147,042 sq mi; 380,838 sq km
LAND AREA	145,552 sq mi; 376,979 sq km
POPULATION	917,621
POPULATION DENSITY	6.2 people per sq mi
MAJOR RACIAL/ ETHNIC GROUPS	90.6% white; 6.2% Native American .5% Asian; .3% African American. Hispanic (any race 2%).
INDUSTRY	forest products, food processing, mining, construction, tourism
AGRICULTURE	wheat, cattle, barley, hay, sugar beets, dairy products

WESTERN MEADOWLARK

BITTERROOT

Did you know?

1. Montana is the only state with river systems that empty into the Gulf of Mexico, Hudson Bay, and the Pacific Ocean.
2. Montana holds the records for rapid temperature changes. In Great Falls on January 11, 1980, the temperature rose from -32°F (-35°C) to 15°F (9°C) in seven minutes, and at Browning on January 23–24, 1916, the temperature fell from 44°F (6°C) to -56°F (-49°C) in 24 hours.
3. Montana has a tribally-controlled college on each of its Indian reservations. Tribes include the Crow, Northern Cheyenne, and Blackfeet.
4. Many dinosaur fossils have been found in Montana, including nests with eggs and juveniles. The nests led paleontologist Jack Horner, consultant to the movie *Jurassic Park,* to conclude that dinosaurs exhibited family behavior.
5. One of the world's highest sports centers is located in Butte, which has an elevation of 5,549 feet (1,690 m).

NEVADA

★ *Silver State* ★

LIKE A BIG PIE SLICE, Nevada angles between California, Utah, and Arizona. The Sierra Nevada, the mountains that give the state its name, rise along the long border with California and block rain and snow moving in from the Pacific Ocean. This helps make Nevada, which averages only about nine inches (23 cm) of precipitation each year, the driest of the 50 states.

Nevada's dry landscape looks like wrinkled paper. Parallel rows of more than 150 north-south mountain ranges rise between at least 90 broad valleys in this Great Basin region. Rivers flowing into these basins dry up in the summer heat. The Paiute, Shoshone, and Washoe peoples and their ancestors roamed this basin-and-range landscape for thousands of years before Europeans and their descendants came to this remote region. In the 1770s the Spanish blazed a trail across the southeast corner to connect their settlements in New Mexico with their missions in California. After the Mexican-American War in 1848, Nevada and much of the Southwest came under U.S. control. Mormons from Utah followed the Spanish Trail in the 1850s to settle in a mountain-ringed valley named Las Vegas ("the meadows"). Here and in other settlements they irrigated crops and raised livestock. Then came mining riches.

Prospectors struck silver and gold in Virginia City, northeast of Lake Tahoe, in 1859. The so-called Comstock Lode turned out to be one of the richest silver deposits ever found. This mineral wealth helped Nevada become a U.S. territory in 1861 and the 36th state in 1864, as hordes of hopeful settlers arrived. Carson City, a nearby mining camp, was made the capital. Though great wealth came from many mines over the next half century, mining created a "boom or bust" economy. Prosperity would be

1843–1845

Lieutenant John C. Frémont, during his exploration of the Great Basin, named Pyramid Lake for this rock formation.

1859

The 1859 discovery of silver and gold led to a rush in settlement, the opening of many mines, and statehood in 1864.

1931

After lawmakers legalized gambling, casinos began to attract tourists, laying the foundation for Nevada's largest industry.

Present day

The U.S. government's plan to make Yucca Mountain a storage site for radioactive waste, is vigorously opposed by many residents.

An Egyptian sphinx, the Eiffel Tower, and the Statue of Liberty can all be seen in replica in Las Vegas (opposite). Gambling, superstar-studded stage shows, and a year-round tourist season have fueled the area's rapid urban growth.

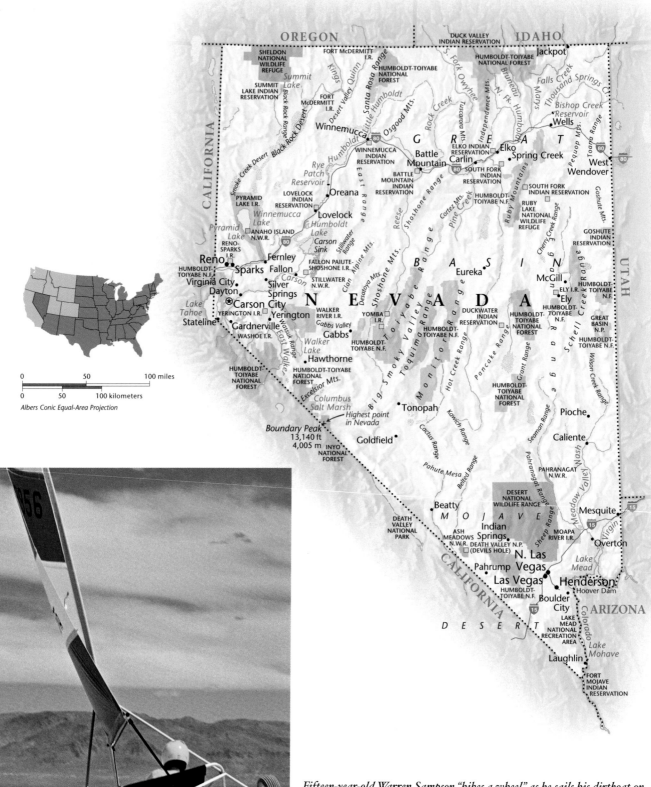

Fifteen-year-old Warren Sampson "hikes a wheel" as he sails his dirtboat on Nevada's Black Rock Desert in 2001. The windy 300-square-mile (777-sq-km) expanse of sand and salt, perfect for racing activities, was a sparkling lake 60,000 years ago. While this sail-propelled buggy might hit 40 miles per hour (64 kph), the world's land speed record of 763 miles per hour (1,228 kph) was set here by a jet-powered car in 1997.

replaced by hard times after each mineral deposit was "played out." Nevada was hit hard by the Great Depression in the 1930s. The state needed to find a more stable base for its economy. Making gambling legal was one answer to the up-and-down mining activity. Water was needed to irrigate desert valleys and provide light to homes, hotels, and gaming tables. Federal money and thousands of imported workers built spectacular 726-foot (222-m) Hoover Dam. The project, which spans the Colorado River, supplies water and power to cities and farms across several states and, by forming Lake Mead, provides water recreation in the middle of a desert, too.

Like a desert flower after a rain, Nevada has blossomed. Las Vegas, Reno, and Lake Tahoe attract millions of tourists each year. People come to live, too. Beyond the cities are cattle and sheep ranches, farms, and mines. The state still produces more gold and silver than any other state.

While Nevada now bets on its gaming wealth, future good luck is not a sure thing. Tourists visit less often when the nation's economy is weak or when the cost of transportation is high, creating a big problem in a state where many wages depend on these visitors. Nevada's population has grown, too, from 1.2 million in 1990 to more than 2.2 million. In 2003, the U.S. Census Bureau announced that Nevada has been the fastest-growing state for 17 years straight. This growth puts stress on already limited water supplies. Nevada must share Colorado River water with neighbor states as well as with Mexico. There is concern, too, about the long-term effects of past nuclear testing on federal land and the plan to bury nuclear wastes from around the country in Yucca Mountain. Whatever awaits Nevada, a good bet is that its people will work hard to keep on winning.

NEVADA
Silver State

STATEHOOD	October 31, 1864; 36th state
CAPITAL	Carson City
LARGEST CITY	Las Vegas Population 508,604
TOTAL AREA	110,561 sq mi; 286,351 sq km
LAND AREA	109,826 sq mi; 284,448 sq km
POPULATION	2,241,154
POPULATION DENSITY	19.8 people per sq mi
MAJOR RACIAL/ ETHNIC GROUPS	75.2% white; 6.8% African American; 4.5% Asian; 1.3% Native American. Hispanic (any race) 19.7%.
INDUSTRY	tourism and gaming, mining, printing and publishing, food processing, electrical equipment
AGRICULTURE	cattle, hay, dairy products

MOUNTAIN BLUEBIRD   SAGEBRUSH

Did you know?

1. In the early days, mail was delivered to Carson Valley by a Norwegian mailman on homemade skis.
2. Samuel Clemens (now better known as Mark Twain) started his career writing for the Virginia City *Territorial Enterprise* newspaper in the spring of 1862 for $25 per week. He later described his salary as "bloated luxury" in his book *Roughing It*.
3. The top-secret U.S. Air Force base known as Area 51, whose existence was denied for years and where believers in UFOs claim alien spacecraft are hidden underground, is located some 75 miles (120 km) northwest of Las Vegas on Groom Lake.
4. Between 1975 and 2000 the population of Las Vegas County grew by almost 250 percent. It is still one of the fastest-growing counties in the nation.
5. More than a thousand atomic bomb tests have been conducted in Nevada by the U.S. Army.

OREGON

★ Beaver State ★

"IF YOU POKE A BROOMSTICK in the ground, it will grow!" To an 1840s farm family looking for a new life in the American West, such words about the rich soils of Oregon's Willamette Valley pulled like a magnet. Tens of thousands of hopeful settlers came by wagon train across the Oregon Trail, generating enough population for Oregon to become a state in 1859. Most Oregonians still call this broad and beautiful valley home.

East of the Willamette loom the giant, snow-crowned volcanoes of the Cascade Range—Hood, Jefferson, and the Three Sisters. To the west, the Coast Range stands shrouded in fog and covered in mossy forest. A string of picturesque fishing towns, jewel-like state parks, and lonely lighthouses stretch along the rocky coast. Howling winds blast the shore in winter, whipping up huge waves that crash against it, chipping away the land. Rocky sea stacks stand as remnants of a long-ago shoreline.

The mountains split the state into two main climate regions. They force Pacific moisture out on the western slopes but block most precipitation from reaching the Columbia Plateau and Great Basin lands to the east. Here, semi-arid lands favor cattle ranching and farming of wheat, hay, sugar beets, and other specialty crops with water from the Snake and other rivers. Oregon's diverse agriculture yields more than 200 different farm products. The state ranks first in production of Christmas trees, hazelnuts, peppermint, raspberries, blackberries, loganberries, and grass seed. That's right, the green grass on a lawn near you may have had its beginnings on an Oregon seed farm.

Trees—big trees!—also love Oregon's climate. They cover nearly half the state. Forests of towering Douglas fir and western hemlock carpet the slopes of the Coast and Cascade Ranges,

Early 1800s

John McLoughlin and his fur trading company helped newcomers settle in the region. He is known as the "Father of Oregon."

1850s

Development boomed with the Donation Land Law of 1850, which gave 320 acres to settlers who farmed land for four years.

Late 1800s

Logging of vast stands of trees began in the late 1800s and provided the basis for the state's forest-products industry.

1990–Present

Since 1990 logging has been banned within 2,000 acres of a known nesting site of the endangered northern spotted owl.

Crater Lake (opposite), at 1,943 feet (592 m) is the deepest in the United States. It fills a depression created when an eruption caused the top of a mountain to collapse. Wizard Island, in the center of the 6-mile- (10-km-) wide lake, is the top of another volcano.

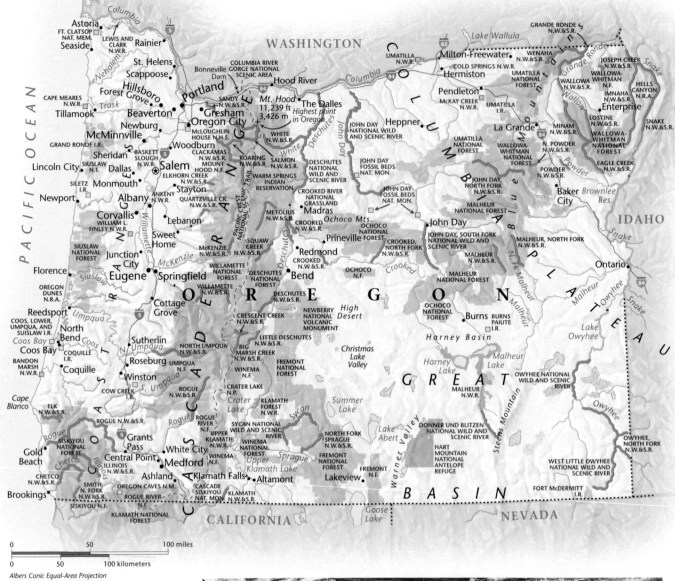

PACIFIC OCEAN

WASHINGTON

COLUMBIA

OREGON

IDAHO

GREAT

BASIN

CALIFORNIA

NEVADA

0   50   100 miles

0   50   100 kilometers

Albers Conic Equal-Area Projection

*A member of the Warm Springs tribe
fishes in the Deschutes River of north-
central Oregon. Net fishing for salmon,
lamprey eels, and other species has been
a way of life here for generations. Today,
sediments from logging, farming, industrial pollution, and dams on Oregon's
rivers have caused the fish populations
to decline, threatening Native American
traditions.*

while ponderosa pines thrive in the eastern highlands. Logging has been at the top of Oregon's economic activities for decades. Although forest protection agreements have reduced the state's tree harvest in recent years, Oregon still leads the country in timber output.

Oregon is more than forests and fields. Where the Willamette River flows into the Columbia, a trading center bloomed into Portland, the City of Roses. Its docks import cars from Asia, and its factories process wood products and computer components. Portland is recognized as a model city for its success in keeping its downtown healthy and active.

Oregon faces challenges in managing its rich natural resources and sources of scenic beauty in a way that will maintain the quality of life that its people long have enjoyed. The Columbia River powers massive hydroelectric plants that generate most of Oregon's electricity and power metal-processing plants. While a boon to industry, the dams have disrupted river flow and contributed to the decline of the state's once-rich salmon fishery. Opportunities in computer and other high-tech jobs have encouraged people to emigrate from California and other states. There has also been an increase in the number of Hispanic and Asian residents. With the population increasing at a rate of more than 50,000 people each year, there is major concern over the loss of agricultural land and the competition for water. Renewed logging of old-growth forests that have been standing for centuries—long before there ever *was* an Oregon—stirs controversy. While the struggle to balance economic growth and preserve the environment will be ongoing, a fine Pacific Coast position and plentiful natural assets hold great promise for Oregon's future.

OREGON
Beaver State

STATE OF OREGON
1859

STATEHOOD	February 14, 1859; 33rd state
CAPITAL	Salem
LARGEST CITY	Portland Population 539,438
TOTAL AREA	98,381 sq mi; 254,805 sq km
LAND AREA	95,997 sq mi; 248,631 sq km
POPULATION	3,559,596
POPULATION DENSITY	36.7 people per sq mi
MAJOR RACIAL/ ETHNIC GROUPS	86.6% white; 3% Asian; 1.6% African American; 1.3% Native American. Hispanic (any race) 8%.
INDUSTRY	real estate, retail and wholesale trade, electronic equipment, health services, construction, forest products, business services
AGRICULTURE	nursery stock, hay, cattle, grass seed, wheat, dairy products, potatoes

WESTERN MEADOWLARK   OREGON GRAPE

Did you know?

1. During World War II, Japan tried unsuccessfully to start huge fires along the Oregon coast by launching fire bombs.
2. Beneath the streets of Pendleton, Oregon, you can tour a labyrinth of tunnels built between 1870 and 1930 by Chinese laborers who were forced to live and work underground to escape discrimination. A Chinese laundry, ice house, and butcher shop are among the businesses restored in 1989.
3. The U.S. Department of Energy's Bonneville Power Administration, headquartered in Portland, provides about 45 percent of the electricity used in the Pacific Northwest. Most of this power comes from 31 hydroelectric plants along the Columbia River.
4. Oregon takes its nickname from the abundant beaver that gave rise to a thriving fur trade in the early 1800s.

UTAH

★ Beehive State ★

"THIS IS THE RIGHT PLACE." So said Brigham Young, as he looked out over the Great Salt Lake Valley from the Wasatch Mountains on July 24, 1847. Young had just led a hardy group of Mormon pioneers to find freedom in the west to practice their religion. From the 1847 group of 1,900 immigrants, Mormon communities grew quickly to 40,000 by 1860. Irrigation helped communities thrive on the thin strip of fertile soil along the Wasatch Front. Today, seven of ten Utah residents are Mormons, and the region between Brigham City and Provo is still the most populated.

Utah brims with scenic landforms. The north-south running Wasatch join the Uinta Mountains, which reach east along the Wyoming border. Topped by Kings Peak at 13,528 feet (4,123 m), the Uintas are the only major range in the Rockies that face east-west. The dry valleys and rugged ranges of the Great Basin stretch west and southwest of the Wasatch. Here, rivers may flow into low areas during spring, but none flow out. Salts carried from the surrounding mountains are left behind as the water evaporates. When mountain man Jim Bridger first tasted the water of the Great Salt Lake in 1824, he thought he had reached the Pacific Ocean! In Utah's southern section stands the Colorado Plateau, a huge raised tableland shared with Colorado, New Mexico, and Arizona. Here the Colorado and other rivers slice down through layers of colored rocks, forming scenic canyon lands.

For thousands of years the Ute, Paiute, and Shoshone peoples lived in small groups in this remote region. But it was the Mormons who settled in great numbers. They dug ditches to channel water from streams to their fields. With hard work and cooperation they turned the desert into productive farmland. Arrival of

1847

Brigham Young, along with about 600 followers, arrived in Salt Lake Valley and established Utah's first Mormon settlement.

1869

The completion of the first Transcontinental Railroad brought settlers and opened new markets for Utah's farm and mining products.

1952

Uranium deposits near Moab provided a basis for weapons development industries that now raise environmental concerns.

Present day

Desert expanses make excellent testing grounds and have helped make Utah a leader in defense systems and aerospace technology.

Millions of years of wind and weather have chiseled away at domes of red sandstone to create the more than 2,000 landforms preserved in Arches National Park. The largest, Landscape Arch (opposite), stretches 306 feet (93 m) end to end.

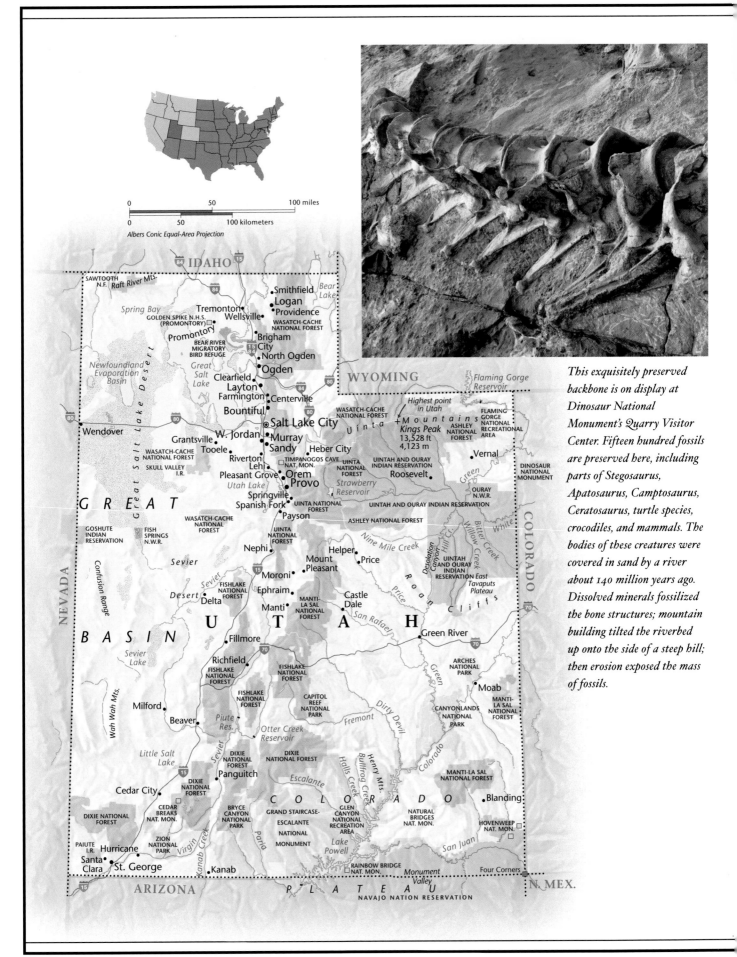

This exquisitely preserved backbone is on display at Dinosaur National Monument's Quarry Visitor Center. Fifteen hundred fossils are preserved here, including parts of Stegosaurus, Apatosaurus, Camptosaurus, Ceratosaurus, turtle species, crocodiles, and mammals. The bodies of these creatures were covered in sand by a river about 140 million years ago. Dissolved minerals fossilized the bone structures; mountain building tilted the riverbed up onto the side of a steep hill; then erosion exposed the mass of fossils.

Albers Conic Equal-Area Projection

the railroad brought non-Mormons and other immigrants. In 1869 the Golden Spike that completed the first transcontinental railroad was driven into the ground near Promontory, north of Great Salt Lake. Mining of copper and other minerals brought more people and wealth to Utah in the 20th century.

Mormons wanted Utah to enter the Union with the name Deseret, meaning "beehive," in recognition of all their hard work. Congress thought that sounded too much like "desert," so the state was named Utah after the native Ute people. But its nickname, Beehive State, honors its Mormon settlers.

Nearly two-thirds of the state is owned by the federal government. Government building of weapons parts and rockets has been important to the economy since World War II. The vast western flatlands make perfect testing grounds for fast cars and missiles. But the government has also helped make tourism a huge industry for the state. Some of the best opportunities for skiing, rock climbing, mountain biking, hiking, and boating are on government land. Manufacturing, especially of computer and other high-tech equipment, is another key industry.

Utah does face challenges. Mormons sometimes argue with non-Mormons over land use, civil versus religious rights, and other issues. Decades of mining and military weapons testing have damaged some land areas. Struggles continue over further mining and building on Utah's fragile natural areas. Drought and water shortages are always a concern, and danger could come from a hidden source. Movement along a fault near Salt Lake City could trigger an earthquake. But with careful planning, Utah should continue to be the "right place" for residents and visitors alike.

UTAH
Beehive State

STATEHOOD	January 4, 1896; 45th state
CAPITAL	Salt Lake City
LARGEST CITY	Salt Lake City Population 181,266
TOTAL AREA	84,899 sq mi; 219,887 sq km
LAND AREA	82,144 sq mi; 212,751 sq km
POPULATION	2,351,467
POPULATION DENSITY	28.2 people per sq mi
MAJOR RACIAL/ ETHNIC GROUPS	89.2% white; 1.7% Asian; 1.3% Native American; .8% African American. Hispanic (any race) 9%.
INDUSTRY	government, manufacturing, real estate, construction, health services, business services, banking
AGRICULTURE	cattle, dairy products, hay, poultry and eggs, wheat

CALIFORNIA GULL

SEGO LILY

Did you know?

1. Rainbow Bridge, in the national monument of the same name, is the world's largest natural stone bridge. It is 290 feet (88 m) high and 275 feet (84 m) across.
2. To support Mormon missionary programs around the world, language classes at Brigham Young University offer Swahili, Tagalog, and many other African and Asian languages as well as traditional French, German, and Spanish.
3. The Great Salt Lake is three to five times saltier than the ocean and the largest lake west of the Mississippi River. It is the remnant of a much larger ancient inland sea called Lake Bonneville.
4. Utah's spectacular scenery is preserved in five national parks, seven national monuments, two national recreation areas, and six national forests.
5. The names Utah, Uinta, and Wasatch all derive from the Ute people.

WASHINGTON

★ *Evergreen State* ★

WET AND MILD, hip and wild. Washington State is all of these and more. While the weather, especially in the western third, is known to be foggy and rainy with mild temperatures, it does not dampen the spirit and creativity of the people who live there. The forces of nature that created its spectacular landscapes are still at work. Washington State residents enjoy the beauty and deal with the wildness.

Washington forms the northwest corner of the Lower 48 states. The Coast Ranges are topped by the towering Olympic Mountains. These slopes are drenched with moisture—an average of 12 to 14 *feet* (3–4 *m*) a year. Temperate rain forests of spruce, hemlock, fir, and cedar thrive there. Just east is glacially-carved Puget Sound where most of the state's residents live. On clear days, they can see majestic, snow-clad Mount Rainier, an active volcano in the nearby Cascade Range. In 1980 Mount St. Helens, in

the southern part of the range, literally blew its top—a dramatic reminder that powerful forces are still at work here. These western mountains block most precipitation from moving to the eastern part of the state, where it is dry enough for sagebrush and short grasses to grow.

Zigzagging from northeast to southwest across the state is the massive Columbia. The largest-volume river in the western U.S., the Columbia is perhaps the hardest working, too. A huge system of dams, topped by the Grand Coulee, spin turbines to create electricity and form reservoirs to provide water for agriculture.

Sea journeys brought early explorers to the area, and sea otters brought fur traders. But it was Lewis and Clark's overland route to the Pacific and the opening of the Oregon Trail that spurred settlement in the mid 1800s. Native Americans, including the Nez Perce, Yakima, and Spokane, fought to keep their lands but

Early 1700s–1781

Spanish explorers were followed by British and American fur traders and merchants. At various times, each claimed the region.

Early 1900s

Riots in Seattle between Chinese workers and white newcomers seeking jobs led to the establishment of labor unions.

1940s

Boeing Company began building military aircraft during World War II. Today it is the world's largest aircraft manufacturer.

1970s–Present

Microsoft, founded by computer gurus Bill Gates and Paul Allen, has greatly enhanced the state's economy, especially in the 1990s.

The observation deck of Seattle's 60-foot- (18-m-) high Space Needle (opposite) provides great views of the entire Puget Sound region as well as stately Mount Rainier, which at 14,410 feet (4,392 m) is Washington's highest peak.

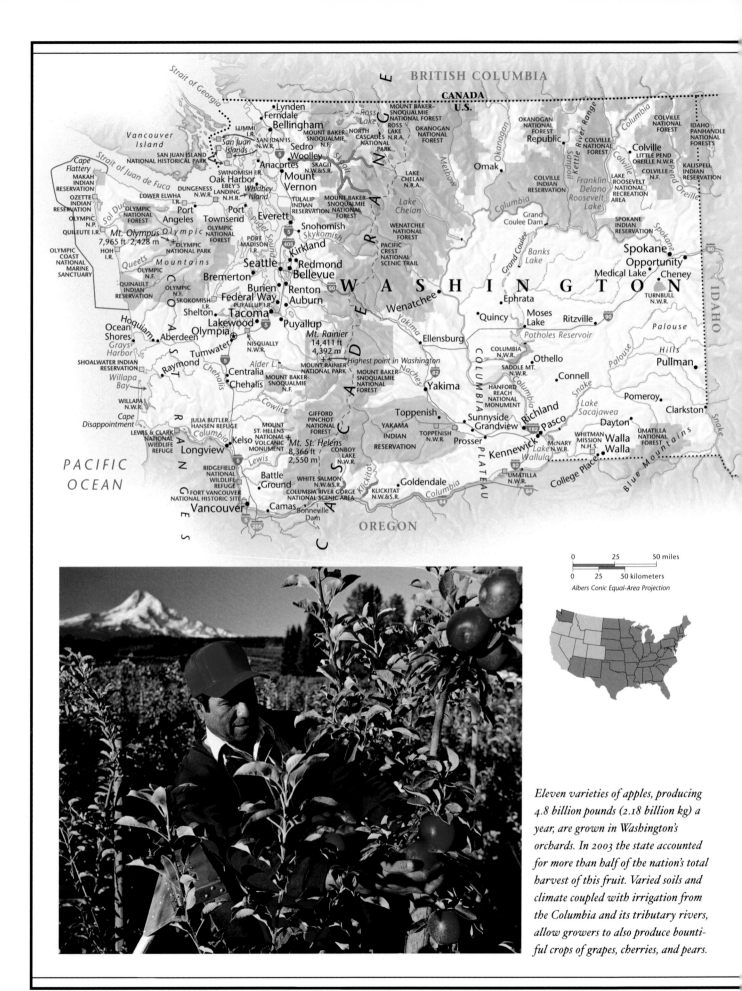

Eleven varieties of apples, producing 4.8 billion pounds (2.18 billion kg) a year, are grown in Washington's orchards. In 2003 the state accounted for more than half of the nation's total harvest of this fruit. Varied soils and climate coupled with irrigation from the Columbia and its tributary rivers, allow growers to also produce bountiful crops of grapes, cherries, and pears.

lost. The first railroad reached the territory in the 1880s, and by the end of the decade Washington gained statehood. When gold was discovered in Alaska in the 1890s, Washington became the shipping gateway to the gold fields. The Evergreen State boomed, growing from 75,000 people in 1889 to 1.25 million by 1920.

Its nickname suits the state, with more than half the land cloaked in forests. Early development centered on logging, along with fishing from coastal waters, cattle and wheat farming in the east, and orchards—especially apple—scattered throughout. Manufacturing "took off" when aircraft builders, aluminum companies, and defense industries set up shop in the Puget Sound area during the two world wars. The success of a coffee company and a computer software giant caused Seattle's population to explode in the 1990s.

Over the years, residents have learned lessons about economic growth and state resources. The state's once-thriving salmon catch has been greatly reduced, in part through over-harvest and dam construction. Concerns about forest preservation have led to less logging, though the forest industry is still huge. Washington's successful aircraft and computer industries face intense global competition. Seattle, regarded as one of the country's most beautiful cities, is jammed with traffic. The discovery in December 2003 that one of the state's dairy cows had mad cow disease raised concerns about the safety of U.S. beef.

Bright spots in the economic forecast for the state include growth in biotechnology research, a likely increase in shipping from Puget Sound ports, and a renewed emphasis on preserving resources through wise management to ensure that future generations of Washingtonians will benefit from the state's natural riches.

WASHINGTON
Evergreen State

STATEHOOD	November 11, 1889; 42nd state
CAPITAL	Olympia
LARGEST CITY	Seattle Population 570,426
TOTAL AREA	71,300 sq mi; 184,665 sq km
LAND AREA	66,544 sq mi; 172,348 sq km
POPULATION	6,131,445
POPULATION DENSITY	91.2 people per sq mi
MAJOR RACIAL/ ETHNIC GROUPS	81.8% white; 5.6% Asian; 3.2% African American; 1.6% Native American. Hispanic (any race) 7.5%.
INDUSTRY	aerospace, tourism, food processing, forest products, paper products, industrial machinery, printing and publishing, metals
AGRICULTURE	seafood, apples, dairy products, wheat, cattle, potatoes, hay

AMERICAN GOLDFINCH   COAST RHODODENDRON

Did you know?

1. Washington is the only state named for a President. As a territory it was known as Columbia, after the Columbia River.
2. Sam Hill built a concrete replica of England's Stonehenge on a bluff overlooking the Columbia River as a memorial to the soldiers from Klickitat County who fought and died in World War I.
3. The Olympic Peninsula is home to the only temperate rain forest in the lower 48 states. It receives 12 to 14 feet (3–4 m) of rain each year. The forest is dominated by Sitka spruce and western hemlock, some of which are 300 feet (90 m) high and 23 feet (7 m) around.
4. Washington has more glaciers than all of the other 47 contiguous U.S. states combined.
5. The northwesternmost point in the contiguous United States is Cape Flattery on the Olympic Peninsula.
6. The first Father's Day was observed in Spokane in 1910.

WYOMING

★ Equality State ★

HIGH, WIDE, AND WINDY—all describe Wyoming. The state is second only to Colorado in elevation, averaging 6,700 feet (2,044 m). It stretches 350 miles (560 km) east to west and 280 miles (450 km) north to south. Winds blow hard across rugged mountains and dry basins, making Wyoming the windiest state. In winter, winds can pick up dry snow, creating "ground blizzards" even on clear days. Wyoming could be described as lonely, too. Though ninth largest in area, the state has the lowest population. More people live in the city of Denver, Colorado, than in all of Wyoming!

Wyoming may be short on people, but it is tall on scenery. Mysterious Devils Tower, which perhaps is more famous for its role in the movie *Close Encounters of the Third Kind* than it is for being the nation's first national monument, is a reminder of an ancient volcanic past. Three hundred miles to the west, heat from Earth's core still reaches the surface. Yellowstone National Park contains more geysers than any other place in the world. These and other geothermal features share the park with canyons, waterfalls, forests, and wildlife. In fact, Wyoming's huge variety of wildlife—elk, moose, pronghorn, bison, bear (both black and grizzly), deer, coyote, mountain lions and eagles—makes the entire state seem like a big game park.

Just south of Yellowstone stand the jagged, glacier-carved peaks of the Tetons, youngest range in the Rockies. Like a teenager, the Tetons are still growing—about a foot every four centuries. Near the end of the Wind River Range, ruts from Oregon Trail wagons can still be seen along South Pass. This natural gateway through the Rockies opened the West to settlement beginning in the 1830s.

Oil was discovered in the Wind River Basin

1825

The Green River Rendezvous was the annual meeting place for trappers who came to trade furs for food and other supplies.

1869

Wyoming's territorial legislature was the first in the U.S. to allow women to vote and to hold office on an equal basis with men.

1880s

By 1887 overgrazing and a series of terrible winters had caused many ranches to fail, crippling Wyoming's cattle industry.

1912–Present

The state's richest oil deposits were discovered at Salt Creek, north of Casper. The oil industry is still key to Wyoming's economy.

The majestic peaks of the Tetons, youngest range in the Rocky Mountains, rise above the Snake River (opposite). Nearby Jackson Hole provides year-round recreational opportunities and is the winter home of the nation's largest elk herd.

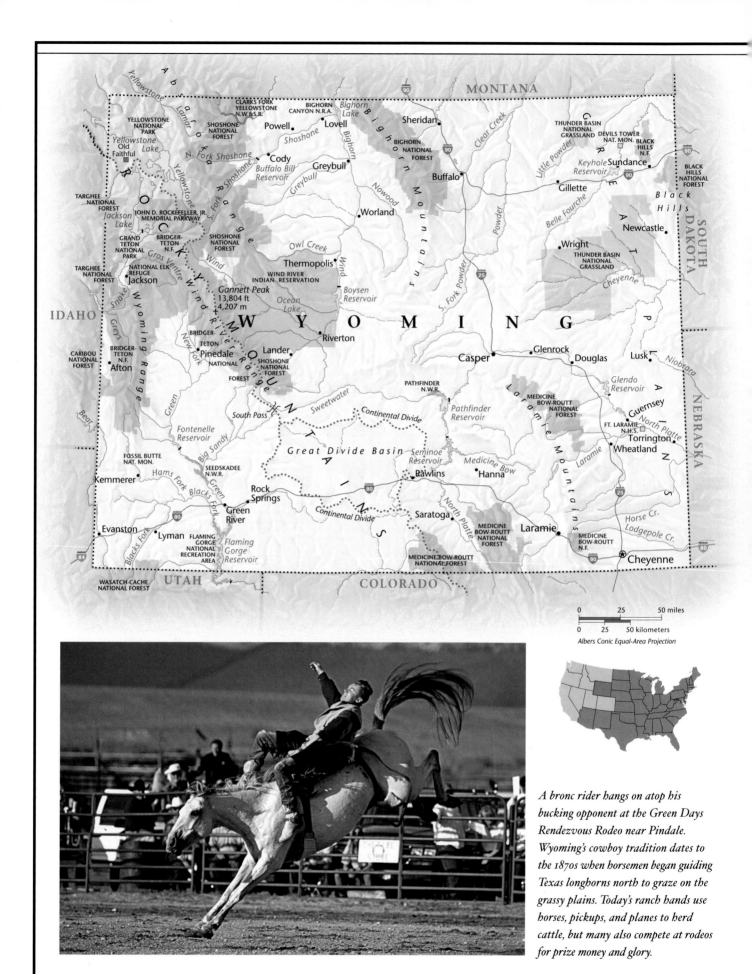

A bronc rider hangs on atop his bucking opponent at the Green Days Rendezvous Rodeo near Pindale. Wyoming's cowboy tradition dates to the 1870s when horsemen began guiding Texas longhorns north to graze on the grassy plains. Today's ranch hands use horses, pickups, and planes to herd cattle, but many also compete at rodeos for prize money and glory.

in 1833. A year later Fort Laramie, the first real settlement in Wyoming, was founded as a trading post on land where Absaroka, Shoshone, and other native peoples had long lived. As a military post, it played a key role both in protecting settlers and in the wars and treaties that eventually gave them control of the land.

The Union Pacific Railroad, which reached Wyoming in 1867, brought a boom in settlement and spurred economic activities that are still important to the state. Ranching became a big business. Cattle, at first longhorns from Texas, were fattened on the open range and then shipped by train to the East. Other homesteaders came to ranch sheep and farm crops. Coal deposits were mined along the early rail route. Now, massive machinery strips vast seams of coal, making Wyoming the nation's largest producer of this resource. Most is exported by rail to eastern power plants.

People came in search of other minerals, too. In 1888 oil was found near Casper. Today, the refining of oil and natural gas is the state's most important industry. Uranium was found in the 1950s. Wyoming is now the nation's top producer.

The opening of Yellowstone National Park in 1872 brought tourists to Wyoming, and this industry is key to Wyoming's future. Visitors come to re-live the Wild West, staying at dude ranches and cheering at rodeos in towns across the state. The U.S. government owns about half the state. Much of this land is used for recreation and tourism, but logging, grazing, and mining are permitted in selected areas. Some people are concerned that these activities could hurt the land and the state's future. Careful management can ensure that Wyoming's wild, wide-open spaces will be around for all to enjoy for many years to come.

WYOMING
Equality State

STATEHOOD	July 10, 1890; 44th state
CAPITAL	Cheyenne
LARGEST CITY	Cheyenne Population 53,658
TOTAL AREA	97,814 sq mi; 253,336 sq km
LAND AREA	97,100 sq mi; 251,489 sq km
POPULATION	501,242
POPULATION DENSITY	5.1 people per sq mi
MAJOR RACIAL/ ETHNIC GROUPS	92.1% white; 2.3% Native American; .8% African American; .6% Asian. Hispanic (any race) 6.4%.
INDUSTRY	oil and natural gas, mining, generation of electricity, chemicals, tourism
AGRICULTURE	cattle, sugar beets, sheep, hay, wheat

WESTERN MEADOWLARK   INDIAN PAINTBRUSH

Did you know?

1. The famous Teapot Dome scandal, which blackened President Harding's administration, concerned oil leases in Wyoming and California. It took its name from the shape of a rock formation above the oil reserves in Wyoming.
2. Butch Cassidy's Wild Bunch gang lived in and around Kaycee, Wyoming, on the Powder River.
3. Wyoming is called the Equality State because it was the first state to give women the right to vote, granted in 1869 when it was still a territory.
4. The horse on Wyoming's license plate is named Old Steamboat in honor of a legendary bucking bronco that no one could ride.
5. Devils Tower was named the country's first national monument by President Teddy Roosevelt in 1906. It is a sacred site of worship to many Plains Indians, who know it as Bears Lodge.
6. Cody, Wyoming, is named for "Buffalo Bill" Cody.

U.S. TERRITORIES

FAR-FLUNG TROPICAL ISLANDS. The United States claims 13 islands scattered across ten time zones as territories, but only the five largest—Puerto Rico and the U.S. Virgin Islands in the Caribbean Sea and the Northern Marianas, Guam, and American Samoa in the Pacific Ocean—have their own governments, cultures, and economies. Each of these was acquired from another country as the result of a war or international agreement, and each is a valued part of the United States.

Residents of all but American Samoa are U.S. citizens, and all except the Northern Marianas have a non-voting delegate in the U.S. House of Representatives. Many island people, seeking new opportunities, have moved to the United States. The country's population now includes 2.7 million Puerto Ricans, and tens of thousands of American Samoans live in Hawaii and other Pacific states. Meanwhile, each year millions of mainlanders are lured by the promise of sun and sand to these distant shores.

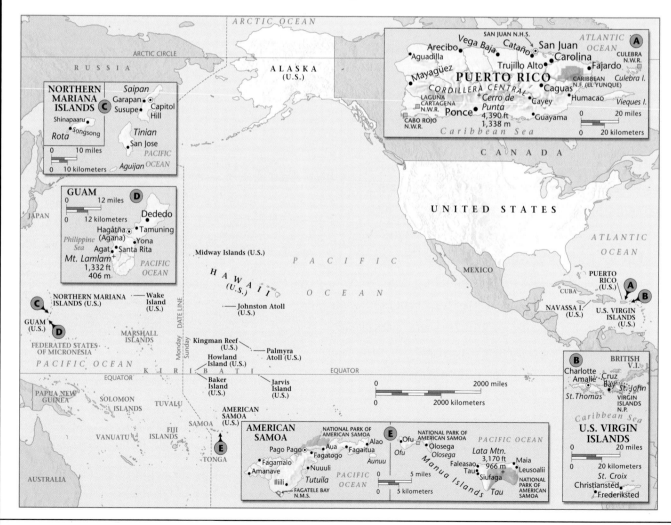

AMERICAN SAMOA (Pop.: 62,000)

Populated mainly by descendants of Polynesian seafarers who arrived here some 4,000 years ago, American Samoa processes huge tuna catches for U.S. markets. Fagatele Bay National Marine Sanctuary (left) serves as a symbol of the concern Samoan people have for the environment.

GUAM (Pop.: 164,000)

Much of Guam belongs to the U.S. military. More than half of its 164,000 people were born elsewhere. Tourism, especially in the form of tropic-seeking Japanese visitors, is the island's most important economic activity. At right, a native Taotao dancer performs at a Pacific Arts Festival.

NORTHERN MARIANA ISLANDS (Pop.: 78,000)

Most people here live on Saipan, the center for commercial and government activities. Chamorros, Indonesians who have inter-married with people of Spanish and Philippine heritage, make up the largest ethnic group. Many islanders farm or hold government jobs. Tourism is growing thanks to fabulous beaches (left).

PUERTO RICO (Pop.: 3,879,000)

Spanish-speaking Puerto Rico has more people than 25 U.S. states. Manufacturing, especially of medicines and electronics, has replaced an agricultural economy based on sugar, coffee, and tobacco. El Yunque rain forest (right) is among the attractions that fuel a thriving tourist industry.

VIRGIN ISLANDS (Pop.: 110,000)

The islands of St. Thomas, St. Croix, and St. John—purchased from Denmark in 1917—make up most of the U.S. Virgin Islands. Sugar-mill ruins (left) are evidence of a past dominated by plantation farming. Today, profits come mainly from tourism and the refining of imported oil.

★ Facts & Figures ★

All 50 States

Capital City
Washington, D.C.

Largest City
New York City
Population 8,084,316

Total Area
3,794,083 sq mi;
9,826,630 sq km

Land Area
3,537,439 sq mi;
9,161,923 sq km

Population 290,809,777

Population Density
81.5 people per sq mi

Major Racial/Ethnic Groups
75.1% white; 12.3% African American; 3.6% Asian; .9% Native American. Hispanic (any race) 12.5%

Top States

Top Ten in Farm Products (by net farm income)
1. Texas
2. California
3. North Carolina
4. Georgia
5. Florida
6. Iowa
7. Nebraska
8. Alabama
9. Illinois
10. Arkansas

Top Five in Fisheries
1. Alaska
2. Louisiana
3. Maine
4. Florida
5. Texas

Top Ten in Minerals
1. Texas
2. Louisiana
3. Alaska
4. California
5. Oklahoma
6. Wyoming
7. New Mexico
8. West Virginia
9. Kentucky
10. Colorado

Extremes

World's Strongest Surface Wind
231 mph (372 kph),
Mount Washington, NH,
April 12, 1934

World's Oldest Living Tree
Methuselah bristlecone pine, California; about 4,700 years old

World's Tallest Living Tree
The "Mendocino Tree," a coast redwood at Montgomery State Reserve in California, 367.5 ft (112 m) high

World's Largest Gorge
Grand Canyon, Arizona; 290 mi (466 km) long, 600 ft to 18 mi (183 m to 29 km) wide, 1 mile (1.6 km) deep

Highest U.S. Temperature
134°F (56.6°C), Death Valley, California, July 10, 1913

Lowest U.S. Temperature
Minus 80°F (-62.2°C) at Prospect Creek, Alaska, January 23, 1971

Highest U.S. Point
Mount McKinley (Denali), Alaska; 20,323 feet (6,194 m)

Lowest U.S. Point
Death Valley, California; 282 feet (86 m) below sea level

Longest U.S. River System
Mississippi-Missouri; 3,708 mi (5,971 km) long

Rainiest U.S. Spot
Waialeale (mountain), Hawaii: average annual rainfall 460 in (1,168 cm)

U.S. Metropolitan Areas with More Than Five Million People
(A metropolitan area is a city and its surrounding suburban areas.)

1. New York, pop. 21,199,900
2. Los Angeles, pop. 16,373,600
3. Chicago, pop. 9,157,500
4. Washington, D.C., pop. 7,608,100
5. San Francisco, pop. 7,039,400
6. Philadelphia, pop. 6,188,500
7. Boston, pop. 5,819,100
8. Detroit, pop. 5,456,400
9. Dallas-Fort Worth, pop. 5,221,800

Map Key

⊛ State capital
+ Elevation
■ Point of interest
—— River
— – Intermittent river
⊥⊥⊥⊥ Canal
—— Interstate or selected other highway
- - - - Trail
••••• National boundary
•••••• State boundary
•••••• Continental divide
⊢—⊣ Lake and dam
⟳ Intermittent lake
Dry lake
Swamp
Glacier
Below sea level
Sand
Lava

City and Town Population:
● New York *1,000,000 and over*
● San Jose *100,000 to 999,999*
● Frankfort *25,000 to 99,999*
● Aspen *under 25,000*

☐ National Battlefield, N.B.
National Battlefield Park, N.B.P.
National Battlefield Site, N.B.S.
National Historic Site, N.H.S.
National Historical Area
National Historical Park, N.H.P.
National Lakeshore
National Military Park, N.M.P.
National Memorial, NAT. MEM.
National Monument, NAT. MON.
National Park, N.P.
National Parkway
National Preserve
National Recreation Area, N.R.A.
National River
National Riverway
National Scenic Area
National Seashore
National Volcanic Monument

☐ National Forest, N.F.
☐ National Grassland, N.G.
National Wild & Scenic River, N.W.&S.R.
☐ National Wildlife Refuge, N.W.R.
☐ State Park, S.P.
State Historical Park, S.H.P.
State Historic Site, S.H.S.
☐ Indian Reservation, I.R.

★ Resources ★

Bibliography

————. *Atlas of North America.* National Geographic Society. Washington, DC: 1985.

——————. *Discover America: A Comprehensive Travel Guide to Our Country's Greatest Destinations.* Reader's Digest. Pleasantville, NY: 2004.

————. *Historical Atlas of the United States.* National Geographic Society. Washington, DC: 1988.

————. *National Geographic United States Atlas For Young Explorers,* Updated Edition. National Geographic Society. Washington, DC: 2004

————. *Webster's New Geographical Dictionary,* 3rd edition. G. & C. Merriam Co. Springfield, MA: 1997.

————. *The World Almanac and Book of Facts 2004.* World Almanac Books. New York: 2004

Barber, Nathan. *Get Wise! Mastering U.S. History.* Peterson's. Lawrenceville, NJ: 2004.

Ciovacco, Justine, et al. *State-by-State Atlas.* DK Publishing. New York: 2003.

Garrington, Sally. *United States.* Facts on File. New York: 2003.

Hakim, Joy. *A History of Us,* 11 vols., 2nd rev. ed. Oxford University Press Children's Books. New York: 1999.

Hintz, Martin. *United States of America,* 2nd series. Scholastic, Inc. New York: 2004.

Johnston, Robert D. *The Making of America.* National Geographic Society. Washington, DC: 2002.

Lyon, James and Andrew Dean Nystrom. *Lonely Planet USA,* 2nd edition. Lonely Planet Publications. Oakland, CA: 2002.

Pogany, Don. *Our Flag Was Still There: 50 States in 100 Days.* Barnes and Noble. New York: 2002.

Rogers, Mary M., ed. *United States—in Pictures.* Lerner Publications. Minneapolis, MN: 1995.

Sedeen, Margaret, ed. *National Geographic Picture Atlas of Our Fifty States.* National Geographic Society. Washington, DC: 1991.

Stewart, George R. *Names on the Land: A Historical Account of Place-Naming in the United States,* 3rd edition. Houghton Mifflin. Boston: 1967.

More advanced texts include:

Boyer, Paul S., et al. *The Oxford Companion to United States History.* Oxford University Press. New York: 2001.

Conzen, Michael P., ed. *The Making of the American Landscape.* Unwin Hyman. Boston: 1990.

Davis, Kenneth C. *Don't Know Much About History: Everything You Need to Know About American History but Never Learned.* Harper Collins. New York: 2003.

Faragher, John Mack, et al. *Out of Many: A History of the American People,* 4th ed. Prentice Hall. Upper Saddle River, NJ: 2002.

Halberstam, David. *Defining a Nation: Our America and the Sources of Its Strength.* National Geographic Society, Washington, DC: 2003.

Hine, Robert V. and John Mack Faragher. *The American West: A New Interpretive History.* Yale University Press. New Haven, CT: 2000.

Hudson, John C. *Across This Land: A Regional Geography of the United States and Canada.* Johns Hopkins University Press. Baltimore, MD: 2002.

Useful Web sites:

State facts: http://www.50states.com
http://www. infoplease.com/states
http://www.ipl.org/youth/stateknow/skhome.html

State Web sites: http://www.state. [state postal abbreviation].us (for example, Alabama's web site is http://www.state.al.us)

State of the State addresses: http://www.nga.org

National Park Service: http://www.nps.gov

U.S. Census Bureau: http://www.census.gov

The United States Mint—50 State Quarters Program: http://www.usmint.gov

Agricultural information, including state rankings from the US Department of Agriculture, National Agriculture Statistics Service: http://www.usda.gov/nass/aggraphs/graphics.htm
http://www.usda.gov/nass/pubs/agstats.htm
http://www.usda.gov/nass/sso-rpts.htm (for links to state offices)

USDA crop data is housed in the Mann Library at Cornell University. For listings of Crop Production Annual Summaries, go to: http://usda.mannlib.cornell.edu/

For mineral resource information, go to the US Geological Survey Web site:
http://minerals.usgs.gov/minerals/pubs/state/

★ Index ★

★ Illustration Credits ★

Key to abbreviations: (le) left; (rt) right; (ctr) center; (lo) lower

Cover (wheat), Darrell Gulin/CORBIS; (mountains), Jeff Vanuga/CORBIS; (sky), L. Clarke/CORBIS; (eagle), Ron Sanford/CORBIS.

Front Matter
2–3, Mitchell Funk/Getty Images; 4 (up), John Henley/CORBIS; 4 (ctr), Siegfried Layda/Getty Images; 4 (lo), Philip Gould/CORBIS; 5 (up), Layne Kennedy/CORBIS; 5 (ctr), Bruce Dale; 5 (lo), Michael Melford/Getty Images; 6, John Henley/CORBIS; 9, Layne Kennedy/CORBIS; 10, Charles O'Rear/CORBIS.

The Northeast
15, James L. Amos/CORBIS; 16, Michael Melford/Getty Images; 17 (le), North Wind Picture Archives; 17 (ctr, le), Bettmann/CORBIS; 17 (ctr, rt), Talladega College; 17 (rt), AP Photos; 18, James Marshall/CORBIS; 20, Courtesy, Winterthur Museum; 21 (le), courtesy Library of Congress; 21 (ctr, le), Hagley Museum and Library; 21 (ctr, le), ©Hulton-Deutsch Collection/CORBIS; 21 (rt), Kevin Fleming/CORBIS; 22, Pat Crowe; 24, Owaki-Kulla/CORBIS; 25 (le), CORBIS; 25 (ctr, le), CORBIS; 25 (ctr, rt), courtesy Maine Historical Society; 25 (rt), Owaki-Kulla/CORBIS; 26, David H. Wells/CORBIS; 28, Medford Taylor; 29 (le), St. Mary's County Museum Division; 29 (ctr, le), Bettmann/CORBIS; 29 (ctr, rt), CORBIS; 29 (rt), David Ball/CORBIS; 30, Pat & Chuck Blackley; 32, Dave Bartruff/CORBIS; 33 (le), Bettmann/CORBIS; 33 (ctr, le), courtesy National Army Museum, Chelsea; 33 (ctr, rt), CORBIS; 33 (rt), Andy Ryan; 35, Robert Holmes/CORBIS; 36, Siegfried Layda/Getty Images; 37 (le), North Wind Picture Archives; 37 (ctr, le), CORBIS; 37 (ctr, rt), Bettmann/CORBIS; 37 (rt), Kevin Lamarque/Reuters/CORBIS; 38, AP Photos; 40, PictureNet/CORBIS; 41 (le), North Wind Picture Archives; 41 (ctr, le), Bettmann/CORBIS; 41 (ctr, rt), Bettmann/CORBIS; 41 (rt), Brownie Harris/CORBIS; 42, Mark Peterson/CORBIS; 44, Alan Schein Photography/CORBIS; 45 (le), North Wind Picture Archives; 45 (ctr, le), Bettmann/CORBIS; 45 (ctr, rt), Bettmann/CORBIS; 45 (rt), Sean Adair/CORBIS; 46, Cosmo Condina/Getty Images; 48, Francesco Ruggeri/Getty Images; 49 (le), Bettmann/CORBIS; 49 (ctr, le), Bettmann/CORBIS; 49 (ctr, rt), CORBIS; 49 (rt), Wally McNamee/CORBIS; 50, AP Photos; 52, Onne van der Wal/CORBIS; 53 (le), Bettmann/CORBIS; 53 (ctr, le), Bettmann/CORBIS; 53 (ctr, rt), Bob Krist/CORBIS; 53 (rt), Mark E. Gibson/CORBIS; 54, Onne van der Wal/CORBIS; 56, Randy Olson; 57 (le), North Wind Picture Archives; 57 (ctr, le), North Wind Picture Archives; 57 (ctr, rt), Vermont Historical Society; 57 (rt), Steven E. Frishling/CORBIS; 58, Kevin Fleming/CORBIS.

The Southeast
63, Bob Clemenz; 64, David Muench; 65 (le), Alabama Department of Archives and History; 65 (ctr, le), CORBIS; 65 (ctr, rt), Bettmann/CORBIS; 65 (rt), courtesy NASA; 66, Richard Howard; 68, Bernie Jungkind; 69 (le), North Wind Picture Archives; 69 (ctr, le), North Wind Picture Archives; 69 (ctr, rt), Bettmann/CORBIS; 69 (rt), ©Reuters/CORBIS; 70, AP Photo; 72, Getty Images; 73 (le), Bettmann/CORBIS; 73 (ctr, le), North Wind Picture Archives; 73 (ctr, rt), Flagler Museum Archives; 73 (rt), AP Photo; 75, Richard T. Nowitz/CORBIS; 76, Gary Randall/Getty Images; 77 (le), North Wind Picture Archives; 77 (ctr, le), Bettmann/CORBIS; 77 (ctr, rt), CORBIS; 77 (rt), ©THIERRY ORBA/CORBIS SYGMA; 78, Inga Spence/Index Stock Imagery; 80, Kevin R. Morris/Getty Images; 81 (le), George Caleb Bingham, "Daniel Boone Escorting Settlers through the Cumberland Gap, 1851–52." Oil on canvas, 36 1/2 x 50 1/4". Washington University Gallery of Art, St. Louis. Gift of Nathaniel Phillips, 1890.; 81 (ctr, le), North Wind Picture Archives; 81 (ctr, rt), Underwood & Underwood/CORBIS; 81 (rt), Randy Duchaine/CORBIS; 83, Kevin R. Morris/CORBIS; 84, Philip Gould/CORBIS; 85 (le), Louisiana Historical Society; 85 (ctr, le), North Wind Picture Archives; 85 (ctr, rt), Bettmann/CORBIS; 85 (rt), CORBIS; 86, Philip Gould/CORBIS; 88, Dave Bartruff/Index Stock Imagery; 89 (le), North Wind Picture Archives; 89 (ctr, le), CORBIS; 89 (ctr, rt), Flip Schulke/CORBIS; 89 (rt), Philip Gould/CORBIS; 91, Richard Hamilton Smith/CORBIS; 92, Randy Wells/Getty Images; 93 (le), North Wind Picture Archives; 93 (ctr, le), Bettmann/CORBIS; 93 (ctr, rt), courtesy US Army; 94, Brownie Harris/CORBIS; 96, Benn & Esther Mitchell/Getty Images; 97 (le), North Wind Picture Archives; 97 (ctr, le), CORBIS; 97 (ctr, rt), George D. Lepp/CORBIS; 97 (rt), Tom Salyer/CORBIS; 98, Tim Dominick; 100, David Muench/CORBIS; 101 (le), courtesy Library of Congress; 101 (ctr, le), The Philadelphia Print Shop; 101 (ctr, rt), Bettmann/CORBIS; 101 (rt), John Madere/CORBIS; 103, Hiroyuki Matsumoto/Getty Images; 104, Colonial Williamsburg Foundation; 105 (le), North Wind Picture Archives; 105 (ctr, le), North Wind Picture Archives; 105 (ctr, rt), Francis G. Mayer/CORBIS; 105 (rt), Virginia Polytechnic Institute and State University; 106, Ann Purcell/CORBIS; 108, Anna Susan Post; 109 (le), Kansas State Historical Society; 109 (ctr, le), The Museum of African American Art, Los Angeles, California, Palmer C. Hayden Collection, gift of Miriam A. Hayden; 109 (ctr, rt), Bettmann/CORBIS; 109 (rt), Kit Kittle/CORBIS; 110, James L. Amos/CORBIS.

The Midwest
115, Layne Kennedy/CORBIS; 116, Adrian Lyon/Getty Images; 117 (le), North Wind Picture Archives; 117 (ctr, le), Bettmann/CORBIS; 117 (ctr, rt), Bettmann/CORBIS; 117 (rt), FermiLab; 118, Richard Hamilton Smith/CORBIS; 120, Ron Goltry/Index Stock Imagery; 121 (le), North Wind Picture Archives; 121 (ctr, le), Bettmann/CORBIS; 121 (ctr, rt), Calumet Regional Archives, Indiana University Northwest; 121 (rt), Reuters/CORBIS; 122, AP Photos/Darron Cummings; 124, Craig Aurness/CORBIS; 125 (le), North Wind Picture Archives; 125 (ctr, le), State Montage; 125 (ctr, rt), State Historical Society of Iowa; 125 (rt), Les Stone/CORBIS; 126, Julie Habel/CORBIS; 128, Joel Sartore/www.joelsartore.com; 129 (le), Bettmann/CORBIS; 129 (ctr, le), Bettmann/CORBIS; 129 (ctr, rt), Bettmann/CORBIS; 129 (rt), courtesy Raytheon Aircraft; 130, AP Photo/Dodge City (Kan.) *Daily Globe,* Michael Schweitzer; 132, Andy Sacks/Getty Images; 133 (le), North Wind Picture Archives; 133 (ctr, le), courtesy Library of Congress; 133 (ctr, rt), CORBIS; 133 (rt), courtesy Kellogg's Cereal City USA; 134, AP Photo/*Traverse City Record Eagle*/John L. Russell; 136, Paul Harris/Getty Images; 137 (le), North Wind Picture Archives; 137 (ctr, le), Minnesota Historical Society; 137 (ctr, rt), Keystone View Company/CORBIS; 137 (rt), Bob Cole; 138, Layne Kennedy/CORBIS; 140, Sam Abell, National Geographic Photographer; 141 (le), Missouri State Historical Society; 141 (ctr, le), Charles Hargens, Pony Express Museum, St. Joseph, Missouri; 141 (ctr, rt), Schenectady Museum; Hall of Electrical History Foundation/CORBIS; 141 (rt), Ralph Krubner/Index Stock Imagery; 142, Randy Olson; 144, Jeff Gnass; 145 (le), North Wind Picture Archives; 145 (ctr, le), Nebraska State Historical Society; 145 (ctr, rt), Bettmann/CORBIS; 145 (rt), Jim Sugar/CORBIS; 146, Richard Hamilton Smith/CORBIS; 148, Annie Griffiths Belt; 149 (le), Michael Haynes; 149 (ctr, le), Minnesota Historical Society/CORBIS; 149 (ctr, rt), Bettmann/CORBIS; 149 (rt), Annie Griffiths Belt/CORBIS; 150, Andy Sacks/Getty Images; 152, Richard A. Cooke/CORBIS; 153 (le), North Wind Picture Archives; 153 (ctr, le), Bettmann/CORBIS; 153 (ctr, rt), Cleveland State University Library; 153 (rt), Wes Thompson/CORBIS; 154, Andy Sacks/Getty Images; 156, Sarah Leen/NG Image Collection; 157 (le), Joslyn Art Museum, Omaha, Nebraska; 157 (ctr, le), CORBIS; 157 (ctr, rt), photo courtesy of the South Dakota State Historical Society-State Archives; 157 (rt), AP Photo/Charles Bennett; 158, Charles Thatcher/Getty Images; 160, Jim Richardson; 161 (le), Wisconsin Historical Society; 161 (ctr, le), Wisconsin Historical Society; 161 (ctr, rt), CORBIS; 161 (rt), Peter Turnley/CORBIS; 162, Layne Kennedy/CORBIS.

The Southwest
167, Lester Lefkowitz/CORBIS; 168, Bruce Dale; 169 (le), Buddy Mays/CORBIS; 169 (ctr, le), CORBIS; 169 (ctr, rt), Bettmann/CORBIS; 169 (rt), Roger Ressmeyer/CORBIS; 170, David Hiser/Getty Images; 172, R.W. Jones/CORBIS; 173 (le), Museum of New Mexico; 173 (ctr, le), Museum of New Mexico; 173 (ctr, rt), CORBIS; 173 (rt), SANTA FE NEW MEXICO/CORBIS SYGMA; 174, AP Photo/Eric Draper; 176, CORBIS; 177 (le), Victor R. Boswell, Woolaroc Museum, Bartlesville Oklahoma; 177 (ctr, le), Bettmann/CORBIS; 177 (ctr, rt), Bettmann/CORBIS; 177 (rt), Anthony Suau/BLACK STAR; 179, Richard Hamilton Smith/CORBIS; 180, Joseph McNally/Getty Images; 181 (le), CORBIS; 181 (ctr, le), Bettmann/CORBIS; 181 (ctr, rt), CORBIS; 181 (rt), courtesy/NASA; 183, AP Photo.

The West
187, Kennan Ward/CORBIS; 188, Michael Melford/Getty Images; 189 (le), Bettmann/CORBIS; 189 (ctr, le), Alexander Alland/CORBIS; 189 (ctr, rt), Horace Bristol/CORBIS; 189 (rt), Nevada Wier/CORBIS; 190, Paul A. Souders/CORBIS; 192, Morton Beebe/CORBIS; 193 (le), CORBIS; 193 (ctr, le), North Wind Picture Archives; 193 (ctr, rt), Bettmann/CORBIS; 193 (rt), Kenneth James/CORBIS; 194, Lester Lefkowitz/CORBIS; 196, David Muench; 197 (le), Richard Frajola; 197 (ctr, le), Bettmann/CORBIS; 197 (ctr, rt), Bettmann/CORBIS; 197 (rt), courtesy NORAD; 198, Paul Chesley/NG Image Collection; 200, Jim Sugar/CORBIS; 201 (le), Richard Cummins/CORBIS; 201 (ctr, le), Bettmann/CORBIS; 201 (ctr, rt), Bettmann/CORBIS; 201 (rt), David Sailors/CORBIS; 202, Reuters/CORBIS; 204, Michael Melford; 205 (le), Doris S. Clymer; 205 (ctr, le), Jo Proferes, graphic from Nez Perce Bicentennial Exhibit; 205 (ctr, rt), courtesy Bureau of Reclamation; 205 (rt), David Stoecklein/CORBIS; 206, Mark Gibson/Index Stock Imagery; 208, Dewitt Jones; 209 (le), North Wind Picture Archives; 209 (ctr, le), North Wind Picture Archives; 209 (ctr, rt), Buffalo Bill Historical Center, Cody, Wyoming; gift of Charles Ulrich and Josephine Bay Foundation, Inc.; 88.60; 209 (rt), Tony DiFronzo; 210, Jan Burchofsky-Houser/CORBIS; 212, Bob Krist/CORBIS; 213 (le), North Wind Picture Archives; 213 (ctr, le), CORBIS; 213 (ctr, rt), Bettmann/CORBIS; 213 (rt), Dan Lamont/CORBIS; 214, Scott S. Warren; 216, AP Photo/*Herald and News,* Ron Winn; 217 (le), Bettmann/CORBIS; 217 (ctr, le), North Wind Picture Archives; 217 (ctr, rt), F. Burns/CORBIS; 217 (rt), Galen Rowell/CORBIS; 218, AP Photo/Don Ryan; 220, George H. H. Huey/CORBIS; 221 (le), Bettmann/CORBIS; 221 (ctr, le), Bettmann/CORBIS; 221 (ctr, rt), Utah State Historical Society; 221 (rt), courtesy NASA; 222, Tom Bean; 224, Joel W. Rogers/CORBIS; 225 (le), Don Crook; 225 (ctr, le), courtesy Museum of History and Industry; 225 (ctr, rt), Bettmann/CORBIS; 225 (rt), James Leynse/CORBIS; 226, CORBIS; 228, Lester Lefkowitz/CORBIS; 229 (le), Alfred Jacob Miller, The Walters Art Gallery, Baltimore; 229 (ctr, le), Bettmann/CORBIS; 229 (ctr, rt), Buffalo Bill Historical Center, Cody, Wyoming; 7.69; 229 (rt), Jonathan Blair/CORBIS; 230, Kevin R. Morris/CORBIS; 233 (up, le), Kip Evans, National Marine Sanctuaries; 233 (up, rt), James Davis; Eye Ubiquitous/CORBIS; 233 (ctr), Michael S. Yamashita/CORBIS; 233 (lo, rt), Wolfgang Kaehler/CORBIS; 233 (lo, le), CORBIS.

Published by the National Geographic Society

JOHN M. FAHEY, JR.
President and Chief Executive Officer

GILBERT M. GROSVENOR
Chairman of the Board

NINA D. HOFFMAN
Executive Vice President. President of Books and Education Publishing Group

ERICKA MARKMAN
Senior Vice President, President of Children's Books and Education Publishing Group

---

Staff for this book

Nancy Laties Feresten
Vice President, Editor-in-Chief of Children's Books

Suzanne Patrick Fonda
Project Editor

Bea Jackson
Art Director

Carl Mehler
Director of Maps

Kay Kobor Hankins
Illustrations Editor

Janet A. Dustin
Illustrations Coordinator

Jennifer Emmett
Virginia Ann Koeth
Editors

Susan Kehnemui Donnelly
Editorial Assistant

Matt Chwastyk
Gregory Ugiansky
XNR Productions
Map Research and Production

Jocelyn G. Lindsay
Text Research

David Lindsay
Research Assistant

Daniel L. Sherman
David M. Seager
Production Design

Mark A. Wentling
Indexing

Heidi Vincent
Director of Direct Response Sales and Marketing

Jeff Reynolds
Marketing Director, Children's Books

Rebecca E. Hinds
Managing Editor

R. Gary Colbert
Production Director

Lewis R. Bassford
Production Manager

Alan V. Kerr
Vincent P. Ryan
Manufacturing Managers

Consultants

NORTHEAST
Sari Bennett
Director, Center for Geography Education University of Maryland Baltimore County

Cathleen McAnneny
Associate Professor of Geography University of Maine at Farmington

Chester E. Smolski
Professor Emeritus of Geography Rhode Island College

SOUTHEAST
Kurt Butefish
Tennessee Geographic Alliance University of Tennessee

Truman Hartshorn
Professor of Geography Georgia State University

Joseph T. Manzo
Geography Department Concord University West Virginia

Robert Morrill
Professor Emeritus Virginia Tech University

Keith Mountain
Kentucky Geographic Alliance Department of Geography and Geosciences University of Louisville

Steve Pierce
North Carolina Geographic Alliance

Bobbie Richardson
Mississippi Geographic Alliance Blue Mountain College

William R. Strong
Alabama Geographic Alliance University of Alabama

MIDWEST
Carol Craig
Missouri Geographic Alliance

Darrell P. Kruger
Illinois Geographic Alliance Illinois State University

John Heinrichs
Kansas Geographic Alliance Fort Hays State University

Kathy Lamb Kozenski
Geography Educators Network of Indiana

David A. Lanegran
John S. Holl Professor of Geography Macalester College Minnesota

Michael Libbee
Michigan Geographic Alliance Central Michigan University

Kay E. Weller
Geographic Alliance of Iowa University of Northern Iowa

SOUTHWEST
Sarah Bednarz
Associate Professor of Geography Texas A&M University

Richard Boehm
Texas Alliance for Geographic Education Texas State University

Ronald Dorn
Arizona Geographic Alliance Arizona State University

Gale Ekiss
Arizona Geographic Alliance

WEST
Jody Smothers Marcello
Alaska Geographic Alliance

Mark Montgomery
Colorado Geographic Alliance University of Denver

Virgil M. Young
Professor Emeritus College of Education Boise State University

To my father, Blaine V. "Buck" Bockenhauer (1926–1995),
who taught me to love life and to learn through travel. Thanks, Dad!—MHB

In memory of Meg Cunha, who introduced me to reading—SFC

Acknowledgments

I've learned much on this fifty states writing adventure. I've marveled at the dizzying diversity across this vast country while appreciating the connections that bind its people and regions together into a single great nation.

I've also learned how rewarding it is to work with the dedicated team of people at the Children's Books Division of National Geographic. I appreciated working with Steve Cunha, who brought energy and creativity to the regional essays. Thanks much to the coordinators of state geographic alliances and other geographers who provided feedback on my state essays. And to former President Jimmy Carter, a special thanks for penning a beautiful Foreword.

I could not have completed this book without the constant support of my family. My freshman son Sam took time from his studies at the University of Wisconsin to compile resources and offer incisive commentary about many state essays. Sixteen-year-old Karen and fourteen-year-old Thomas read drafts, found useful Web sites, and organized resources. Now and then one of them would read a passage and say, "A middle-school kid won't understand *that*, Dad!" I needed that. I also valued weekly phone calls of support from my mother, Dolores. Most of all, my wife, Nancy, not only provided daily encouragement but agreed—when impossible deadlines loomed—to draft many of the timeline legends for the book. Without her I wouldn't be writing these lines.

Published by the National Geographic Society
1145 17th Street, NW
Washington, D.C. 20036-4688

Library of Congress Cataloging-in-Publication Data

Bockenhauer, Mark H.
  National Geographic our fifty states / written by Mark H. Bockenhauer and Stephen F. Cunha.
    p. cm.
  Includes bibliographical references and index.
  ISBN 0-7922-6402-9 (trade edition)
  ISBN 0-7922-6992-6 (library edition)
  1. U.S. states. 2. United States—Geography. 3. United States—History, Local.
I. Title: Our fifty states. II. Cunha, Stephen F. III. Title.
  E180.B635 2004
  917.3—dc22

                                        2004001190

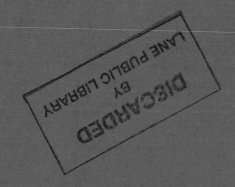